Durocher's Cubs

The Greatest Team
That Didn't Win

Durocher's Cubs

David Claerbaut

Taylor Publishing Company

Dallas, Texas

Copyright © 2000 by David Claerbaut

All photographs courtesy of AP/Wide World.

Designed by Barbara Werden

Published by Taylor Publishing Company
1550 West Mockingbird Lane
Dallas, Texas 75235
www.taylorpub.com

Library of Congress Cataloging-in-Publication Data
Claerbaut, David.
    Durocher's Cubs : the greatest team that didn't win / David Claerbaut.
        p.   cm.
    Includes bibliographical references (p.) and index.
    ISBN 0-87833-177-8
    1. Chicago Cubs (Baseball team)—History. 2. Durocher, Leo, 1906– I.Title.
GV875.C6 C52 2000   00-022184

10   9   8   7   6   5   4   3   2   1

Printed in the United States of America

*To Craig Lynch, Sam Psimoulis,
and Greg and Kay Yoder—four
of the Cubs' most faithful.*

Contents

Acknowledgments

Books are always cooperative efforts. More cooperated most graciously in completing this work than I can cite with proper justice. Several truly do stand out. I owe special thanks to George Castle, who was most helpful with his time and connections, and to Les Grobstein, who contributed selflessly to this effort, in addition to Randy Lambert and Ken Triphahn, whose practical help was especially valuable.

Durocher's Cubs

The Best Team That Didn't Win

Position by position, it was nearly an all-star team.
Dick Selma, on the contending Cubs

In what year did the Cubs last win a pennant?

Few committed Cub fans do not know the answer to that question. Its answer—1945—bears testimony to the main reason that devoted Cub fans are renowned nationwide for their loyalty, a loyalty which has gone largely unrewarded.

In fact, even that last pennant is a bit tarnished. It was won in a war year, one in which such National League diamond luminaries as Stan Musial, Enos Slaughter, and Johnny Mize, among about 300 others, were wearing military khakis rather than baseball double knits. Scratch 1945 and the Cub time machine spins back to 1938 when last the beloved Bruins were perched at the top of the league, and then to 1908 for their last World Series triumph.

It has been a tough century. Particularly the last half.

Remove the 1967 through 1972 seasons, and for half a century this organization, last to install lights in its beloved ballpark, has labored in near total baseball darkness. During those 55 years, the team has won just two isolated divisional titles and posted but one wild card entry. The club has had six winning seasons—none back-to-back.

And that's what makes those bittersweet, magical, never-to-be-forgotten 1967–1972 years shine so brightly in the memory of Cub fans. That team, the nucleus of which spanned that entire six-year patch of baseball sunshine, was arguably the best baseball team that never won.

No other National League team posted six consecutive winning seasons over that stretch. In fact, only one other team in all of baseball, the equally snakebitten-by-history Boston Red Sox, accomplished that feat. And they did manage a pennant in 1967. The Cubs turned in 515 victories, finished second three times, never lower than third, but won not a single flag of any kind—not a World Series, not a pennant, not even a divisional championship.

The team was led by the intensely controversial Hall of Fame manager Leo "the Lip" Durocher. Durocher came to Chicago after having won three pennants and a World Series in New York. By the time he was through as a skipper, Leo was one of only seven managers to win over 2,000 games, and he was but a single victory shy of finishing an aggregate 300 games above .500 for his 24-year career.

Three Hall of Fame players graced the squad.

Mr. Cub, Ernie Banks, though at the end of his career, managed to hammer no less than 78 home runs and knock in 184 runs between 1967 and 1969. (When his battered knees gave way in 1970, his place at 1B was ably taken by Jim Hickman. "Hick" drilled 32 taters and sent home 115 tallies in that all-star season.)

Leftfielder Billy Williams played in all but nine games during the six-year run. Inducted into Cooperstown in 1987, sweet-swinging Billy batted .302, averaging 33 home runs and 104 RBI over the span. He led the league in hits and runs in 1970 and added a batting title two years later.

Ferguson Jenkins, a 1991 inductee, averaged better than 21 wins a campaign from 1967–1972, never failing to post at least 20 triumphs. Jenkins, the 1971 Cy Young Award winner, threw two dozen shutouts over those years and led the league in complete games in three of the seasons. He paced the loop in wins, strikeouts, and innings pitched once each. Fergie logged more than 300 innings four different times and registered an ERA of under 3.00 on three occasions. He posted a 2.99 ERA for those six years, a genuinely remarkable feat, considering that roughly half his starts were in hitter-happy Wrigley Field.

And there was one likely future Hall of Famer on the team.

Perennial all-star third baseman, Ron Santo, averaged 25 homers and

99 RBIs over the six-year stretch. Never playing in less than 154 games from 1967 through 1971, the diabetic slugger hit .300 and led the loop in walks twice in those six seasons. Defensively excellent with five Gold Gloves, he led NL third sackers infielding in 1968, posting a .971 mark.

Though not yet inducted, Santo was, without doubt, a Cooperstown caliber player. He appeared in nine all-star games during his 15-year career. Just a notch below the legendary Brooks Robinson with the glove, Santo was a far better offensive performer. He totaled 342 homers, driving in better than 1,300 runs over his career. He hammered 30 or more homers, hit the century mark in RBIs, and led the league in walks four times each. Twice he was the slugging champion and once he led the league in three-baggers.

Inexplicably overlooked thus far, Santo is almost certain to be inducted eventually. In fact, his case is so compelling that ranking baseball scholar Bill James, whose the *Politics of Glory* tome is the definitive book on the Hall of Fame, claims that Santo is the best player not currently in Cooperstown.

But there is still more.

Four additional players made a total of 11 all-star appearances for the Cubs over the 1967–1972 span, a combined 9 of them by stalwart 2B Glenn Beckert and SS Don Kessinger. That keystone combo, along with Santo at third, were clearly the best at their infield positions over the period.

In short, the team was loaded with talent. Twice it sent five players to the all-star game in a single season. In fateful 1969, the entire infield plus durable catcher Randy Hundley went. Moreover, pitching all-star Ferguson Jenkins was not their only mound ace. Bill Hands averaged better than 15 wins per season during his five campaigns as a full-time starter (notching 20 in 1969), and lefty Ken Holtzman posted two 17-win years, going 63-53 as Chicago's number 3 hurler from 1967 through 1971. Holtzman also threw two no-hitters during those seasons. And there was reliever Phil Regan who twice won in double digits and led the league in saves in 1968.

A team with such a glittering collection of personnel that could fall short of at least one divisional flag is historically unprecedented in modern times. Between 1946 (the dawn of the postwar modern baseball era) and 1972, eight National League and five American League teams have had at least a trio of Hall of Famers playing major roles together for at least three consecutive seasons. Every one of those thirteen won at least one title, most more than one.

Every one but the Cubs.

• • •

Having looked at the Cubs, the following table compares the remaining twelve teams and their shining years, with their key players listed in the second column. Note that although each player listed may not have played throughout the entire period cited, each team did have at least three Hall of Famers playing regularly during the years noted.

NATIONAL LEAGUE

Team	Player	Accomplishments
St. Louis 1946–1953	Stan Musial Red Schoendienst Enos Slaughter	1 pennant in 1946, 8 straight winning seasons
Brooklyn 1948–1956	Jackie Robinson Duke Snider Pee Wee Reese Roy Campanella Walter Alston*	5 pennants, 1 world championship
Milwaukee 1954–1964	Hank Aaron Eddie Mathews Warren Spahn	2 pennants, 1 world championship, 5 second places
San Francisco 1962–1971	Willie Mays Orlando Cepeda Willie McCovey Juan Marichal Gaylord Perry	1 pennant, 1 division, 10 straight winning seasons
St. Louis 1967–1971	Lou Brock Bob Gibson Steve Carlton Orlando Cepeda	2 pennants 1 world championship
Cincinnati 1971	Pete Rose Joe Morgan Johnny Bench Tony Perez Sparky Anderson*	1 divisional title
Atlanta 1969–1970	Hank Aaron Orlando Cepeda Phil Niekro	1 divisional title

AMERICAN LEAGUE

Team	Players	Accomplishments
Cleveland 1948–1954	Lou Boudreau Bob Feller Bob Lemon Larry Doby Early Wynn Al Lopez*	2 pennants, 1 world championship, 6 ninety-win seasons
New York 1948–1963	Joe DiMaggio Mickey Mantle Whitey Ford Yogi Berra Phil Rizzuto Casey Stengel*	13 pennants, 9 world championships
Chicago 1958–1962	Nellie Fox Luis Aparicio Early Wynn Al Lopez*	1 pennant, 5 winning seasons
Baltimore 1963–1971	Brooks Robinson Luis Aparicio Robin Roberts Frank Robinson Jim Palmer Earl Weaver*	4 pennants 2 world championships
Oakland 1969–1972	Reggie Jackson Catfish Hunter Rollie Fingers Dick Williams*	2 divisions, 1 pennant, 1 world championship

*Manager

Clearly, some of these squads had far more daunting barriers to victory facing them than those of the Cubs. The Cleveland team of the early 1950s, and the go-go White Sox a few years later, had to fight off the mighty Yankee dynasty to post a flag. Moreover, the St. Louis Cardinals, from the late 1940s through the early 1950s, had to contend with the vaunted Brooklyn Dodgers, as did the Milwaukee Braves in 1957 and 1958.

If we count Santo as a future Cooperstown figure and push the bar up to four Hall of Famer players per team, only seven contingents other than the Cubs still qualify. All, however, won at least a pair of flags, and two of them—the Cincinnati Reds and Oakland A's—were just assembling their dynasties by 1972.

Tightening the entrance requirements to baseball elitism still further, by making the presence of a Hall of Fame manager a criterion, two more teams disappear, leaving just five teams other than the Bruins still qualifying.

Look at the consistent six-year record. The Hall of Famer performers. The all-stars. The picture is clear. The 1967–1972 Chicago Cubs were more than an outstanding team, they were the best team that didn't win.

Two

THE WILDERNESS

**Bert Wilson taught me to believe that even if you're
behind 16–0 with two outs in the 9th, there is still
a chance.**
Jim Langford, the legendary announcer's
optimism amid Cub futility

I grew up about an hour north of Milwaukee, cutting my baseball
teeth on the Milwaukee Braves. In 1953 my dad took me to County Stadium. We sat in the upper deck, where to my unaccustomed eyes every fly
ball looked initially like a home run. My in-person introduction to major
league baseball was a 3–2, 14-inning Milwaukee victory over (who else?)
the Chicago Cubs in the Braves' inaugural season in beertown. I was
hooked.

From then on, I strengthened my jaws by chewing bubble gum, committing to memory the statistics on the backs of the baseball cards that
came with the pink chew. I would hold forth for hours as my amazed peers
fired names at me, in hopes of unearthing some major league regular
whose batting average I might not know.

Although the Braves were the love of my life, they were heartbreak-
ers over those early years. They finished second to the hated Dodgers in
1953, came in third the following year, and then a distant second again in
Brooklyn's great 1955 season. That set up 1956, certainly the year of the
Braves.

It looked like a championship season for Milwaukee right into the final week of the season. Then disaster struck as my heroes stumbled in the last few games, coming in but a single agonizing game behind those same Brooklyn Bums.

My faith was rewarded during the glorious summer of 1957. With Elvis, Ricky Nelson, and Pat Boone dominating the pop music charts, and *The Adventures of Ozzie and Harriet* considered topflight television entertainment, the Milwaukee Braves marched to the pennant and a World Series victory over the seemingly omnipotent New York Yankees.

Then my baseball life changed.

A grade school classmate, Donny, who was a deeply devoted Cubs fan, began beseeching me to consider switching my rooting loyalty to the Cubs. He recited their glorious pre-1950 history and pointed to big days ahead with the team's acquisition of several veteran power hitters in addition to young Ernie Banks.

I was sorely tempted, as there were no more worlds to be conquered by the Braves. Moreover, I already enjoyed listening to the exciting play-by-play diamond descriptions of Cub announcer Jack Quinlan and reveled in watching the team's games on WGN television. The timing seemed right so I made the switch. Little did I realize I was joining a nationwide cult of long-suffering zealots, a group destined for decades of pain and disappointment.

A major reason Leo's Cubs are so memorable for baseball followers around the world is that they emerged from such depths. In fact, appreciating the excitement of those years necessitates knowing the length and intensity of the baseball drought that preceded it.

The Forties

During the war years of 1943 to 1945, baseball was hardly big league, with so many of the game's stars on the battlefield rather than the baseball diamond. Hence, when WWII ended, the 1946 season marked the real commencement of the modern baseball era.

Coming off the pennant of 1945, the Cubs' wanderings in baseball's wilderness began, lasting 21 very long years. From 1946 through 1966, the Cubs were indisputably the worst team in the National League. With the exception of the first year, 1946, when the team did finish third at 82-71, the Cubs were permanent, uninterrupted occupants of the league's second division, finishing seventh or worse 15 times. They turned in but one winning season after 1946 and were an aggregate 431 games under .500.

In 1947 the team dropped to a sixth-place 69-85 status. The 1948 cellar-dwelling season of 64-90 provided a sober indication of how far the little bears' fortunes had slipped. Stars were few. Phil Cavarretta was winding down, and neither Andy Pafko nor pitcher Johnny Schmitz was ticketed for superstardom. The 1948 offense was so impotent that when a scout wired Jolly Cholly Grimm—the 1945 pennant-winning skipper then in his fifth year at the throttle—"Spotted a pitcher who stopped a good team cold for nine innings. Only one ball hit out of the infield and that was a foul fly," the skipper allegedly wired back, "Forget the pitcher. Send the guy who hit the foul."

So disappointing was the Cubs' second straight losing season that after drawing over 1.2 million fans, owner P. K. Wrigley published an ad in the Chicago papers.

> TO CHICAGO CUBS FANS
>
> The Cub management wants you to know we appreciate the wonderful support you are giving the ball club. We want you fans and Charlie Grimm to have a team that can be up at the top—the kind of team that both of you deserve.
>
> We also know that this year's rebuilding job has been a flop. But we are not content—and never have been—to just go along with an eye on attendance only. We want a winner, just as you do, and we will do everything possible to get one. If one system does not work, we will try another. Your loyal support when we are down is a real incentive for us to try even harder to do everything in our power to give us all a winner.
>
> Thanks,
> The Chicago Cubs

Trying harder was not the answer. In 1949 the Cubs lay prone again in the National League, with a 61-93 mark. In June Grimm was headed upstairs for a vice presidency, and the old Gashouse Gang teammate of Leo Durocher, Frankie Frisch, was given the task of filling out the lineup cards. Grimm vanished from the organization before the opening of the 1950 campaign, owing to a lengthy feud with longtime General Manager (GM) Jim Gallagher.

The Fifties

Jim Langford, in his delightful book *The Game Is Never Over,* points out that the Cubs opened the new decade with the objective of building a strong farm system. As such, they hired Wid Matthews away from Dodger wizard Branch Rickey to take over personnel matters. Matthews proclaimed a Five-Year Plan, aimed at restoring Chicago's North-siders to glory. On the field, however, the 1950s opened ominously. While Pafko, burgeoning outfield star Hank Sauer, and shortstop Roy Smalley combined for 89 home runs and 280 RBIs, the club finished last in runs scored, posting a sorry 64-89 log. The team's top pitcher, Bob Rush, lost 20 games.

The 1951 season was another bomb, with the squad occupying the league's garden apartment owing to a 62-92 measure. Frisch's chips were cashed in midway though the 1951 campaign and hometown hero Phil Cavarretta was handed the baton. The following year, 1952, offered promise. Hank Sauer won the MVP award, smashing 37 round-trippers and delivering 121 RBIs. Bob Rush, Warren Hacker, and Paul Minner were a combined 46-31, as the team divided their 154 games evenly.

With slugging Ralph Kiner coming over from Pittsburgh to join Sauer, 1953 promised a return to "those glorious days of yesteryear," as the voiceover for the then popular *Lone Ranger* horse opera would enthusiastically intone each week. That promise was not kept. The team skidded into seventh place with a 65-89 record. While Kiner and Sauer bashed a combined 63 home runs, the pitching blew out again in 1954 under yet another new field general, Stan Hack, as the team went 64-90.

In 1955 hope was resurrected as a spindly 24-year-old shortstop, Ernie Banks, hit a whopping 44 home runs, and the Bruins climbed to a less disturbing 72-81. The optimism was short-lived. With big things expected of Banks, 1B Dee Fondy, and newly acquired Monte Irvin, Chicago's 1956 diamond fortunes headed southward with a last-place 60-94 campaign. Wid Matthews had now completed the seventh year of his Five-Year Plan, and he and Stan Hack's services were no longer desired.

New front-office chief John Holland and field manager Bob Scheffing did not prove to be the elixir, as 1957 brought more of the same. Despite Banks's 43 circuit shots and the 28 wins rung up by pitching youths Dick Drott and Moe Drabowsky, the Cubs won just 62 outings.

The 1958 season, however, provided reason for me to believe that I had made a prudent emotional investment in moving my rooting interests to the Cubs. Despite injuries to Drott and Drabowsky, a retooled Bruin team finished within 10 games of .500 at 72-82, in a season filled with power. Banks was the league MVP, clouting 47 homers and sending home 129 runners. The team led the league in home runs with 182. Five Cub sluggers delivered 20 or more dingers. Moreover, the Cubs broke out of the gate so quickly pennant talk lasted all the way into July. There was plenty of excitement as the team's attendance vaulted upward, falling just short of the million mark. Cub fortunes were clearly on the ascendancy, I reasoned. With a return to health by Drott and Drabowsky in 1959, the team was almost certain to leave the second division in the rearview mirror.

Another MVP season by Banks was the highlight of 1959. Though neither Drott nor Drabowsky reemerged, the team hit another 163 homers and the still young pitching staff placed in the middle of the league statistically, as the Cubs tied for fifth yet again, this time at a slightly improved 74-80.

With that, the 1950s were over. Despite times of great promise, reality suggested the decade had been a bust. Its stark nature is revealed in these numbers. The team went 672 and 866 (.437) over the ten years, with no winning seasons, two eighth and four seventh-place finishes in the eight-team league.

Despite my disappointment with the on-field misadventures of the Cubbies over those 1958 and 1959 seasons (while the Braves were going 92-62 and 86-70, with another pennant, might I add), my allegiance to the Bruins was sealed by the captivating style of Cub play-by-play radio announcer "Handsome" Jack Quinlan. No one rejoiced more passionately over a Chicago triumph, nor suffered more poignantly from a defeat. He was the Cub fan's perfect emotional companion during the journey through the wilderness.

When the 1958 minirenaissance contained a melange of early season come-from-behind victories, Quinlan luxuriated in these "Frank Merriwell finishes." After one stirring 9th-inning win, he observed that Cub fans "were walking into walls," resulting from the glorious shock into which their heroes had sent them. Moreover, if a Wrigley Field tilt went into extra innings, there were "going to be some late dinners around Chicago." Daily, he invited listeners, coast-to-coast, to tune in to Cub games on WGN radio, "a clear-channel station."

Quinlan would often employ somewhat understated sarcasm when the team would lapse into a baseball coma and lose dishearteningly.

A pitcher who had just been shelled—a frequent occurrence for a Cub hurler—would be described as having "left a little bit to be desired" on that particular day. If after having thrown a few quality innings, a pitcher got utterly bombed in say, the 5th, the moundsman was said to have done rather well before he "ran into a buzz saw in the 5th."

Moreover, Handsome Jack would make no secret of his despair or disgust when the team would fall on its own baseball sword and engender an excruciating defeat. Once, during an early 1960s 19-1 defeat at the hands of the even more inept New York Mets, Quinlan described a botched foul fly with emotionless disgust thusly: "There's a high foul pop up the first base line, the catcher and the first baseman are converging on it . . . the ball falls between them and they knock each other over."

I recall a Cub-Reds game in Crosley Field in which Frank Robinson came to the plate in the 9th with the game on the bases. It was truly the defining moment of the game. Either the Chicago reliever would retire the Cincy slugger and close out a nail-biting Cub win, or the Reds would bail one out at the Cubbies' expense. Quinlan verbally prepared the listener, sketching the scene with a drama befitting Alfred Hitchcock. I recall Quinlan's utter dismay when Robinson sent a rocket out of Crosley and into the Cincinnati night. Quinlan anticlimactically followed his high drama "And here's the pitch . . ." with an unforgettably cryptic, monotonic six-word sentence. "He swings and hits a home run." Not, "Robinson swings and hits a long drive, deep to left, way back . . ." No, just "He swings and hits a home run." It was uttered quickly, flatly, and dripping with disgust.

Quinlan's sidekick, Lou "Good Kid" Boudreau, was ever the halting yet obedient straight man. As much out of his element behind the mike as an ineloquent former player/manager can be, poor Lou would constantly park on certain phrases. Without exception, any player who delivered a two-bagger either stood up or slid into second "with a double to his credit." Lou's "Leadoff Man" pregame show was similarly littered with verbal ruts. The benediction for every guest was identical, "Continued success, my friend," Lou would say. Moreover, the departing guest was almost without fail then described to the listeners as a "fine gentleman," as in, "Our guest, ladies and gentlemen, has been Lee Walls, fine gentleman and rightfielder of the Chicago Cubs."

Seemingly timeless and eternal Jack Brickhouse handled the TV chores. No matter how incompetently the Cubs conducted themselves on the diamond, Brickhouse could find a silver lining. There was always something to feel good about. The Cubs were adjudged to have been merely "a day late and a dollar short," after one of their myriad defeats. Any Cub homer—often hit by Banks—no matter how meaningless, was celebrated with a high-pitched "Hey, hey, attaboy Ernie." If it was a game winner, you were almost certain to hear a falsetto "Oooowheee!!!"

For Brickhouse, no glass was less than half full. No opponent's lead was insurmountable, no game hopelessly out of reach, and unless mathematically eliminated, no amount of games behind the league-leading team totally expunged hope of the Cubs' seizing the pennant. Life was good. If one was thirsty, there was always Hamms, "the beer refreshing from the land of sky blue waters," and if money was needed, one need only call "friendly Bob Adams" at Household Finance.

When the Cubs would suddenly blow what appeared to be a certain lead, Brick would allow himself an "Oh, brother." Should perhaps that wholly unanticipated loss owe to an enemy round-tripper, turning triumph into sudden tragedy, TV Jack would simply utter, "What a revoltin' development."

Like Quinlan, Brick rooted openly for the Cubs. When the last batter in Don Cardwell's 1960 no-hitter hit a sinking liner in the direction of iron-footed leftfielder Walt Moryn, Jack's concern was undisguised. "Watch it . . . there's a drive on the line to left. C'mon Moose! He did it! He did it!" the shiny-faced communicator howled. Brickhouse also did the play-by-play for the Chicago Bears, teaming with legendary columnist Irv Kupcinet. On one occasion in which the often perpetually penalized, excessively aggressive Bears had forced its opponent into a punting situation, Jack wedged in a fan-based admonition in midplay. "There's the snap to the kicker," Brick announced, "let's don't be roughing the kicker now, guys, there's the boot. . . ."

Any Chicago victory was concluded by rendering the "happy totals"; a defeat, by reciting the "sad totals." In either case, the Cubs were not brought to the fans by WGN-TV, but on "good 'ol channel nine," and played their games at "beautiful Wrigley Field," which by itself likely drew more fans than the dreary baseball contingents that inhabited what Banks loved to refer to as the Friendly Confines.

Wrigley Field is the seamless web that ties the sorry past to the present. The almost unchanged cozy, pastoral setting has an even stronger grip on baseballdom now than in previous eras. "They say Cooperstown is the baseball shrine," says John Mutka of the *Gary Post-Tribune*, "but this is the baseball shrine."

Current star Jay Bell is struck by Wrigley. "It is much, much different from most ballparks in baseball. If you had to narrow it down to just a few, probably Wrigley Field, Fenway Park, and Yankee Stadium are the three that really stand out as having the ambience of what baseball really is.

"When you come to Wrigley Field and see the ivy on the walls, and the way the fans support their team—good or bad—it certainly exemplifies what baseball is all about."

Moreover, Wrigley is not really a stadium. "It is a true, pure ballpark," says FOX sportscaster Thom Brennaman. "From the press box (and upper deck), you can see the field, the stands, the city skyline, Lake Michigan, and the sailboats out on the water. What can be better than to watch a game at Wrigley Field? This is truly a ballpark, not a multipurpose stadium."

My parents took me on my first pilgrimage to the hallowed park in my baptismal season as a Cub fan, 1958. As my dad was driving east on Addison Avenue, I was looking for indicators that a major league stadium was proximal, such as a huge wraparound parking lot. Driving through a residential community, I was suddenly stunned to encounter the front wall of Wrigley Field situated directly on the corner of Chicago's Addison Avenue and Clark Street, a veritable baseball throw from nearby city homes. Rather than being surrounded by an enormous parking expanse in a lowly populated suburbanlike setting, its right-in-the-neighborhood location was no different from any other home or business building.

Clark Street intersects to the north with Waveland, a street that runs just outside the left-field wall, while Addison intersects east with Sheffield Avenue just outside the right-field wall. The old ballpark is such an integral part of the residential community that no less than 60 feet separates the back wall of the stadium to the steps of the brownstone residential building across Waveland Avenue.

It is also cozy inside. Wrigley Field is a simple two-decked structure, with 48 rows in the larger lower tier. In addition, it is less than 40 feet from the box seats to home plate. Hence, nearby fans are closer to the batter than the pitcher is. Moreover, the fans behind the first and third base dugouts are less than 30 feet from the respective bases.

The dugouts are simple brick enclaves, devoid of stainless steel and modern amenities. Six steps below field level, the view of the action from the dugout is faulty. A small water fountain, a bat rack, and steps going to the clubhouse separate the two wooden benches on which the players sit. The bat rack is a rather crude green wooden apparatus with slots. Rust spots peek through the green paint that covers almost everything.

The bullpens are in full view, down the left- and rightfield lines, positioned roughly midway between the bases and the walls. The foul lines are so close to the stands that fans can easily converse with players sitting on the bullpen bench or warming up on the sideline mound. In fact, they are less than 10 feet from a pitcher heating up in anticipation of entering the game. The foul territory all but disappears as one reaches the outfield walls, with almost no space between the yellow foul poles and the stands in the left- and right-field corners. About 60 feet from the leftfield foul line, the outfield wall juts in, as a catwalk gives way to bleachers. A similar bend in right gives the park a pleasing symmetrical look. In summer, the brown, brick, unpadded outfield walls are covered with freshly watered ivy in full bloom.

Towering above the centerfield bleachers is the old manually operated scoreboard, with a clock at the top. Above the clock is an American flag, with National League team pennants arranged according to current divisional standings immediately below.

Cub broadcaster Chip Caray captures the charm of the baseball shrine well. "It is so different from every other ballpark. It's very intimate—the fans are on top of you—hence the term "Friendly Confines." What I like most is that it is a throwback park with no advertising, no signage inside. It's baseball in its most pure form. It says a lot that they when they build these new ballparks, the first place they come to is Wrigley Field, and the second, Fenway Park. They go to the retro ballparks first, not the new ones to find the prototypical baseball stadium. I hope there will never be another Wrigley Field. I hope it stays this way for a long time."

The Sixties

The adage, What goes around, comes around, applied to Cub skipper Charlie Grimm. Good 'ol Jolly Cholly was recycled for what figured to be a rousing 1960 campaign. With the team having gone 146-162 during the previous two seasons, Ernie Banks still in his prime, and the addition of a number of veterans, Quinlan, Brickhouse, and countless other Cubs fans—me included—just knew 1960 would be the breakthrough year.

The team broke *down* rather than *through,* however, finishing but a game in advance of the hapless Phillies at 60-94. Grimm's tenure lasted 17 (6-11) games, before "Good Kid" himself, Lou Boudreau, left Jack Quinlan's side in the broadcasting booth and headed for the dugout. A little arithmetic will tell you that he went a sorry 54 and 83 as head mentor. The pitching was the worst in the league, and after Banks, no Cub drove in more than 64 runs.

Right here, P. K. Wrigley came to the startling conclusion that the conventional role of manager was not one that had served the team well. Certainly one could say that the position had proved problematic, with seven occupants in ten years and nary a winner to show for those many personnel alterations. The cure, however, was truly Cublike—bizarre. Wrigley concluded that what the team needed was not a manager, a person in charge, but rather a "college of coaches."

The logic behind this head-scratching maneuver was that this collection of mentors would circulate throughout the entire Cub system and so offer uniform direction to Cub players and prospects at every level. The corollary to this notion was that it would speed the development of young players in the farm system, offering the Cubs much-needed big league help more rapidly. Terming this eight-man motley assemblage a college, perhaps Wrigley believed a higher level of intelligence would emerge.

It didn't.

Rather than being led more comprehensively, the team was without leadership. Ron Santo remembers it as a degrading experience. "We were the laughingstock of baseball. . . . When we stepped onto the field, you knew the other team was smirking . . . the club was so disorganized other professionals could sense it. It hurt," he wrote in his autobiography, *For Love of Ivy.*

A young man from Whistler, Alabama, named Billy Williams, did brighten 1961 with a Rookie-of-the-Year campaign. He and 21-year-old Ron Santo combined for 48 homers, while Banks and George Altman belted 56 more. But it did little good, as the pitching remained dormant and the team improved by but four games to 64-90.

The late Washington Redskins owner, Jack Kent Cooke, once said after a disappointing season that he had learned that "no matter how bad things get, they can always get worse." This is a truism Cub fans of the 1960s knew well. The two previous 90-loss campaigns were followed with an even more lifeless 59-103 mark in the expansion year of 1962. Only Casey Stengel's amazin' Mets were worse at a ghastly 40-120.

From 1957 to 1964 the desert wilderness was littered with painful mirages—illusions of hope. First there were the pitchers. Perhaps the most devastating of the pitching mirages showed up in the Cub desert in 1957. He was a 21-year-old right-hander from Cincinnati, named Dick Drott. Yearning for pitching, the Cubs handed young Drott the ball and he threw it very, very well. Fifteen wins against just 11 defeats to go with 170 strikeouts and a 3.58 ERA in 229 innings—all on a team that finished 62-92. Moreover, he punched out 15 first-place Braves on May 26, 1957, setting a Cub record. The next year he had a convenience store mark, 7-11, and a sore arm. Drott, who appeared as impressive as Tom Seaver did a decade later, won just five more games the rest of his career.

To make it even more cruel, rookie Drott was paired with another fuzzy-cheeked can't-miss hurler, Moe Drabowsky in 1957. Moe, having pitched but 50 innings in the bigs the previous year, went a near Drott-matching 13-15—with an even better 3.53 ERA. But that was it. Drabowsky registered a sad 17-22 over his next three seasons at Wrigley, with his ERA never lower than 4.51 before being unceremoniously dispatched to Milwaukee in 1961. He later resurfaced as a relief ace for the Baltimore Orioles in the mid-sixties.

The 1958 season provided another mirage. Glenn Hobbie, also a starboarder, went 42-39 and averaged 220 innings with an ERA consistently under 4.00 for three losing Cub squads between 1958 and 1960. Twice he won 16 games before he also broke down. Hobbie went just 20-42 during his remaining four seasons in the major leagues.

Also in 1958, the Cubs picked up lefty Taylor Phillips from the Milwaukee Braves. Given an opportunity to start, he tossed 170 innings and posted a 7-10 mark that, though mediocre, suggested better things to come. Phillips won only one more game in his big league career.

In 1959 the aforementioned Hobbie was paired with yet another righthander, Bob Anderson. In 1959 big Bob was 12-13, with a 4.13 ERA in 235 innings. Hobbie and Anderson were on the verge of helping Cub fans forget the Drott-Drabowsky heartaches of seasons previous. Anderson came back with a 9-11 log in 1960. He then won only nine more big league encounters and was out of baseball after the 1963 campaign.

There's more. In 1961 the Cubs featured a junkballing southpaw named Jackie Curtis. Throwing 180 innings for a 64-90 squad, Curtis contributed 10 wins against 13 defeats, one of which came after pitching brilliantly against Warren Spahn in the legendary lefty's 300th win. Curtis hurled just 99 more frames in the bigs and won only four more games after 1961.

Jackie Curtis was followed by "Cub phenom Calvin Koonce," as the broadcasters termed him. In dreadful 1962, Cal roared out the starting blocks and seemed virtually unbeatable in the early going. He finished 10-10, with a 3.97 ERA for a 59-103 Chicago team. Koonce then went 19-22 over the next five seasons for Chicago, never posting more than 7 wins in a single season.

As for the position players, easily the highest touted was a 17-year-old Irish bonus-baby named Danny Murphy. In a city so dominated by those of Irish descent that the Chicago River is still dyed green on St. Patrick's Day, a lad like Murphy excited many. So can't-miss was this young outfielder in 1960, the Cubs unveiled the adolescent at their first opportunity. Murphy did miss—immediately and completely—contributing just 23 hits in 130 big league at bats over that and the next several seasons. Nine years later Murphy tried to catch on as a hurler for the crosstown White Sox, but with similar lack of success.

Billy Cowan, a righthanded slugger with ostensibly great power and topflight defensive skills, was given the centerfield job in 1964. Cowan did smack 19 jacks, but drove in only 50 runs in over 500 plate appearances. Moreover, the youngster fanned 128 times while drawing but 18 bases on balls. Cowan was out of Chicago by 1965 and never again got more than 174 at bats in a big league season.

If Dick Drott is one bookend, then Ken Hubbs is the other. Hubbs, the National League Rookie of the Year at just 20 years old in the otherwise grim 1962, handled 418 errorless chances over 78 straight games, both major league records at the time. He hit .260 in his first campaign. By the end of the following season, Hubbs was established as a coming star in the Cubs infield.

He was dead before the opening of spring training in 1964.

Hubbs's plane crashed in the ice near Provo, Utah. Ironically, and sadly, he had gotten his pilot's license in an attempt to overcome a flying phobia.

Just as the wilderness journey seemed the bleakest, an oasis arrived. The 1963 Cubs, on the strength of the league's second-ranked pitching staff, improved by 23 games over calamitous 1962, turning in an 82-80 season under burly Head Coach Bob Kennedy. While lefty Dick Ellsworth won 22 and lost only 10, and Lindy McDaniel paced the league in saves, Santo and Williams were making their mark as rising stars for an oncoming team.

Despite the overall success of the team, however, infielders Andre Rodgers (SS), Ron Santo (3B), and Ken Hubbs (2B) combined for an unconscionable 83 errors, plaguing the pitching staff.

In any case, the 1964 season couldn't come soon enough for Cub followers. It did come, and it went too—76-86, good for a disappointing 8th-place finish.

Few baseball fans, let alone Cub backers, who remember the 1964 season will forget what is simply referred to as the Trade. Lou Brock for Ernie Broglio. Brock left to help lead the St. Louis Cardinals to a pennant that year and went on to total over 3,000 hits and 938 stolen bases in his career, eventually settling into Cooperstown immortality, while Broglio headed for obscurity. The Trade has forever been the barometer by which subsequent disastrous transactions are compared.

Curiously, at the time, it was considered a steal, except the Cubs were the bandits. At 25 years old, Brock had already been labeled a bust. By trade time in 1964, he had spent all or part of four years with the team. A leadoff man, Brock had never hit over .263, had not posted an on base percentage (OBP) even equal to the league average, nor had he hit over 9 home runs in a season. Broglio, seemingly in midcareer 28, had already posted a 21-win season and 18 gamer. Three times he had registered ERAs of 3.00 or under. When he came to Chicago with a career record of 70-55 over five-plus years with middling Cardinal teams, Cub fans rejoiced.

He also, apparently, came with a sore arm.

The Cub heist, then, was just another mirage. Broglio won just 7 games for Chicago and was out of the league by 1966.

Hoping that 1964 was a mere aberration after the previous year's banner campaign, better things were expected for 1965. Then the entire mood chilled because of an occurrence having nothing to do with the team's on-the-field exploits. On March 19, 1965, Jack Quinlan, lover of Notre Dame and the verbal soul of Cub fans nationwide, was killed in a car crash near Mesa, Arizona. Brickhouse cited Quinlan's singular brilliance when he wrote in his *Thanks for Listening* memoir, "If he had lived, Jack Quinlan, in my opinion, quite possibly would have established himself as the best sports announcer ever." Jack Quinlan was just 38 years old.

Brickhouse's television partner, Vince Lloyd, picked up the fallen microphone. He was good, very good, but he was not Jack Quinlan, and for many fans the Cub radio experience would never be the same.

Back on the field, the 1965 number was 72-90, another eighth-place occupancy. With that, the members of college of coaches faculty were granted the Cub version of emeritus status. When the lab closed on the collegial experiment, the final grades were 353 and 459, the won/lost totals, respectively.

Could it get worse? Cooke's words echo in Cub fans' mental ears. The sorry two-year backslide was followed by a 59-103 tenth place-brownout in 1966.

Through 1966 things had proven even more calamitous in the 1960s than in the abysmal previous decade. The team was 472-646 for those seven seasons, "good" for a measly .422 winning percentage. It never finished above seventh, and was eighth or worse four times.

There you have it. Twenty-one wretched years of wilderness wanderings, cruel mirages, second-division finishes, and just plain losses. Lifelong Cub fan Greg Yoder puts it well. "I started (as a Cub fan) in 1953. I got my hopes up every year and only to become disappointed, because they had some great players."

The final 21-year log reads 1420 triumphs and 1851 surrenders, a .434 success rate. By the end of 1966 the Cubs were no longer a team with a glorious tradition. They were baseball's lovable losers.

THE LION

Stick it in his ear!
Durocher to a pitcher, hollered from the
dugout, audible to the batter

After watching attendance dwindle to under 650,000 for the 1965 season and repeatedly accused of not caring about the fortunes of his team, the venerable owner P. K. Wrigley had had a bellyful. He was tired of coaching colleges and losing seasons. He wanted someone who truly knew the game and was willing to take charge.

The man he and GM John Holland settled on was Leo "the Lip" Durocher.

Leo Durocher had last managed a major league team in 1955 when he guided the New York Giants to an 80-74 third-place finish. That was fully 11 years previous, so long ago there was no longer a New York Giants baseball team.

So much had changed since then that 1955 seemed eons ago. On the national landscape, the Eisenhower years had given way to Kennedy's Camelot and then his assassination. The nation was no longer solely concerned with communism and Russia's military buildup. The United States also faced a growing civil rights movement—justifiably aggressive attempts at racial desegregation, a shift from innocence toward drug use and sexual experimentation among teenagers, as well as an ever-expanding war in Southeast Asia.

Baseball itself had undergone its own changes. It had seen Ruth's magic 60–home run number surpassed by a tormented Roger Maris in 1961, and irascible Ty Cobb's seasonal stolen base mark eclipsed by Dodger shortstop Maury Wills the following summer. Moreover, there had been a near complete changing of the superstar guard. Mickey Mantle, Eddie Mathews, Duke Snider, Ted Williams, Warren Spahn, and Stan Musial were either beginning to fade, fading, or gone. The era's main-stage performers now included Frank Robinson, Hank Aaron, Bob Gibson, Sandy Koufax, and Maury Wills.

Speed and the stolen base had increased in value with the advent of new larger parks, and with the exploits of Chicago's Go-Go White Sox in 1959, the Maury Wills-led Dodgers of the early 1960s, and of course the St. Louis Cardinals, led by now Cub nemesis Lou Brock. The Yankees were on the way down as both leagues were becoming more balanced. Further, the Milwaukee Braves were on the brink of extending baseball's reach into the South, and more important, the game had four new teams, owing to a brand-new phenomenon called expansion.

About the only baseball constant since 1955 was that the Cubs continued to lose.

Leo Durocher's baseball biography long predated even 1955. His playing career began with a cup of coffee in 1925 with the New York Yankees. By 1928 he was in the majors for good, appearing in his first of two World Series. From the legendary Ruth-Gehrig Yankees he moved to Cincinnati and then on to St. Louis as the shortstop for the famous 1934 Gashouse Gang. A banjo hitter though a slick fielder, the 5 foot 10 inch, 160-pound Durocher was named to three all-star squads in a playing career that lasted until 1945.

Durocher's first managerial endeavor involved the then Brooklyn Dodgers back in 1939. As player-manager, his team won 84 of 153 games. Two years later the beloved bums won 100 games and a pennant, followed by a 4-out-of-5 World Series victory. By the end of the 1946 season, Durocher had managed winning teams in seven of his first eight big league seasons, finishing third or better in each of those winning campaigns.

Out of baseball in 1947 and fired by the Dodgers the following season, Durocher moved across town to lead the hated New York Giants. In seven full campaigns there, he turned in five more .500-plus seasons, two pennants, and another World Series title.

Player or manager, Leo Durocher was a stone winner.

He was also many other things.

There are few personalities in baseball history about which more has been written and less truly known than that of Leo Ernest Durocher. Most writing about Leo is far more descriptive than analytical, driven by either the writer's admiration or more likely contempt for him, rather than by an effort to understand.

Coming into the world on the kitchen table of a wooden home in West Springfield, Massachusetts—90 miles from Boston—on July 27, 1905, Durocher was the incarnation of the classic underdog, a status he seemed to be subconsciously driven by as he battled his way through life.

His spiritual life was cyclical. It started as an altar boy at St. Louis de France Church and finished with a spiritual awakening in his closing years in Palm Springs, California, where he returned to the church and the confessional, sincerely seeking spiritual counsel to overcome a lifelong habit of swearing.

Claiming poverty so severe that he "never had a Christmas tree," Leo came to love the grand old game early. Constantly toting a glove, Durocher idolized another diminutive shortstop, Rabbit Maranville of the Boston Braves, and sought to play catch with anyone who would engage him. When not tossing a baseball, young Leo tossed marbles. It was likely his first encounter with gambling, a near lifelong addiction for Durocher.

According to Gerald Eskenazi's definitive biography, *The Lip,* by age 12, marble throwing gave way to pool hustling. Leo worked the local pool halls with estimable success as a teenager. Rarely doing conventional work, he would borrow several dollars and then run his winnings upward to pay off the debt, only to lose his own winnings in an impulsive desire for continued action. He attained local celebrity status as a top-notch player at Winterborn's, a loud, foul, alcohol-laden hangout where the top players matched skills. As for school, according to Durocher's somewhat fictional autobiography, he was on the verge of gaining a baseball scholarship to Holy Cross, but his secondary educational career ended after having hit a teacher. In reality, there is no record of Durocher ever attending high school.

Durocher clearly suffered from a severely addictive personality, a major key to understanding so many of his often self-destructive antics. Early on, the addictive pattern was set. Education and reflection had given way to gambling and action.

Durocher's gambling addiction ruled him well into his sixties. According to Lynn Walker Goldblatt, it cost Durocher his 12-year marriage to her. Having left Leo for good in 1981, she is quoted by the late Rick Talley in *The Cubs of '69* as saying, "It was a disease with him. Leo was a degenerate gambler."

Durocher's gambling took many forms—pool hustling, dice rolling, card playing, horse betting, and possibly baseball betting. Though never indicted nor publicly implicated, Durocher was investigated for gambling by the commissioner's office during Bowie Kuhn's tenure. According to Talley, Leo had reportedly won $60,000 betting against the Cubs in a September 9, 1969 game against the Mets. Moreover, he had sent his ace, Ferguson Jenkins, to the hill on just two days rest and then let him hit for himself in the 5th, with the Cubs already down 6-1.

Though this dubious managerial strategy was hardly grounds for nailing Durocher with a treasonous gambling rap, his gambling addiction and its related associations were a troubling cloud under which Leo labored throughout his baseball life. Durocher had made a career of keeping public company with unsavory characters, a practice that cost him a yearlong suspension as far back as 1947 and was likely the reason the FBI kept a file on him. Moreover, he navigated in and out of trouble with legendary Branch Rickey because of his penchant for high-stakes clubhouse card playing and other similarly questionable behaviors.

Joyous as it is, gamblers are not addicted to winning. They are addicted to action. Life on the edge. This need for risk-taking action—courting disaster—was a major element of Durocher's personality. There is no better evidence than in Leo's constantly empty pockets. He lived on the brink financially. Despite hefty salaries, throughout his adult life, Durocher was always broke, endlessly borrowing money to pay off gambling debts to keep in the action.

Adventurous sex was another apparent high for Leo, who bragged about his conquests. Openly adulterous throughout his marriages, he was charged by Ray Hendricks as a corespondent in Hendricks's divorce from Laraine Day. In 1964 a Middlebury, Vermont, man charged Leo—then already 58—with alienation of affection, claiming Durocher had stolen his wife while dating the man's 26-year-old daughter. Well into his sixties, with the wedding cake of his marriage to Goldblatt hardly sampled, Durocher— according to Ken Holtzman by way of Talley—took up with a Montreal usherette for a one-night stand. Approaching 72, while living with a woman nearly 40 years his junior, Leo had a penile implant in an effort to sustain his sexual performance.

This risk-taking and action-seeking streak expressed itself in other ways. Pugnacious to a point of fault, fines and suspensions were familiar experiences to Durocher. Moreover, Leo did not limit his brawling to the baseball diamond. On three occasions, he was charged by fans with assault and battery. When once accused of stealing Babe Ruth's watch, Durocher denied it, claiming, "If I had wanted Babe's watch, he would have given it to me." No one has raised the more likely scenario that Durocher did in fact pilfer the Bambino's watch not for material gain, but for the sheer excitement and drama such a caper would bring.

Extremely impulsive, Durocher provided a telling insight into his personality when he wrote in his autobiography, *Nice Guys Finish Last,* that among the cardinal tenets by which he lived was "If you feel like doing it, do it, and it will all come out right in the end."

This addictive, adrenaline-seeking streak accounts for much of Durocher's robust managing style. Durocher was renowned for his take-no-prisoners approach to the game. Leo "came to kill you," as he loved to put it. "If I were playing third base and my mother was rounding third with the run that was going to beat us, I would trip her," bragged Durocher. Hitting-and-running, base-stealing, scuffing a baseball, falling on top of a sliding runner to prevent him from taking an additional base were all maneuvers Leo reveled in.

So enamored of action-driven baseball was Durocher, he openly charged that it was largely Dodger manager Walter Alston's conservative approach to the game that cost Los Angeles the 1962 pennant. At that time the team's undermining third-base coach, Durocher boasted of ignoring Alston's take signs and turning hitters loose, disregarding bunt messages and flashing the hit-and-run directive. As for Alston's tendency to quell the Dodgers' Wills-driven running game, Durocher had this to say. "Forget the signs. Speed overcomes everything. Let them run."

In fact, one of Durocher's biggest complaints during his tenure with the Cubs was that their personnel did not favor the high-action running game he so enjoyed. "Right in the middle of the lineup, I had two men who couldn't run. Santo and Banks," noted Leo. Though he could hardly gamble in playing style, he showed his daring with bold personnel moves early, going with youngsters like Don Kessinger, Bill Hands, Kenny Holtzman, Ferguson Jenkins, Adolfo Phillips, and Randy Hundley, while later taking chances on veterans with checkered pasts like Milt Pappas and Joe Pepitone.

Moreover, the skipper's addictive bent often gave way to impulsivity and impatience. By the time he came to Chicago, he no longer possessed the measured approach he employed in bringing along Willie Mays 15 years earlier. "Leo had always been impatient, especially with young players," wrote Ferguson Jenkins in his book *Like Nobody Else.* "He could never wait for them to mature, which is why so few of them made good with the [Cub] team while he was managing it. I recall his berating Bill

Stoneman, who was with us in 1967 and 1968 before he went on to become a fine pitcher at Montreal. Leo would yell at Stoneman, 'I didn't bring you up to the big leagues to throw a curve ball. Throw your fastball. We're not paying you to throw that junk.' Later, with Montreal, Stoneman threw one of the best breaking pitches in the game."

Durocher gave the envelope an additional shove by feuding with the popular broadcaster Jack Brickhouse; by disrespecting radio color man Lou Boudreau who hosted Leo's pregame show "Durocher in the Dugout" throughout the Lip's Chicago tenure; and by infuriating beat writers with insults, refusals to talk, and lies about who his starter on a given day might be. "I felt he went out of his way to slight me and the rest of the broadcasters and sportswriters who covered his exploits daily," pointed out Brickhouse.

The research on addictive personalities is replete with references to shaky self-esteem and emotional insecurity. Despite cunning attempts at bravado and daring, Durocher tipped the shaky side of his less than secure psychological hand in a number of other ways. Close associates claim he never spoke about his childhood, suggesting the experience was characterized more by emotional pain and deprivation than pool-hustling glories. Further, he concealed his insecurities under a facade of braggadocio. Hence, on the rare occasions when Leo did speak of his childhood, he did so in the form of embroidering events in self-congratulatory ways or of spinning self-glorifying tales that had no possible basis in fact.

As one prime example, Eskenazi cites Leo's fable about having an opportunity for a college scholarship when there is no record that he ever attended high school. Another is Durocher's claim of once having ice-skated 90 miles to Boston and back on the Connecticut River, which would have been a truly Olympian feat inasmuch as the Connecticut River did not go in that direction.

Leo rarely saw a microphone or camera he didn't like. Jack Brickhouse put it well: "He was very quotable and at times probably didn't let the facts stand in the way of an otherwise good story."

Indeed Durocher often went well beyond exaggeration. Legendary baseball columnist Jerome Holtzman referred to Durocher as a "pathological liar." Hall-of-Fame umpire Jocko Conlan told the *Tribune*'s Dave Condon, "I've got to give Durocher credit for being great. He could have been one of the all-time greats. My gripe with Leo was that he just wasn't truthful. No sir, Leo wasn't truthful."

Moreover, the little man from West Springfield could not abide anything other than being the center of attention. He fed this insatiable craving by saying and doing outrageous, attention-getting things. Writer Tom Meany tells the famous story of Leo's first spring-training trip in 1926 as a Yankee prospect. The flashily clad Durocher took a seat in the veterans' poker game aboard a Pullman train.

"What's the name, keed?" queried the Babe himself.

"Leo Durocher," the 20-year-old replied.

"It was our first introduction to this rookie shortstop," Meany recounted later, "but so help me, Durocher wasn't in that poker game more than five minutes before he was telling the Babe how to run it."

The need for center stage compelled Leo to constantly demean the one player whose Chicago profile was always larger than his own—Ernie Banks. Whether in interviews at the time or in the derisive "Mr. Cub" section of Durocher's book, these attempts are generally regarded as thinly disguised examples of Leo's jealousy of #14's greater celebrity.

"He disliked Ernie from the go. It was just that Ernie was too big a name in Chicago to suit Durocher," claimed Brickhouse. Brickhouse recounts a game at the end of Banks's career when Leo humiliated him by letting him hit against a tough, side-arming right-hander, only to pinchhit a fellow right-handed batsman, Jim Hickman, for him later when a southpaw took the hill. Wrote Brickhouse, "Hickman told me later it was one of the toughest things he ever had to do."

Durocher was "a bald man with a rasping voice and cold blue eyes," according to Ferguson Jenkins. Leo, however, had a thirst for elegance. He luxuriated in wearing expensive, tightly tailored suits. He regularly placed his baseball cap on a hat blocker, citing the need "to look professional." Then traveling secretary Blake Cullen shed light on Durocher's megadose of vanity, telling Talley, "Leo took care of himself. He went to the Mayo Clinic every year. He dressed like a million bucks. He was the only guy I ever knew who carried spare teeth. He had these two false front teeth and he always carried two spares in this little jeweled cuff link box, just in case somebody took a swing at him and knocked out his teeth."

When the attention turned negative, however, Leo's epidermal layer became paper-thin. While his acrimonious relations with writers is public record, he could be incredibly cruel even to fans. A colleague of mine heard Leo on a radio call-in show and related to me what happened when a fan sought to critique the skipper.

When the host tried to cut the caller off, Leo snookered the unsuspecting soul. "Let the man speak, give him his say," Leo encouraged the host, feigning graciousness. When the fan had completed his uncomplimentary review of the manager, Leo asked the fan what he did for a living and how much he made. When the caller took the bait, replying with a rather conventional occupation and compensation to match, Durocher had him in his sights. "Is that all?" the lion roared. "I wouldn't walk around the block for that kind of money! Look, pal, they'll never have to do any benefits for me."

Durocher's hunger for an elite social status extended to the vicarious. He never tired of name-dropping. His penchant for publicly referring to his friend "Frank," although few can recall Sinatra ever reciprocating, smacked of a pathetic, adolescentlike attempt to impress rather than of a description of a peer relationship. Beyond Sinatra, Durocher made certain all in earshot knew he lived with then famous actor George Raft during one of his early but not infrequent baseball sabbaticals.

His in-your-face verbal style earned him the moniker "the Lip." His feuds and confrontations with umpires are a part of baseball lore. In fact, few mementos meant more to Leo than renowned artist Leroy Neiman's portrait of him, jawing with an umpire.

Durocher displayed a devastating wit in getting the last word with an arbiter. No one enjoyed telling stories of his disputes with umpires more than the Lip himself, and there were plenty to choose from.

In one instance, George Magerkurth, a hulking umpire who chewed tobacco, got into it with Durocher, and in his zeal to make a point, inadvertently splattered some of his chaw on Leo.

Durocher spit back.

"That'll cost you, Durocher, you spit on me," asserted Magerkurth.

"What do you think this is, all over my face," bellowed Durocher, "smallpox?"

"My spitting was an accident," the umpire stated firmly.

"Mine wasn't," barked Leo, ever getting the edge.

In another imbroglio, the skipper roared out of the dugout to confront the great Beans Reardon over a tight call, and while deliberately kicking lime on Reardon's pants, demanded, "Was that ball fair or foul?"

"I guess it was a fair ball," answered the umpire.

"You guess? You guess!" barked Durocher. He then strutted away mouthing some uncomplimentary remarks about Reardon's ancestry.

Taking the bait, Beans chased after Leo and challenged, "Just what's that you called me?"

The Lip then sprung the trap, replying in a condescendingly sweet tone, "Well, guess what I called you, Beans. You've spent the whole afternoon guessing at everything else."

The unvarnished reality is that under all the smoke and fire, Leo

Durocher was hardly a complex entity. He was a basically insecure, embattled little man who emerged from a less than stable childhood with a variety of addictive needs. Charged by some as being amoral—calculating every act solely in terms of what would most benefit to him rather than conforming to more noble standards—Durocher's self-centered behavior seems much more motivated from the fears and insecurities inevitably arising from a highly addictive personality and need to survive.

That survivalistic orientation made him a user, and even abuser, of others. Myriad players—from Cal Koonce to Adolfo Phillips, from Bill Stoneman to Ted Abernathy—had the experience of being lauded by Leo at one point, only to be scorned when they could no longer perform, according to his arbitrary judgment. "What have you done for me lately?" could easily have been the diminutive skipper's epitaph.

Leo was nonetheless blessed with a strongly intuitive sense and an incredible survival-driven resourcefulness on which he relied to mask his many character defects behind his colorful, controversial and bold exterior. And it was this cunning, this skill to maneuver and manipulate, that propelled Durocher to the forefront of baseball managers in his time.

His was a precomputer, prestatistical era, a period during which the truly effective field leaders were gut managers, men with well-honed instincts who had the daring to go with their hunches. No one had a better feel for the flow of a baseball game or the capacity of a given player than Leo. Moreover, his street smarts as well as his unwillingness to yield the p.r. throne to anyone under him served Leo well in keeping his players in line. Throughout his managerial career, Durocher did everything to ensure his superstardom. If a player's performance dwarfed him, as in the case of Willie Mays, Leo would take credit for developing him.

In raw baseball terms, Leo Durocher had several outstanding managerial attributes. First, he had a nose for talent. Leo does deserve substantial credit for identifying Mays as a coming star when Willie was but a struggling 20-year-old in 1951. And it was Durocher who sensed that an alcoholic outfielder, Dusty Rhodes, could play a pivotal role for his 1954 champion Giants.

It was Durocher again, recognizing the potential of Jackie Robinson, who openly resisted the prevailing racism of his day and supported Branch Rickey's "Great Experiment." Furthermore, although GM John Holland had a strong hand in acquiring much of the young talent mentioned, it was Durocher who had the ability to sniff out their true value and the resourcefulness to deploy them effectively.

Despite his polarizing personality, Durocher could charm and inspire or ride and drive when he wanted to. His charisma and presence—and reputation as a winner—could instill enthusiasm and elicit extra effort from many players. He had a street-level skill in transmitting to his players his own intensity to win. A stickler for fundamentals, Ron Santo recalls that team meetings under Durocher, though rarely called, were "usually because we weren't executing on fundamentals. Leo wasn't the kind of manager who would ride you if you were in a slump. But if you didn't hit the right cutoff man or execute a bunt, he'd be all over you."

Beyond that Leo was decisive. According to Santo, Leo asserted himself on the first day of spring training with these words. "I want all of you to know one thing: I am THE manager." He exuded certainty in running a game. Whether truly confident or not, Durocher was well-practiced in projecting an assured persona. It is likely, however, that for Durocher—given his lifelong commitment to the game and managerial success in it—the dugout was indeed his comfort zone. It was the one place in which his image as a successful leader was firmly established early on.

Finally, Durocher had sharp baseball intuitions. That sense for how a game was going and the gambler's bent to play those hunches set him apart. Hence, his aggressive, daring, often hunch-driven strategic maneuvers were frequently brilliant. Lean lefty Rich Nye, who at 55 still looks as if he could hurl an inning or two, remembers the already 60-year-old Durocher's diamond acumen. "He could still anticipate moves made by the opposition. He had no idea of how a given hitter performed historically against a certain pitcher. He managed by intuition and he was right most of the time."

To understand Leo's Chicago tenure, however, necessitates comprehending two very different Durochers. The Lip entered the Windy City younger than his 60 years, a vibrant, keen-eyed baseball opportunist. He exited simply an old man. The same daring man who in his early years shook the Cub organization to the core by importing, developing, and playing young talent was also the manager who after 1968 refused to give the ball to a young pitcher and who deployed the same position players in the same lineup spots not for days, or weeks, or months, but for seasons. He went from a lineup shaker who froze the opposition with the element of surprise to an entrenched, predictable, conservative manager who by 1970—in the face of a proven lack of success—would not budge from using the same batting lineup, same pitching rotation, and same bullpen roles year after disappointing year.

Durocher came to Chicago because he was a proven problem solver, a laser-eyed baseball man who could analyze a team's strengths and weaknesses instantly, capitalizing on the former and addressing the latter head-on. And he did exactly that the first several years of his stay. He turned over the roster, injected a harder, winning edge in his charges, filled the holes, and shifted the roles resourcefully. He was on top of things. Then he stopped managing. Problems went unsolved, and proactivity gave way to the previously noted passivity.

Age and the complaceny of increasing celebrity brought about a change after 1967. "When I arrived, Leo was already old, but still pretty sharp," says Nye, "but as things went on, he got distracted—1968 was a transition year. He was no longer putting forth the effort on a daily basis. His mind was no longer in the game. He wasn't getting pinch hitters or pitchers ready. He wasn't adjusting, utilizing his personnel. You see how teams win a World Series, having a guy on the bench ready to go in. In 1968 he'd let a player sit for weeks and then throw him into a crucial situation."

Moreover, Durocher began his Chicago sojourn welcoming the challenges of building a winner, encouraging, inspiring, and shaping his baseball personnel into victorious competitors. He left amid near open rebellion and alienation. The brash declarations of "I come to kill 'ya" and "Nice guys finish last" were replaced by nostalgic references to the "olden days" and bitter laments about the unmanageability of the modern players, "guys [who] are going to do their thing."

The Cub players were in awe of Durocher when he walked through Chicago's North Side baseball door, openly attempting to curry his favor. He left the game (actually in Houston in 1973) with players derisively mocking him and openly deriding his references to "Frank." From a man whose baseball acumen and fire turned the "lovable losers" into a respected baseball club, he became an often distant figure who would forget he gave a player the hit-and-run sign.

In sum, the game eventually did pass him by. He all but admitted as much in his book. "It isn't the game I used to know. In the first place, there are the players. They're a different breed. Everything has to be done their way. . . . You can't tell them what to do. They have to be consulted; they want to know why. Not how but why. The battle cry of today's player is, I don't have to."

Nonetheless, one thing was certain when P. K. Wrigley, after decades of defeat, looked for a way out of the baseball wilderness. Leo Durocher was indeed the man the Chicago Cubs needed to turn things around.

Four

SEEDS OF A TURNAROUND

**Leo's hiring in 1966 made complete sense. You could
see our ball club was coming together.**
Ron Santo

The Chicago baseball air was filled with anticipation. After the 1965
season, Leo Durocher joined the Impossible Missions Force, the group
that tried unsuccessfully to turn baseball's lovable losers into winners
again.

After eight painful years as a Cub fan, the thrill I felt upon hearing of
Durocher's hiring was nearly physiological. Suddenly the madness seemed
over. The Cubs were in the hands of a winner.

I wasn't the only one with that sensation.

"I was ecstatic," enthused Chicago's WSCR talk-show host Les Grobstein, 14 years old at the time. "Up to then, the Cubs were weird, management was strange, and we fans were sick and tired of finishing in the
second division."

Craig Lynch, whose character was immortalized in the stage play
"Bleacher Bums," had been all but weaned on the Cubs of the wilderness
years. "My first Wrigley Field experience was on May 15, 1955 when I was
6—a doubleheader with the New York Giants," recalls Lynch, who still
turns off any Cub broadcast in which his beloved Bruins are hopelessly in
arrears, before hearing the last out. "It was the era of Ernie Banks and Dee
Fondy. After the Cubs won the opener, my dad and I left in the fifth inning

of the second game, with the Cubs getting pasted. I listened to as many games as I could. The first year I listened was the last year for Bert Wilson as the play-by-play man. I can still remember his famous line, 'The ball game's not over till the last man is out.'"

Having become conditioned to disappointment, Lynch responded to Durocher's arrival with controlled excitement. "I was intrigued and filled with anticipation when Durocher arrived, because we were ready for something good to happen. But I was holding back. He hadn't been in baseball as a manager for better than 10 years."

That last point was the stickler for many. "Many fans didn't want Durocher," says legendary Chicago sportswriter and raconteur Bill Gleason, recalling Leo's being regarded by some as a baseball dinosaur. The players, however, viewed Leo's entry as a potential turning point. "When we heard the word," recalls Cub immortal Billy Williams of Durocher's arrival, "we knew that Durocher was a good manager. He had been with the Giants and had been on NBC talking baseball."

From the midwinter luncheon on, Leo became a one-man marketing machine. He was wholly uncritical at the outset, praising the talent and potential of the squad. He wouldn't trade Billy Williams, who would hit for the cycle in St. Louis later that season, "for three Frank Robinsons," and he claimed southpaw Dick Ellsworth (who would be traded after the season) was "the best left hander in baseball after Sandy Koufax." Upon meeting Ron Santo, Leo said, "I know you're the captain of this team. You can continue to be the captain. You're my kind of player. I've watched you for some time and I just want you to know that you're my man."

Durocher was particularly conscious of how he was working the sensitive Santo. "The kid never had anything but good to say about me. . . . He became my biggest booster in the clubhouse," Leo later wrote. "For my part, I made him my field captain to try to instill more confidence in him."

The manager was especially fond of several young players on the team. Pointing out the organization's reputation for failing to hang on to developing young players—an uncamouflaged slap at the denizens of the front office—he indicated he would make this raw material perform.

Durocher would focus on fundamentals, mental sharpness, and the honing of a keen desire to win. No move forward was too small to take, the manager asserted. When the organization picked up light-hitting Ty Cline, hardly a cornerstone on which to build a juggernaut, Durocher defended the move, pointing out that any improvement was worthwhile because it was another step toward winning.

Having skidded from 82 wins in 1963 down to an eighth-place 72 in

1965, Durocher was undaunted by the team's regression. According to Santo, Leo pointed out to the players that winning and losing were both habits, telling the players, "Right now you are in a losing habit. We need to get into a winning habit."

This, according to Jenkins, was Durocher's objective. "I've got to get these guys to believe in themselves," he recalls Leo saying. "It's going to take more than a year. First they have to begin believing that they can win. Then they have to go out on the field knowing that they're going to win, that they're the better club on the field. What has been beating this club is simple—stupid mistakes and a lack of confidence. I'm here to get rid of the mental mistakes and get twenty-five men believing they will win."

The players loved it. Here was a living, breathing nationally famous baseball dynamo, willingly committing himself to them and their mutual success. The hustle was evident as Leo himself hammered hot ground balls at his infielders. And he was in charge. "When asked what his title was, I remember Durocher saying, 'I'm giving myself the title of manager,'" recalls hard-core Cub fan Grobstein.

Santo felt energized. He noted that "from the first day with Leo as manager, we didn't feel like losers any more."

"We knew Mr. Wrigley wanted him to come in because he said the ball club had a country club atmosphere," says Billy Williams, looking back three decades later. "He wanted somebody to come in and put the hammer down and say, 'Let's play baseball, and let's do a good job, and let's give a hundred percent every day.' Mr. Wrigley knew Leo would come and be the man. He would get everybody playing to the best of their abilities."

Santo recalled Durocher's words. "What goes on on this field I am in charge of. Make no mistake. I am THE boss. You have any complaints, you come to me." Durocher's Vince Lombardi-like proclamations invigorated the eager Cubs. Wrote Santo, "When we stepped on the field with Leo as manager, we commanded respect. Leo was the kind you loved to have on your side, hated to have against you. He would protect his team, his hitters. Our pitchers would throw at someone if they threw at us. It was just automatic."

With the limelight focused on the club's strengths and a blind eye turned toward its deficiencies, hopes once again soared as the new season arrived. "This is no eighth-place team," Durocher allegedly crowed in the team's official roster book (although publicist Blake Cullen claims to have originated the quote). Opening Day could not come soon enough.

It came with the first of what seemed daily defeats. Los Angeles and San Francisco, which finished 1–2 in the National League in 1965, were the first opponents. The 1966 Cubs opened the season on the West Coast, only to have those same two teams visit Wrigley Field to help commence festivities in Chicago. From the opening loss—during which Durocher appeared to have flulike symptoms—to the end of the season, the Cubs never made an impact in the won-lost column.

They lost seven of their first eight games. The defeats to the Dodgers had to be especially galling, because Leo's former Los Angeles boss, GM Buzzy Bavasi, had dismissed him by claiming Durocher was too old and "the game had passed him by." Chicago was 10-24 by the last week in May, 20 games under .500 in early June, and closed the dreary campaign at 59 up and a whopping 103 down. They finished dead last.

Not eighth. Tenth.

It was a painful and humbling first year for Durocher. "In 1966 the pressroom in Wrigley Field was turned into a postgame bar," recounts columnist Gleason. "We'd sit around until nine-thirty, ten o'clock at night after some of those day games, and Durocher would be there with us. He was a very intelligent man. He was sort of lonely, he was out of his element. He was new and trying to get the feel of Chicago. He was there all through that 1966 season. Then, once he established himself, he rarely came up anymore. He didn't need us anymore. That was the kind of guy he was," recounts a chuckling Gleason.

"We had a terrible year," confesses catcher Randy Hundley, "trying to learn how Leo wanted us to play the game."

That year, and the previous wilderness wanderings, were difficult for Williams. "It was tough during the down times," Billy Williams recalls of those pre–free agency days. "We were always out of the race by August and the only thing you had to look forward to was the salary drive. You were out there inspired to play a great brand of baseball only because you knew if you played well and put up a lot of numbers, you were going to get a better contract next year."

Jenkins noted the team's long-standing reputation of being soft. "The Cubs were known as the 'good guys' of the league. We were the habitual last-place club, never the spoilers. We just showed up for games and if we lost, well, it really did not disturb us. The situation was seen to change, but in 1966 the 'good guys' reputation still hung over us. We did nothing to dispel it. We plodded along in last place, and, as always in a such a situation, during the latter part of the season, most of the players concentrated on hitting at least .270, and the pitchers tried to get above .500 in their won-lost record.

"We really did not have a bad team. We could stay with other clubs about seven innings. But all of a sudden in the eighth or ninth we would make a couple of errors or give up the long ball, and we would end up second best."

Durocher was surprised. "The fact of the matter is that while I hadn't thought the team was as good as I had been trying to convince the players it was, I hadn't thought it was that bad either."

The age issue, however, was curious. When the Cubs were facing a battery of defeats early in the season, a magazine article portrayed Durocher as old and beaten, making no small issue of his turning 60 in July. Leo had snookered the media again, and without their knowing it. Already 60, Durocher allowed a printed error early in his career indicating a 1906 nativity to stand.

Noted Santo, "Leo wasn't crazed during that difficult 1966 season when we lost all those games." He was too busy revamping the ball club, investing in the future with talented young players.

Durocher opened the season with just eight spots set. Santo, 26, and Williams, 28, were now in their prime. Banks at 35 still had a strong bat. Glenn Beckert, a promising 1965 rookie, was at second base. As for the pitching staff, the season opened with four veterans, right handers Larry Jackson and Bob Buhl, lefty Dick Ellsworth, and another young right hander, Calvin Koonce.

Although W's and L's are ultimately what count, a closer statistical look reveals that the team's 1966 performance wasn't quite as bad as the record indicated. There is a proven formula in the world of sabermetrics (the statistical analysis of baseball data) called the Pythagorean method, which measures to what extent a team's record is an accurate reflection of its quality.

It works like this. First, you simply square the number of runs a team and then the opponents' score (644 for the Cubs and 809 for their opponents when squared are 414,736 and 654,481, respectively). In the case of the Cubs, you divide the square of their runs by the sum of both squares (414,736 divided by 1,069,217) This yields a .388 percentage, which when multiplied by the number of games the team played (162) determines how many games the team actually should have won. For the 1966 Cubs, that number is 62.8, or rounded off, 63 predicted wins.

The Cubs won 4 fewer games (59) than the research formula would have predicted. For 1965 the formula indicates 71 wins, one less than the Cubs actually won.

The point is simply this. In reality, in 1966 the team won 13 fewer games than in 1965, whereas the research suggests they were actually only 8 games weaker. Compare the basic statistics of the two years and it's startling. The team was really stronger offensively in 1966 than the previous year.

BATTING COMPARISON

	Runs	Doubles	Triples	HR	SB	Bat Avg	Slugging	OB Pctg
1966	644	203	43	140	76	.254	.380	.315
1965	635	202	33	134	65	.238	.358	.309

From runs scored to on-base percentage, the numbers are better in pitiful 1966. Now let's look at pitching.

PITCHING COMPARISON

	Inn	Hits	H/GM	HR	BB	SO	H&W/GM	Runs	ERA	Saves
1966	1458	1513	9.3	184	479	908	12.5	809	4.33	24
1965	1472	1470	9.0	154	481	855	12.1	723	3.78	35

The problems in 1966 were more hits, more hits per game, more homers, more runners per game (H&W/GM), many more runs allowed, and an ERA half a point higher. But there's more and the clue is in the last column, SAVES. The 1965 squad racked up 11 more saves than their 1966 counterparts, indicating much greater bullpen strength and bearing out Jenkins's remark that things would fall apart late in the game. By separating the starters' numbers from those of the relievers, the story is told.

STARTERS

	W	L	Saves	PCT	INN	HITS	BB	SO	ERA
1966	33	59	7	.359	831	830	229	556	3.89
1965	48	56	3	.462	836	883	223	441	3.93

The numbers compare the top four pitchers from the two years. Look at it. The 1966 group, despite having a much lower winning percentage and 3 new starters, clearly outperformed the 1965 rotation, doing much better in preventing hits and delivering strikeouts, edging them in earned run average, with walks a wash.

Virtually the entire 1965 pitching edge was generated by two firemen, Lindy McDaniel and Ted Abernathy. Note their combined numbers.

MCDANIEL & ABERNATHY IN 1965

W	L	Saves	INN	HITS	BB	SO	ERA
9	12	33	265	228	103	196	2.55

Neither were available for 1966. McDaniel had been dealt to San Francisco, and Abernathy, after a woeful start (6.18 ERA), was sent packing to Atlanta at the end of May. Having no established reliever of note in 1966, Leo pressed starter Calvin Koonce into 40 appearances out of the pen. Despite their desultory record, the team was making progress. They were better offensively, and they were both younger and better in starting pitching. The 1966 drag factor was the bullpen.

Leo was definitely putting a team together.

Moving decisively, he essentially turned over half the position players. Twenty-three-year-old Don Kessinger had hit just .199 in 110 games over two previous seasons. Durocher played him, however, in 150 games, making him a fixture at shortstop, where he hit .274. Kessinger did see considerable action in 1965, but his .201 batting average had left him unproven. Randy Hundley, brought over from San Francisco in the Lindy McDaniel deal, was just 24 years old. He set a rookie record for games caught (149), having played in only eight games prior to 1966. Though hitting but .236, he cranked out 19 homers.

In the outfield, Adolfo Phillips, 24, who was acquired early in the season, played in 116 games, 60 more than his two-year major league total up to then. He contributed 16 round-trippers and a .348 on base percentage, 35 points above the league average. Another outfielder, Byron Browne, had played in just 4 big league games before 1966. Counted on to bring big power, he hit 16 of them out in 120 games but struck out 143 times in 419 at bats, while drawing just 40 walks. Durocher, not a patient man, wrote Browne off for 1967.

Three out of four isn't bad, but the pitching moves were even better. Southpaw Kenny Holtzman, only 20 years old, caught Leo's eye. Holtzman had pitched a total of four big league frames before Durocher had him hurling 221 innings in 1966. Starting 33 times, he went 11-16, with a promising 3.79 ERA. Bill Hands appeared to be a throw-in in the San Francisco deal. He had tossed just 6 innings in the bigs before Durocher went to work on him. Moving Hands from the bullpen to the rotation early in the season, Durocher started him 26 times in his 41 total appearances. Though his numbers were unimpressive—8-13 with a 4.58 ERA—the career of Bill Hands had finally taken root and was ready to bear fruit.

On April 21 GM John Holland made the most important deal during Leo's tenure. In a bold and risky transaction, he traded their ace starter, Larry Jackson, who had gone 24-11 for the club just two years previous in 1964, along with Bob Buhl, who posted a 51-51 log for the team during the past five seasons (during which the Cubs were a cumulative 70 games under .500) to Philadelphia. In exchange, the Cubs received utility out-fielder/first baseman John Herrnstein, centerfielder Adolfo Phillips, and a 22-year-old right-hander who had but 15 innings of big league experience. His name was Ferguson Arthur Jenkins.

On the face of it, the deal appeared as potentially disastrous as the Brock-for-Broglio travesty. It seemed the organization had tossed in the competitive towel for 1966—and perhaps their sanity as well—after starting the campaign so wretchedly. With Koonce in the pen, left-hander Dick Ellsworth was now the lone rotation holdover from 1965.

Durocher had obviously come to the conclusion that "the arrow was pointing downward," as he loved to put it, on the then departed hurlers' careers. And he was right. Though Jackson did win 41 games for the Phillies through 1968, he lost 43 and left baseball before the start of the 1969 season. Buhl won just six more major league games and was out of baseball a year after the deal. While Herrnstein was not long for the Cubs' world, the arrow was reversed for Adolfo Phillips—a factor from 1967 to 1969, and especially Jenkins.

Durocher, who never tired of using the pronoun "I," liked to infer that he was the driving force behind the team's transactions, letting one believe that Holland was a virtual handmaiden who simply did the paperwork on Leo's deals. Reading Durocher's autobiography, one would believe that Leo all but sat at the table, wheeling and dealing with other clubs'

GMs at off-season hot stove gatherings. Holland, a quiet, nondescript man who preferred the background, did little to quell Leo's less than subtle attempts at claiming hegemony. Nonetheless, it was Holland who pulled the trigger on the trades involving the reshaping of the team.

"After a certain time, Durocher would make trade recommendations," says Gleason, in asserting that Holland was the man. "Holland was criticized much too often," states Gleason. "He made some great deals. You think of Fergy Jenkins and Bill Hands—who became the number 2 pitcher—and they were Holland trades."

Gleason recalls that Durocher scarcely knew the elements of the Jenkins acquisition: "He was up in one of our sessions in the pressroom. This was marvelous because he would talk with us about everything. He said, 'Well, I just got the word that we got these two kids from the Phillies. One thing I know, the centerfielder can really fly. We also got a pitcher. I don't know what I'm going to do with him. I don't know if he's a starter or reliever.' And that was Fergy Jenkins."

Nevertheless, GM Holland and Durocher collaborated well, as there is little hint of friction between the two during Leo's tenure. Even if Holland had been the chief architect, Leo deserves major credit for implementing the personnel changes. Going so fully with youth as he did was a gutsy gamble on Durocher's part.

Jenkins paid near immediate dividends, hitting and pitching the Cubs to a victory over the Dodgers and Don Sutton just a few days after being acquired. Edgar Munzel, the beat writer for the *Sun-Times* noted Jenkins's contribution in glowing terms:

> A star was born at Wrigley Field Saturday. Ferguson Arthur Jenkins, a big rawboned pitcher the Cubs acquired in a deal with the Phillies Thursday, made a sensational debut as he led the Wrigleys to a 2-0 triumph over the Dodgers. Fergie, as he prefers to be called, was virtually a one-man gang. He not only won in relief with $5\frac{1}{3}$ innings of superb relief pitching, but also knocked in both runs with a homer and a single.

Jenkins appreciated the Lip's upbeat style. "Leo and I got along fine," Fergie stated. "Whenever I won, he would always be out to shake my hand, which as an acknowledgment of success, I was always happy to have. 'Good ballgame, Fergie, that's the way to pitch,' Leo would bark. If I got in trouble on the mound and looked like I needed help, Leo would march out there and size up the situation immediately. If I said confidently that I felt good, he would leave me in. If I seemed a little apprehensive, he would take me out. I learned to be positive with him and say, 'I feel great.' If I had made a mistake on a hitter, Leo would let me know right away. 'You're not thinking out there, Fergie,' he would say, 'you're not doing the things you should. You've got to concentrate a little more.'"

Leo used Jenkins 60 times in 1966, 48 of which were in relief. He was only 6-8 with 5 saves, but threw 182 innings and turned in an eye-catching 3.31 ERA. Jenkins would never be a relief pitcher again. That provides an interesting insight into Durocher's thinking. Clearly, he placed the importance of building a four-man starting rotation above everything else, moving both Hands and Jenkins out of the pen to do so. A 1965 starter he did not believe in, Cal Koonce, was left to do fire duty. Koonce was dispatched to the Mets early the following season. Interestingly, it was just this tendency to ignore the building of a quality bullpen that ultimately contributed to Durocher's undoing.

Phillips, who would prove enigmatic, was a sensitive young man, bubbling with talent. A run-in with the fiery Santo after the outfielder loafed after a ball provides insight into the two players' characters as well as into the club's now intense focus on turning around its baseball fortunes.

"What kind of play do you call that? Where do you come off walking after the ball?" rebuked the Cub captain. "What do you talk about?" the Panamanian responded. "Don't give me that language bit, you know what I mean," rejoined the angry Santo. "When you pull a trick like that, you're not just letting down Durocher. You're letting down 24 players on this club. We don't want guys like you here." "Go kiss yourself!" Phillips shot back.

With that Santo grabbed him, and the manager had to intervene.

The next day GM Holland called Durocher and told him Phillips had been in his office. "There were tears streaming down his face," Holland explained. "He says nobody here loves him."

The manager turned on his charm in a talk with Phillips, assuring him of his worth, but to little avail. "When he left," said Leo, "I knew I wasn't getting through to him." Phillips ended the season hitting an unsatisfying .260, with the Cubs hoping a breakthrough would occur the following summer.

Nonetheless, by the end of 1966 the seeds were planted. A 10-player nucleus was now there, 6 of which took root during seemingly calamitous 1966:

SS Don Kessinger
2B Glenn Beckert
LF Billy Williams

3B Ron Santo
1B Ernie Banks
CF Adolfo Phillips
C Randy Hundley
RH Ferguson Jenkins
RH Bill Hands
LH Ken Holtzman

And they were young. Of the ten, only two (Banks and Williams) had seen their 27th birthday, half were younger than 25.

Regrettably, the fans took little notice. A meager 635,891 paid to see the carnage, actually 6,530 down from 1965. Often the games were played in virtual secrecy. "It wasn't much fun," Williams remembers sharply. "Anytime you play a game, you like to play with a lot of people in the stands, cheering and inspiring you to do well. When I came here in 1959, Ernie Banks was hitting 40, 45 homers a year, but still there weren't many people coming to Wrigley Field."

Hard-core Cub follower Grobstein would do imaginary broadcasts at the park in 1966. "I would go to open areas in Wrigley Field with my tape recorder to do my play-by-plays, and there were many open areas. Just me and the pigeons," he recalls.

Rich Nye, up for a "cup of coffee in 1966," remembers the dearth of fan support. "In 1966 I remember a game with 420 fans," he recalls, "fewer fans than vendors. You wondered if they hadn't opened the gates yet."

The 103 defeats on the heels of so much preseason optimism was sharply painful for many fans of Chicago's North-siders. Grobstein tells of the abuse he received from school chums who were White Sox fans. "See, here comes Durocher, and the team is still last," they would taunt.

Understanding the Cubs/Sox divide is basic to comprehending Chicago sportsdom. "I have friends of my generation who have never been in Wrigley Field, whose children have never been and never intend to be. Even a World Series would not draw them," says razor-sharp septuagenarian Gleason.

"It's rigid—very deep and sociological," explains South-sider Gleason. "It's the difference between the South Side with the stockyards and heavy industry, and the light industry up on the North Side. There were no big manufacturing plants on the North Side like the steel mills, and there were more ethnic people on the South Side out to East Chicago, Whiting, and Gary, Indiana. The one thing Durocher did was call attention to the Cubs after people had all but ignored them. A good part of the Sox attendance in the fifties was from the North Side—Cub fans coming down because the Sox were in their ascendancy and rooting for them to get beat by the Yankees, Cleveland, or Detroit."

Even players experienced the divide. Former Sox and Cubs hurler Steve Trout, whose father, Dizzy, was a pitching standout with the White Sox, was raised in South Holland and spent many days and nights in the old Comiskey Park. "I grew up in White Sox park. I knew every tunnel, every part of that old stadium. I hardly knew the North Side existed," says Trout. Then before the 1983 season, after having spent the early part of his career with his beloved White Sox, the left-hander was traded to the Cubs. Some Cub fans held his tenure with the Sox against him. "I wasn't prepared for the hostility on the part of a couple of guys in the bleachers," he recalls. "I felt like an intruder."

Durocher, however, was strictly National League, and the Cubs gave him plenty to worry about. The 1966 season had proved an embarrassment. After munching unhappily on those words "This is no eighth-place team," in the preseason, all Leo would say about 1967 was, "We are not going to win the pennant."

"I cannot say that we felt optimistic about the future," wrote Jenkins. "We knew we were not going to sweep through the league the following season."

Williams, however, sensed change in the air. "Going into 1967, I felt good things were going to happen. We had young pitchers like Bill Hands and Kenny Holtzman, and Ernie Banks was still hitting."

Despite tentativity about the future, for Jenkins, life with Leo in 1966 was indeed a turning point. "We were getting used to each other, learning and adjusting to one another's habits. We were laying the groundwork for better team play, which we hoped would carry over into the next season. We were hoping we could build a winning atmosphere on a club that had been a loser for twenty years."

One thing was certain. It was a different team from the one representing Windy City baseball fortunes just a year before Leo came. *Total Baseball* presents year-by-year rosters for each team going back to 1871. For 1965 there are 20 players cited on the Cub roster. By 1967 15 of them were gone, most of whom were dispatched after Durocher had been named manager prior to the 1966 season. Only Kessinger, Beckert, Williams, Santo, and Banks (curiously, the first five slots in the batting order) remained.

Indeed, the Cubs had a new look going into 1967.

Five

THE RENAISSANCE

**One sign read "Flower Power and Cub Power." The whole
fan atmosphere became visual.**
Craig Lynch, commenting on 1967

Protest was in the air as the mood of the country was slowly taking a
negative turn toward the draining war in Vietnam. Long hair, love beads,
and peace signs were everywhere, serving as private codes for resistance
against the war and for support of civil rights at home. Incense, marijuana,
and draft cards were being burned by the alienated across the nation. The
youth culture, amid the agony of war abroad and civil insurrections at
home, was promoting brotherhood among races and nations.

> *C'mon, people, now smile on your brother; everybody get it
> together, try to love one another right now.*
> —*The Youngbloods*

It was 1967, the summer of love and war.

For the Cubs, the spring training mood was upbeat right from the
start. "The attitude in camp that year was tremendous, everybody working hard and feeling sure we were going to improve greatly," noted Fergie
Jenkins. "I could see the difference," echoed Ron Santo.

Cub fans, regardless of political persuasion, however, were not buying just yet. The 1966 brownout was quite enough to keep them from
anticipating great things from the denizens of the Friendly Confines. *Tribune* beat writer Ed Prell saw the Bruins coming in eighth in the 10-team

National League, with San Francisco beating out Pittsburgh and St. Louis for the flag.

In addition, he had specific words of caution for any unrealistically optimistic Cub fans. "Readers of the *Tribune* have been heartened by dispatches from Arizona noting a new spirit among the Cubs, who are under the expert guidance of Leo Durocher. If he leads the Cubs into eighth place, ahead of the Mets and Astros, no more can be expected. If the Cubs finish seventh, a baseball miracle will have been accomplished."

The big question for the opener against Philadelphia was whether Ken Holtzman or Ferguson Jenkins would get the call? For sure, however, Mr. Cub, despite efforts by the Lip to supplant him, would be in the starting lineup.

And Durocher had indeed tried to supplant him. "Durocher hated Ernie Banks," states Les Grobstein. "While for GM John Holland, Adolfo Phillips was the key man in the 1966 trade with the Phillies. For Leo, it was John Herrnstein. He hoped Herrnstein would force the old man out. Each saw Jenkins as a throw-in."

By spring of 1967 it was Herrnstein who was out, along with several other Durocher wannabes. The press loved it, openly rooting for Banks. "He hit .370 in exhibition games and despite everything that Leo Durocher, abetted by John Boccabella, could do, he [Banks] won the starting first baseman's job," wrote an admiring Bob Markus in the *Tribune*.

Markus and others noted that throughout spring training, rumors spread about other first base candidates, much of them likely initiated by Durocher himself. Nonetheless, as the team readied itself to head north, #14 occupied the first baseman position, much to the pleasure of fans and media alike, who hoped his stay was permanent.

"We hope so," wrote Markus unabashedly. "Ernie has never met a man he didn't like, and we've never met a man who didn't like Ernie."

Durocher, for his part, was generally upbeat and supportive of his team. He held a 40-minute meeting at the close of spring training praising the players' efforts. He told the team, "You are far and away in better physical condition than when the season started a year ago. You cut down on your mistakes. Your spirit was wonderful. But you've got to keep bearing down the way you did in Arizona."

Later, in a press conference, after being told that most experts tabbed his charges for 8th in the league, the doughty skipper took it personally and proclaimed defiantly, "I don't care where they pick me. When the bell rings, that's when it counts. I just hope all the players feel as good about the season coming up as I do."

The campaign opened with a bang as Ferguson Jenkins hurled a route-going 6-hit victory, 4-2, over the Phillies and their ace Jim Bunning before 16,462 Wrigley Field well-wishers on April 11.

Philadelphia opened the scoring with 2 in the 2nd. In the 5th, however, 31-year-old Dick Bertell—playing for Randy Hundley, who had a leg injury—hit a three-bagger to the right-field wall. Adolfo Phillips knocked him in with a double. In the 6th, Glenn Beckert singled and Billy Williams sent him to third on a base hit of his own. Ron Santo fanned. Then with a 3-2 count on Ernie Banks, Durocher showed his daring by sending the runners. Banks struck out, but Beckert scored after catcher Clay Dalrymple threw to second and Cookie Rojas's return heave to the plate was late and high, enabling Williams to advance to third. A bloop single by Lee Thomas then sent Billy home. Glenn Beckert's homer run in the 8th added another tally.

Fergie, with his father and (blind) mother present, had gotten word of his starting assignment just two days before Tuesday's Opening Day. He had been nervous. "I stayed up until one o'clock in the morning watching television, just sitting around trying to keep busy," confessed the Canadian pitcher.

Electricity indeed was in the air. The morning *Tribune* reported, "A few minutes after the finish, young Bill Wrigley (owner P. K. Wrigley's son) knocked at the door of Leo Durocher's office, which fronts on the walking area near the exit to Waveland Avenue. The manager peered through a peephole, which has been installed so he may decide who's in and who's out. Once inside the manager's quarters, Wrigley stuck out his hand and exclaimed: 'Bee-yoot-iful!'"

The Cubs were a .500 team after the next day's game, as the Phillies prevailed 5-4 in 11 on a wild pitch by reliever Bill Hands. This despite a Banks home run in front of the sparse crowd of 2,690.

The Cubs then won two more, gaining their third win on the strength of a 5-run 8th-inning outburst against the Pirates. It had taken the team 11 games to register three wins a year ago. "We're beating the Pirates at their own game," chortled Santo after the Cubs' show of power.

On April 16, the Bucs scored 4 in the 9th to defeat the North-siders 6-5. Ferguson Jenkins turned his ankle in the 7th, backing up a play, leading 5-1. Lefty John Upham, in his first major league appearance, gave up an infield single and took the loss after Joe Niekro, also making his big league debut, yielded a 2-run triple to Matty Alou.

The *Tribune* noted that Leo had gone with newcomers in the loss. He and pitching coach Joe Becker had been intrigued by Niekro, lefties

Upham and Rich Nye, and fellow rookie Tom Manville, the former three making the team. "Durocher does not coddle or protect his players," the paper reported. "He gives them full rein to do or die. He wants to find out the quickest way whether they have it."

The *Trib* went on to say that Durocher, piloting a squad of which little was expected, was in a rather advantageous everything-to-gain, nothing-to-lose circumstance. As such, he had the "luxury of letting these untried youngsters see it to the end, through thick or thin."

After a day of rain, the Cubs won number 4, downing Philadelphia on the road, 8-4. Adolfo Phillips victimized his old mates with a triple and a homer, as Kenny Holtzman went 6 innings, giving up only one earned run, after which Bill Hands worked three shutout frames. Following an off day, it was on to Shea Stadium in New York. There the Cubs lost 6-1, encountering an unknown rookie named Tom Seaver.

The auspicious start did not generate much turnstile action, as the Cubs returned to Wrigley Field for a date with Pittsburgh before a paltry 2,974. Ray Culp was trounced 6-1 by the Bucs, leveling the season mark at 4 and 4. Through eight games, Phillips was all the rage while Ron Santo slumped. "Cream will come to the top," stated hitting coach Pete Reiser. "It's just a matter of Ron regaining his rhythm. I think he's been overcautious at the plate."

Phillips, in an emotional funk the previous season, seemed like a different person. Durocher had sent the moody outfielder to Arizona during the winter telling coach Pete Reiser, "See what you can do about getting through to him. God knows I tried."

Leo claimed he saw the outfielder three times in winter league play that off-season. "I didn't say a word to Adolfo," he claimed. "I didn't suit up. I was just a visitor."

Leo had visions of Willie Mays, watching Phillips hit, field, and run the bases with zest. "Pete and Joey Amalfitano did a great job with him down there," said the skipper. "I don't know how they did it, but they did it. They loosened him up. They brought him out of his shell."

Santo, hearing glowing reports, was still skeptical after his confrontation over Phillips's low-energy effort in the outfield the previous season. Phillips, however, broke the ice. He came over to Santo in spring training and said, "You were right. I should have run after the ball. Anytime you think you should bawl me out, you do it."

Frozen out on Saturday, Ferguson Jenkins fanned 10 in flattening the Pirates in the snow and cold the following day 7-3. A three-run home run by 28-year-old rookie rightfielder Norm Gigon—his first major league hit—was the headliner. It was so cold in Chicago that Jenkins wrapped his hand around a hot water bottle in the dugout. "It made my hand sweat," said the Canadian, "and it got cold when I started pitching. So after the fourth inning, I just put on a glove to keep warm. This was picnic weather up home."

April ended with a 4-1 win at Houston on a three-run shot by Santo, his second. It was the first major league win for southpaw Rich Nye (1-1) who was sporting a 1.93 ERA. Such success was a heady experience for the youngster fresh off the Berkeley campus, where he had been only the number three hurler on the college staff.

"It was a fantasy," says Nye today. "I never really believed I had the ability to operate at that level. At the end of 1966 the team brought up three left-handers—Freddie Norman, Dave Dowling, and me. By 1967 I was the only one left. So with the team having only one other left-hander who stuck—Kenny Holtzman—I had time and opportunity."

The 8-6 Cubs were clearly not the same team as the 1966 contingent, which had closed April at 3-12. With Cincinnati leading the pack at 15-5, followed by St. Louis (9-6) and Pittsburgh (7-5), the 4th-place Chicagoans were but four games out.

Fans, like high schooler Grobstein, were elated. "It was just incredible from Opening Day—when Fergie Jenkins beat the Phillies—on. My tormenting Sox friends would say, 'They'll never stay up there, they'll never last.' I just wanted them to stay over .500 and be a winning team. I ditched class after class that spring to go to Wrigley Field."

Offensively, Lee Thomas was hitting .400, Billy Williams .352. Despite the Cubs as a team having an ERA of 2.88, there were again concerns about the relief corps. The starters had gone 7-2 with a 2.70 ERA. Fergie (3-0) and Kenny Holtzman (1-0) had hurled a combined 64 innings, posting a glittering 1.83 ERA. The firemen, however, were just 1-4, with a hefty 4.78 mark.

Pitching coach Joe Becker was pinning his relief hopes on one-time Bosox fireballer Dick Radatz, newly acquired from Cleveland where he was attempting to pull his career out of reverse. "I'm hoping—and keeping my fingers crossed—that Dick Radatz will go a long way toward solving the bullpen problem," stated the coach. "I've been delighted at the big guy's attitude. He is determined to make a comeback and is a willing worker."

Nye remembers Becker as a diligent coach. "His best contribution was his conditioning. He worked us out every day, and had us throwing every other day."

"Becker was an old catcher and he took no bull from anybody," says fellow former backstop Randy Hundley fondly. "He was with his pitchers all the time, and ran them every day."

"He constantly worked with pitchers on new stuff," relates Nye with a smile. "One day in 1967 he got me up in the bullpen during a game and said, 'I'm going to teach you a new pitch.' He slapped some vaseline on my wrist and told me to throw. I had absolutely no success. Several balls took off over the bullpen catcher's head and rolled toward home plate. The game actually had to be stopped to get the baseballs off the field. 'I guess the spitter won't be your pitch,' Becker said, and that was it."

Though Nye—ever the student of the game—respected Becker, he had a special allegiance to minor league instructor Freddie Martin, the man who later taught Bruce Sutter the split-fingered fastball. "Martin was treated poorly by major league baseball," states Nye, "but he was a wonderful instructor. You know the difference between Freddie Martin and Joe Becker? Martin was a pitcher and Becker was a catcher. Catchers understand pitching philosophy, but pitchers understand mechanics."

After a pair of losses, the team returned to Chicago and a 5-3 victory over St. Louis. Moreover, a three-run 7th broke a 23-inning scoring drought. Ernie Banks knocked in his first run in his last 49 times up. Ron Santo, still in a slump and dropped to fifth in the lineup, went 1 for 4 with an RBI. Ken Holtzman (2-0) turned in 7 innings, with Bill Hands working the final 2.

On May 19, with the Cubs at 16-13, 34-year-old veteran George Altman rejoined the team from Tacoma. Altman's return, though hardly significant, marked the beginning of Durocher's movement away from what *Tribune* scribe Prell termed the "all-out youth movement." Now that the club had demonstrated the capacity to win, the preference was to supplement the youthful nucleus with veteran help rather than rookie promise. For the record, Altman was the third veteran addition, following Radatz and outfielder Ted Savage, who the team picked up from the Cardinals. Radatz was particularly important to the Cubs, who were hoping he would regain his radar, freeing Bill Hands to fill in as a starter.

Although acknowledging the still fuzzy-cheeked composition of the team, Prell observed change in the wind. "Nine potential phenoms who were on the roster are gone," he noted, "some on option, others with all strings cut. In this list are pitchers Chuck Hartenstein, Dave Dowling, and Tom Manville; outfielders Byron Browne, Bob Raudman, and Don Young; and infielders Norm Gigon, Clarence Jones, and Felix Manilla."

"Durocher couldn't communicate with young players," Nye points out. "In fact, the way we found out where we stood was through the papers.

He'd tell the writers what he thought and they would print it. When Leo would come out to the mound in perhaps the 7th inning, he wouldn't say anything to me. He'd turn to Hundley and ask, 'Randy, how's he throwing?' 'Well, he doesn't have the same stuff he had when he started,' Randy would answer. Without even looking at me, Durocher would say, 'That's it. Here,' opening his palm for the ball."

Hundley corroborates Nye's recollections. "That's about the truth," says the former receiver. "After my first year, Leo started counting on me a lot."

Though Durocher generally did not deal directly with his pitchers, Nye remembers the exercise of going over the opposition's hitters before a game. "Once Curt Simmons got Roberto Clemente out four times. I'm sure Leo, when he asked him what pitch he was getting Clemente with, was surprised by the answer. 'Nothing. A nothing pitch,' Simmons said. 'I just threw it right down the chute.'"

Unfortunately for Nye, Clemente could adjust even to nothing pitches. "Several years later when I was pitching in Montreal," a chuckling Nye recalls, "I faced Clemente. I remembered what Simmons had said and got him out twice on off-speed stuff. The third time, with a runner on second, he hit a triple off the screen."

Early inning exits were not well received in the 1960s. "In that era," says Nye, "you were expected to go nine if possible. They gave you the ball and you didn't look at the bullpen. I remember one game in Wrigley against Houston," says Nye. "It was my worst outing of the season. It was boiling hot, with a gale wind ripping out. The game opened with a scratch double, then a seeing-eye single. Jimmy Wynn then hits what looks like a routine fly to left. Billy gradually moves back, pounding his glove to make the easy catch. The next thing I see is the ball landing on the catwalk. After a couple of outs and two more baserunners, I could hear Durocher's voice in the dugout yelling to Becker, 'That's all, Joe, I'm getting him out of there.'"

Nye's mention of the gale wind calls up what is perhaps the Windy City's North Side baseball facility's most distinctive feature. "The first thing you did as a visiting player when the team bus dropped you off in front of the ballpark," says FOX-Sports broadcaster and former San Francisco Giant catcher Bob Brenly, "is run up one of the tunnels and see which way the wind was blowing. Depending on which way the flags are blowing, pitchers have been known to develop a very rapid case of tendinitis, while hitters all but pull muscles in their haste to get their uniforms on when the wind is blowing out."

Hall of Fame pitcher Don Sutton, who in one midcareer stretch just could not win a game in the Friendly Confines, said he would rather sell cars than pitch in Wrigley Field.

Did the wind change how pitchers thought on a hot, windy day? "Absolutely," states Brenly, authoritatively. "It would get in your head as a pitcher. Dave LaPoint, a guy who pitched briefly for the Giants in the 1980s and also for St. Louis, was so psyched out by Wrigley Field that Whitey Herzog would not start him here. He would skip his spot in the rotation and bring a reliever in to pitch the game because Whitey knew that LaPoint had no chance of getting anybody out in this ballpark. On the other side, when the wind was blowing in, I saw many pitchers take advantage of it. Mike Krukow, a Cub of the 1970s, said, 'When the wind is blowing in, you just throw the ball up and out over the plate and let them hit it as hard as they can, because it's not going anywhere.' The wind can inflate and deflate some offensive numbers. In actuality, the wind blows in off the lake a lot more than it blows out. If you ask pitchers, they'll say it blows out 90 percent of the time, and if you ask hitters, they'll say it blows in 90 percent. It all depends on your viewpoint."

The Cubs fell to 16-14 when sidewinding right-hander Don Drysdale of the Dodgers shut them out 8-0. A hitless Santo watched his average drop to .203. Moreover, Rich Nye was bombed for the first time and Joe Niekro relieved. Durocher was tossed in a rhubarb over a rule in which the pitcher must take his sign while standing on the rubber. "I told Niekro he would have to take his sign from the catcher while on the rubber and not back of it," stated plate umpire Augie Donatelli. "Durocher yelled to his pitcher that he didn't have to take it there." Donatelli, stationed off third base, could not help but hear the leather-lunged skipper. "This game is too big for one man. Durocher defied us," he explained.

The next game, however, was a laugher. Ken Holtzman, ordered to report for army duty due to the war, was the winner. Given the uncertainty of the nation's military involvement, no one knew what the lefty's availability would be. "The game was such a blowout that in the 7th, with the score 19-3, Don Drysdale waved a white towel from the bullpen," recalls Grobstein. "I wanted the Cubs to get to 20, but when Glenn Beckert hit a routine fly to left to all but close the team's chances, I gave up. Then, amazingly, the outfielders collided, the ball rolled to the wall, and Beckert circled the bases." The final score was 20-3.

A crowd of 29,903, the largest of the season, saw the Cubs split a pair with LA the following day. Ray Culp was up 1-0 in the 7th inning of the opener until LA got to him and to reliever Bob Hendley for four big runs to win. Dick Radatz, fast showing he was not the answer to the team's problems in the pen, continued wild and ineffective. Fergie, however, beat Don Sutton 2-0 on a three-hitter to take the nightcap.

Now 18-15, the Cubs had registered 42 losses in 1966 before gaining their 18th win.

By now I was an enthusiastic believer in the Cubs as well, and on Memorial Day my Dad and I made the three-hour drive to Chicago from our home in little Cedar Grove, Wisconsin, to watch the Cubs play two, with Hank Aaron and the Atlanta Braves. There was a fresh feel to Wrigley Field that day. The long-standing air of defeat seemed expunged as 28,919 roared when the Cubs took the field in the opener, with Jenkins heading to the mound. They won 12-5, with Fergie fanning a dozen in the process. Williams and Santo chipped in with round-trippers. Despite witnessing the Braves come back to beat Joe Niekro 4-1 in game 2, I left that day sensing an anticipation among Cub fans of good things to come.

May ended with Nye defeating the Reds in Cincinnati 6-5, contributing three hits of his own to the win. Durocher stuck with the youngster until Cincy put three across against him in the 6th to make it a 1-run contest. The skipper then summoned Red-killer Cal Koonce, who ran his shutout innings against Cincinnati to 7 in his three appearances against them for the season.

Going 14-13 in May, after two months the Cubs were 22-19 and in fifth place, 4½ lengths behind the 30-18 Reds, but just 2½ out of 2nd, held by the 24-16 Cardinals.

The team opened June with two straight losses, dropping to 22-21. Through 43 games, the Cubs were hitting .245, the league median, but were near the top in runs scored, with 4.44 per outing. Billy Williams was hitting .317, Banks .314, and Phillips .300. Lee Thomas, however, had fallen to .234, Santo .225, and Don Kessinger was hitting a puny .180. Four players had at least five homers and in excess of 20 RBI.

On the hill, Bill Hands at 2.28 and Kenny Holtzman 2.33 were at the top in ERA. Fergie and Holtzman led the staff with five wins each, the latter undefeated, while Culp and Nye each had three victories.

Two galling losses on the 6th sent the Cubs back to .500 at 24-24. The bullpen was clearly a continuing problem. After tying the opener at six in the 8th, Chuck Hartenstein and Koonce failed in their half of the frame, yielding two and dropping the contest. The nightcap was even worse, another bullpen blowout. Up 8-1, the Cubs then watched the Phillies pick up 3 in the 5th, 2 in the 7th, and then 3 more in the 8th to win 9-8. Nye, Koonce, and Culp couldn't help Niekro.

On June 7, however, the Cubs began a hot streak, with Jenkins halting the slide by dealing the Phils a 3-hitter, 3-1. Entering a June 18 double-header with the Mets, the Cubs had run off seven wins in nine games, and were five over the .500 mark at 31-26. Craig Lynch and legions of other Cub fans were now crawling on the Bruin bandwagon in earnest.

"I started going regularly to Wrigley Field in 1967 after graduating from high school," says Lynch, in charting the transition of the fans from skeptics to believers. "On Opening Day we got out of school at two o'clock. I arrived at Wrigley Field in the bottom of the 5th and got a box seat in the sun. There were only 16,000 fans in the park. They were happy but not quite into it yet. The excitement built slowly that year, not many people thought the Cubs would do well. Fans started believing after the team got off to a much stronger start and were still playing well in June."

By the end of June the team was really sizzling, having won 19 of their last 23, and 11 of their last 12. They had gone 21-10 for the month and were now perched in second place. Their 43-29 log was just 1½ games behind the Cardinals' 44-27.

Author and sports talk-show host George Castle, then a young Cub devotee, also felt the pain might finally be over. "As a youngster, I never lived more than five miles from Wrigley Field," says Castle, who was a regular attendee at Wrigley Field, "and it was in June, when Phillips got hot and the Cubs went on a tear, that I really believed the Cubs had turned it around. I cut class after class that year to go to Wrigley Field."

Although Ferguson Jenkins was beaten in Pittsburgh 4-3 by strong-arming Bob Veale, the Cubs were coming on. The next night Twiggy Hartenstein, the 155-pound 26-year-old right-hander, whose frame seemed the male counterpart of the pencil-thin British celebrity Twiggy, gave indications that he might be the answer to the team's bullpen puzzle. Taking over for starter Joe Niekro in the 5th with a man on and a 4-3 lead, he held the powerful Pirates scoreless in a 5-3 triumph. The Cubs were again 5 games above .500, winning 4 of their last 6, and 9 of 12.

The team's average had vaulted to .259, a near 15-point jump in a month. They were now averaging 4.83 runs per game, having averaged 5.3 runs per contest for the month. Phillips was now hitting .319, Banks .308, and Williams .290. Banks had 15 homers, Williams and Santo 14, and Phillips 13. All four had more than 40 RBI. On the mound, Jenkins was 10-5, Hands 4-3, with both carrying ERAs well under 3.00. Rich Nye was 6-3 and Ken Holtzman (5-0), now in the army, had still not lost.

On the final day of June the team downed the mighty Reds 7-5 before 14,588 at Wrigley Field. Bill Hands lasted into the 7th with Hartenstein again finishing. Moreover, an epidemic of Cub fever was now breaking out all over the Windy City. With the weekend coming, the organization expected huge crowds for the next two confrontations with 3rd-place Cincinnati.

"All roads lead to Wrigley Field," wrote the *Tribune*'s Dave Condon, "where the Cubs suddenly have emerged as full-grown, growling Bruins after two decades of hibernation. This weekend, if the weather remains favorable, fans will converge upon the North Side baseball palace by bus, auto, foot, and elevated railway. The trickle of fans has suddenly become a flood."

Rich Nye witnessed the dramatic response on the part of the fans once they sensed the turnaround was real. "There was nothing more exciting. At that time the players parked their cars near the firehouse across the street from the left-field wall and walked across Waveland to the clubhouse entrance. By 9 o'clock people were lined up for bleacher seats, and you couldn't get through without being besieged by autograph seekers. The excitement was phenomenal."

Columnist Condon went on to quote Jack Maloney, Cub ticket boss. "We'll have a full house Sunday, for sure . . . in fact, we probably will sell out Saturday [as well]."

Although no one was conceding the pennant to the Cubs, Condon wrote, "The Chicago Transit Authority already is flying the championship bunting. On many of their elevated trains discharging fans at Addison Street, the trainman signals the station stop by announcing 'Home of the National League champions.' Much of Chicago feels the same way."

The Cub concessions department was now selling color photos of the Cubs and reaping huge profits. "This is the first year those color photos have sold big," said Cub photographer Barney Sterling. "Banks is the biggest seller; Ron Santo's photo runs second. But it'll surprise you who is getting the biggest rush these last few days—Manager Leo Durocher. Now Durocher is hotter than a Chicago pizza."

"It's absolutely fabulous," said legendary public address announcer Pat Pieper of the city's enthusiasm. "I give most of the credit to Leo Durocher. I think Durocher is our greatest manager since Joe McCarthy. Leo has the fellows all pulling at one end of the rope. I always thought Mr. Wrigley made a mistake with that rotating coach system, because no one ever knew who was in charge. You sure know who's in charge now. That's Mr. Durocher. He has become the personality in town." Pieper certainly had a sense of history, having served the organization since 1916.

On July 1, the beat went on as the hometown heroes vanquished the Reds again. The *Tribune* blared: "Five in a Row! Ten out of 11 on the

Home Stand! Twelve of Their Last 13! Sixteen in the Last 18! That's the way the statistics scored yesterday while the 31,833 spectators in Wrigley Field and a national television audience of millions watched those amazing Cubs whip the Cincinnati Reds 6-3."

The Cubs had continued to display "power, speed, great fielding, and the zeal to win," in pulling to within but a half length of the front-running St. Louis Cardinals. Moreover, the triumph put them three games up on the Reds, who had broken out of the gate so strongly in the early season.

Nye (7-3), helped by Twiggy, won on Ron Santo's two home runs, giving him 16 for the campaign. Leo couldn't get over the fans' enthusiasm, saying "Well, I gotta tell you. They were sending chills up and down my spine." The mob roared right from the outset when Chico Ruiz grounded to Kessinger for the first out.

Santo, remembering the wilderness years, was especially appreciative of the fans. "The crowds are great. They really help us. I mean it. When we used to get crowds of five, six thousand in August and September, you'd be surprised how hard it was for us to play."

All this only set up the series finale, to be pitched by ace Ferguson Jenkins.

"It was almost impossible to get to the park that day," says Lynch. "Traffic was backed up. We never got to our seats and had to sit on the steps in the aisle, something they don't allow now. It was the ultimate game of the year."

The Cubs didn't disappoint, and the *Tribune* headlines were the team's marketing arm, with the following bannered lines:

Charge of Leo's Light Brigade Reaches the Top
CUBS WIN 4-1: TIE FOR LEAD!
40,464 Watch Jenkins Hurl 3-Hit Game
Crowd Goes Wild after Victory

"It is fortunate," the article began, "for the physical well-being of North Side fans and others who have succumbed to Chicago's newest pastime—watching the Cubs play ball—that this most incredible team is leaving town."

Indeed watching and rooting for the Cubs was becoming the Windy City pastime. Not only did the game sell out, but 10,000 fans were turned away, with admission tickets sold out 30 minutes before the first pitch was thrown.

"I'll bet there were 46,000 in Wrigley that day," says Grobstein, "but [owing to safety violations] the Cubs will never admit it. When the Cubs put up the score that the Mets had beaten the Cardinals in the first game of a doubleheader, the crowd roared. Then, with the fans milling in the park after the game, they rearranged the pennant flags on top of the scoreboard, putting the Cubs on top of the league, and the fans went nuts as they chanted 'We're Number One!'"

"The Cubs went into first for the first time since God knows when," recalls Bruce Miles, now Cub beat writer for the *Daily Herald*, but only 10 years old at this time. "After two decades in the second division, there was all this pent up anticipation, anxiety, and frustration being let out all at once."

The players were in peril amid the fan hysteria. "I never witnessed anything like it," says Lynch. "Ernie Banks had been spiked the previous day by Pete Rose and was out of the lineup. He was up in the broadcast booth leading the cheers. On the radio they were telling him to be careful not to fall out of the booth with the fans grabbing after him."

The *Tribune*, assessing Leo's leadership, remarked, "Nobody plays a hot hand like Durocher. That is his reputation. That is his way of life. He is a gambler, and the good gambler pushes his luck. Durocher pushes hard."

Moreover, the old man was sharp. "Leo did a lot of shouting on the bench," wrote Jenkins. "He was always yelling at the infielders as he positioned them for each batter and each game situation.

"Leo positioned the outfielders by waving them in or out, to the right or to the left, with a white handkerchief. . . . Leo had an uncanny sense of where the ball was going to be hit. It was amazing how accurately he shifted the outfielders."

Now the Midwest was Cub bumper-sticker land. "Cub Power" salutations adorned myriad vehicles. Eventually, a visual sticker appeared suggesting one was to "Put his [picture of a valentine heart] into the Cubs or get his [picture of a donkey] out of here."

July continued apace, with a 12-6 win at Atlanta behind Ray Culp who evened his record at 6-6. Williams, Santo, Beckert, and Hundley all connected and Don Larsen (of World Series perfect-game fame) put in a cameo appearance. Hartenstein again finished. The streak was now at 7 straight, 14 of 15, with the overall mark 46-29.

Back in Chicago, fans were delirious with Cub fever. "There was just a tremendous buzz in Chicago," recalls Castle. "I was twelve years old on that July third and I remember running through our West Rogers Park apartment and letting out a war whoop after the game-winning homer.

"It was just a wonderful, exhilarating feeling—destiny's darlings spurred on by Adolfo Phillips and Ferguson Jenkins went into first place without going through the growing pains."

The fans were now truly back. "The team had some off-seasons when they drew maybe 600,000 a year," says Miles, "but all of a sudden, they started to do well and then there were 35,000, 40,000 people here on the weekend."

"By July the park was always full on weekends, and even on weekdays there were bigger crowds," states Lynch. "It was the first year you really started expecting the Cubs to win."

The media was saturated with Cub fodder. Legendary Chicago *Sun-Times* columnist and nationally syndicated talk-show host Irv Kupcinet noted the electric atmosphere. "Kup wrote that if the Cubs and the also-contending White Sox were to meet in a subway series, Ed Sullivan would do his show in Chicago," recalls Castle.

Superjock Larry Lujack, of Top 40 WLS radio fame, now regularly referred to the Cubs as "the Addison Street miracles."

The fourth of July saw the end of the streak as the Cubs took two on the noggin in Atlanta. Phil Niekro beat brother Joe (3-3) by a 4-3 count in the opener, and Pat Jarvis took down Hands (4-4) in the nightcap. The Cubs, 46-31, were now a half length behind St. Louis at 46-30.

From the fourth to the all-star break, times were tough for the team as the Cubs dropped seven straight, the final a 6-0 rip by Don Wilson in the Houston Astrodome. Rich Nye (7-5) was the loser.

Nonetheless, no one was complaining. After 82 games, this team, ticketed for eighth place, was second. Their 46-36 mark placed them just 3½ games behind the 49-32 men from St. Louis.

At this point, however, only the surprising Phillips was hitting over .300, at .306. Banks (.299), Hundley (.296), Williams (.282), and Santo (.280) were next in line. Santo, Banks, and Williams, however, were each at least halfway to 30 homers, with Santo's 53 RBIs leading the pack.

The pitching staff missed Ken Holtzman. Jenkins, 11-6 and 2.82, was clearly the ace. Fergie had worked better than 149 innings; no other hurler had even worked 100. Rich Nye's seven wins was second, but his ERA was near 4.00 (3.95), while Ray Culp's six wins were exceeded by his seven losses. His 4.24 ERA was also unimpressive. Bill Hands, however, was beginning to emerge. Just 4-4, he had a 2.71 ERA for his 63 innings.

No one exploited the Cubs' renaissance more than their celebrated skipper. "That year the all-star game was played in Anaheim," says Grobstein, "and during the team's rush to first in late June, Durocher accepted an invitation to appear on the Joey Bishop Show opposite Johnny Carson's

Tonight Show, the night after the game. Of course, just before the break, the Cubs went into a slump. When Leo appeared on the show and Joey brought up the skid, Durocher played along. 'I feel like killing you,' said Leo, 'we haven't won a game since you asked me on the show. I'm blaming you.'"

After the all-star game, at which Ernie Banks and Ferguson Jenkins represented the Cubs, the team snapped out of its collective doldrums, setting up another moment of glory. Having won 9 of its next 13 and now but a game out, the Cubs headed into St. Louis to face the front-running Cardinals in Busch on July 24.

It was high drama. "When the Cubs went to St. Louis, you knew it was a big game because WGN-TV, which only telecast home games then, went down to do the game," says Lynch. "The Cubs were actually contending for first in late July, amazing."

Up-and-down right-hander Ray Culp (7-8) drew the daunting Monday night assignment before more than 40,000 in rainy St. Louis. With the Cubs leading 3-0 through 6th, the skies poured down precipitation, resulting in a 51-minute rain respite. Despite the lengthy hiatus, a gritty Culp went back to the hill in the 7th and finished off the Redbirds over the final three frames for a 3-1 victory.

The Cubs were now dead even with St. Louis at 56-40. It would be Culp's last hurrah. He did not win again as a Cub and was unceremoniously dispatched to Boston at season's end. The Chicagoans also made a southerly turn, losing five of their final seven for the month, finishing one below .500 (15-16) for July. The 62-40 Cardinals won their last six, hammering Nye (9-7) and his mates 9-2 in Wrigley Field on the final day of the month. Nonetheless, the Redbirds were still within reach, just 4½ in front of the second-place 58-45 Chicagoans.

On August 1 the Bruins closed the gap to 3½ behind Jenkins, 3-2, who hurled a gem before 25,439 appreciative observers for his 14th win against eight losses.

The key win set up the most critical confrontation of the season, a twin bill with the front-running Redbirds in the Cubs' nest.

The *Tribune* reported the result well. "The big day, long-awaited by Cub fans and the country over, went down the drain as a total loss yesterday—except at the turnstiles and concession stands."

On the field, the opening verdict was 4-2 with Culp (8-9) taking the loss. Recent acquisition Bob Shaw took the hit in the 7-1 nightcap. The disastrous date drew 37,164 and pushed the team's attendance ahead of the 1966 total.

More bad things followed such that after a 6-4 loss in St. Louis on

August 15, the club had all but fallen out of the race with a fifth place 64-57 mark, 11 down to the super-heated 73-44 Cardinals. An 11th-inning pinch single by Al Spangler helped the team end August on an up note with a 2–1 win over the Mets. Hartenstein, now 7-4, finished the game in relief of Nye and Bill Stoneman.

Back in third place, the Cubs' record now stood at 72-62, 11 games in arrears of the 83-51 Cardinals, and just 1 under the 73-61 Reds. July and August were the team's worst two months, going 29-33 over the 62 contests. The Cardinals picked up 9½ games over the same span, on a 39-24 roll.

The problems were mainly at the plate. The following table shows the team's record and hitting performance through June 30 as compared with July and August.

Period	Games	W-L	RUNS	R/GM	HR	HR/GM	AVG
Apr–June	72	43-29	348	4.83	72	1.0	.259
July–Aug	62	29-33	234	3.77	36	0.6	.242

Only two regulars did better in July–August as compared with the first 72 games. One, Ron Santo, improved mainly in average. The third sacker hit .332, blasting 13 homers and driving home 36 during the latter 62 games, after hitting .279 with 14 and 47 over the earlier 72. The other, Don Kessinger, hardly merits mention inasmuch as almost any July–August batting mark (his was .250) would be an improvement over his .209 early-season number.

The following table for five key players compare their performances over the first 72 games with that of the 62 encounters played in July and August. In each case, the falloff is substantial. As for Phillips, it's alarming.

Player	Period	HR	RBI	Avg
Beckert	April–June	3	18	.281
	July–August	2	13	.246
Hundley	April–June	8	32	.308
	July–August	4	17	.242
Banks	April–June	15	44	.308
	July–August	5	30	.256

Player	Period	HR	RBI	Avg
Williams	April–June	14	41	.290
	July–August	5	25	.260
Phillips	April–June	13	48	.319
	July–August	3	14	.201

There won't be many men on base when a team's 1 and 2 hitters (Kessinger and Beckert) combine for a .248 average—with precious few walks—as table-setters. Runs will be particularly hard to come by when hitters 3 and 5 (Williams and Banks) combine to hit just 10 home runs and bat .258 over 461 at bats. Clearly, Santo's tear kept the offensive ship afloat.

The pitching numbers continued to be strong. Jenkins and Hands, for example, kept their ERAs under 3.00. Nonetheless, together they were just .500, Jenkins at 6-5 and Hands 2-3. Rich Nye's ERA, in fact, was more than a point better during July–August (2.80 vs. 3.92), yet he was 5-6 during the period as opposed to 6-3 earlier.

The Cubs played .500 ball for the first half of September, going 8-8. On September 15 Fergie turned in his 18th win in a 7-1 rout in Atlanta. In the game, he set the team's single-season strikeout mark with 206.

Now 13 behind the 92-56 Cardinals, the Cubs were playing largely for pride. Just two more wins would ensure a winning campaign, three would give them their largest number of victories since the 1945 war-tarnished pennant.

They won seven more games. Moreover, a triumph in Cincinnati in their next to last game clinched a third-place finish, a nose ahead of the fourth-place Reds.

"We used to play a lot of laid-back baseball. Now we're making things happen," said Billy Williams in 1967.

"If 1966 was the last year of the dark ages for the Chicago Cubs," wrote Ron Santo, "1967 was the beginning of the Renaissance." Clearly, the single season turnaround of 28½ games was a reversal of miraculous proportions.

For some observers, there remained concern. Indeed, one can look back on the team from two different vantage points. One view sees the 1967 Cubs as a team simply playing over their collective heads in the early season while finding their true level later on. They did, after all, go just 41-45 in their final 86 games, after winning 46 while losing just 29 of their first 75.

From another vantage point, however, this was a team that could play with the best. They posted a heady 50-39 log against teams with .500 records or better. This included a woeful 6-11 mark against the all-conquering Cardinals. They were just 37-35 against losing clubs.

A way of settling these divergent views is by using the research formula explained in the previous chapter. Employing that method, the Cubs should have been 90-71, actually three games better than they were. Often when a team's wins fall short of its statistical projection, the explanation can be due to bullpen failures, generating too many close losses. Such seemed to be the case in 1967, with the team posting just 28 saves, fourth among the six teams winning at least half their games and one below the NL average.

In any case, this was a good team. Offensively, it had a banner year. The Cubs led the league in runs scored with 702. Even with a statistical adjustment for the scoring friendliness of Wrigley Field, the team scored 13 runs more than would be expected. They hit .251 (two points above the league average), with an on base percentage (OBP) of .319 (7 over the league's .312), and registered a .378 slugging percentage, 15 points over the league.

Individually, Santo ranked third in runs scored (107), tied for third in homers (31), and fifth in total bases with 300. Leading the league in walks, his OBP of .401 was also fifth, and he knocked in 98 runs. Williams was fourth in total bases with 305, delivering 28 round-trippers and 84 RBIs. Banks drove in 95 to go with his 23 home runs.

One major problem already glaringly evident in 1967, however, and one that Durocher either did not discern or simply failed to address throughout his tenure in the Windy City, was the absence of table-setters at the top of the lineup. With the 3,4,5 spots manned by true baseball greats—Williams, Santo, and Banks (later Hickman and Pepitone)—the offense all but cried out for players in the 1 and 2 slots who could, above all, get on base.

Kessinger clearly could not. In 1967 the Cubs leadoff man's OBP was an unbelievably puny .279, fully 33 points below the league average of .312. (His batting average of .231 was 18 under the league norm.) Solid performer though the fielding ace was, Kessinger was not a leadoff man. Moreover, the nonwalking Glenn Beckert, all but coronated by Durocher as the definition of the ideal number two man, had an OBP of .314, despite hitting .280. What Beckert could do was avert the strikeout and execute the hit-and-run, but these are secondary skills when compared with the import of getting on base.

In fairness to Leo, OBP was not a publicly discussed baseball statistic and little was written about it when he managed. Nonetheless, it was widely accepted that the role of occupants at the top of the order was to reach base somehow. Moreover, even as the science of baseball research later exploded with new statistics, retrospective evidence in the managing styles of the great field generals, whose tenures long preceded the now published data, reveals their intuitive understanding of the game's inner workings shown by the new numbers.

In Durocher's time, the top of the order was often filled with speedsters. With Beckert stealing 10 bases and Kessinger only 6, it was obvious neither ran particularly well. In fact, aside from Adolfo Phillips who stole 24 of 34 bases, the team swiped just 39 sacks while being gunned down 40 times.

Despite the slugging of Williams, Santo, and Banks, Kessinger scored just 61 runs, Beckert 91. Both scored less often than league-leading Santo and Williams (92), supposedly the hitters directed to drive the former pair in. Had the two got on just 33% of the time, low for players in the 1 and 2 spots, the team would likely have scored about 20 more runs. An OBP of .375 would have added nearly 40.

For Santo, it was another outstanding campaign. *Total Baseball* employs a statistic called Total Baseball Ranking (TBR). The MVP of statistics, it ranks players by total runs contributed in all areas of endeavor. The Cub third sacker was the TBR leader in 1967 for the second consecutive season.

Defensively, the team was excellent, leading the loop infielding percentage at .981 and tying for fewest miscues at 121. Although the team ERA (3.48) was 10 points over the league average, the staff actually yielded 10 fewer runs than expected, considering their home games were in Wrigley.

Ferguson Jenkins's 20 wins were second in the league, as was his strikeout total of 236. He led the league in complete games with 20. Moreover, Rich Nye (13-10) and Joe Niekro (10-7) gave the team two more solid starters, both of whom finished the season with ERAs below the league norm at 3.20 and 3.34, respectively. The top three winners posted a combined 43-30 mark for the team.

Bill Hands, though just 7-8, had a 2.46 mark in his 150 innings, while the wiry Hartenstein won 9 and saved 10 against just 5 setbacks, with an ERA of 3.08.

Baseball fans, particularly those in Chicago, let the organization know by their Wrigley Field presence that the corner had been turned. The team barely missed the million mark, drawing 977,226, a more than 50% increase from 1996. The still bright-eyed former slugger Billy Williams points to the dramatic growth in fan support in 1967 as an indicator that the organization at large had truly emerged from the wilderness years. "The crowds in 1967 showed the team was making progress off the field as well as on," says Williams.

For then rookie Nye, the 1967 experience was overwhelming. "Anywhere you'd go, fans noticed. Even in restaurants, people would come over filled with excitement. Chicago went crazy for baseball." Now a veterinarian at the Midwest Bird and Exotic Animal Hospital outside Chicago, Nye says he is still warmly greeted by people who became Cub fans in 1967.

"From the end of the 1967 season until the start of spring training in 1968, the city began to change its attitude toward our club," wrote Santo. "After years of frustration, fans began to feel what we as players had already felt. And entering spring training in 1968, I really felt we could do it."

For the first time since 1946, Cub fans looked confidently to the future.

Six

ESTABLISHING A WINNER

Don't fear, this is the year.
Ernie Banks, looking forward to 1968

It was arguably the most memorable year in the second half of the twentieth century. The nation was heading for what some observers called a collective national nervous breakdown. Amid the raging Vietnam War were the sudden decision by President Lyndon Johnson not to join the presidential race, the assassinations of Martin Luther King Jr. and Robert Kennedy, the frustrations boiling out of control on the streets of major cities, and the tumult encapsulating the Democratic National Convention in Chicago's Amphitheater.

It was 1968.

Wrigley Field was expected to be a welcome oasis from the conflict and confrontation, debate and dissension, riot and revolt that enveloped the nation. Jack Brickhouse's invitation to "forget your worries and come out to Wrigley" was never more inviting for Cub fans, who finally had genuine reason for optimism, with their young team coming off an invigorating 1967.

Dick Dozer, the *Tribune* beat writer affirmed this sentiment. "The Cubs can win the pennant. But so can a half a dozen other teams in the NL. . . . The Cubs could finish as close to first place as they did last year—14½ games back—only to find more teams ahead of them than the two [St. Louis and San Francisco] that were up there in 1967," he wrote. Despite the optimistic lead, Dozer had the Cubs finishing fifth in the 10-team circuit behind Cincinnati, Pittsburgh, St. Louis, and San Francisco.

Sensing Cub fever among the faithful, Dozer remarked, "It's unfair to expect the Cubs to win the pennant, but unfortunately, their ecstatic fans are likely to do just that. Their stock rationalization sounds something like this: 'We passed up six teams last year, and Kenny Holtzman was around for only half the time.' No question about it. But Holtzman somehow won nine games without a loss, and you get the idea that this superb 22-year-old pitching prospect is expected by some to have a record twice as good. But Holtzman won't be 18-0 this year even if he becomes the best pitcher in the league."

Nevertheless, the 1967 absence of Holtzman was, in Dozer's opinion, a blessing in disguise, as it opened the door to other young arms. Rich Nye and Joe Niekro had broken through as starting hurlers, and there was simply no way of knowing how good either or both of them might become. Each had pitched the team 3 games over .500 the previous year and had combined for 23 victories, more than 25% of the team's 87 triumphs.

Combining Nye and Niekro with Holtzman and bulwark Ferguson Jenkins gave the Cubs as formidable a group of young arms as could be found anywhere. Dozer felt it was "genuinely possible that these four young hurlers some day will become the game's best 'big four' since Cleveland's collection of Feller-Garcia-Wynn-Lemon."

Despite Dozer's and others' cautions to rein in their enthusiasm, expectations were high among Cub fans. Add that pitching to an offense that led the NL in runs scored and fielding in 1967, and it was indeed hard to avoid visions of World Series action in Wrigley Field from dancing in their heads.

The ever loyal Les Grobstein couldn't wait for 1968. "I thought they'd win it all," says the talk-show host. "In fact, I was in Miami Beach that winter for a special Boston Celtics-St. Louis Hawks game. Harry Caray was the Hawks' broadcaster, and someone remarked about seeing him back at the World Series that October. 'Hey, the Cubs are going to be in the Series this year,' I broke in. Harry was nice about it and said, 'Yeah, the Cubs have a good team, they'll be tough.' "

"I was a freshman at DePaul," says diehard Craig Lynch, "and I wrote a column that the Cubs would win the pennant."

"After '67," says Grobstein, explaining his Miami bravado, "I thought the Cubs would be good for years to come. What bothered me is that the White Sox were still stealing their thunder."

So fired up was Grobstein, he and fellow Cub–addicted friend David

Heller decided to witness the final preseason games, played in the North against the hated White Sox. The two drove from Chicago deep into Indiana, then all the way up to Milwaukee where the Sox played some home games each year, and finally back to Chicago to catch the preseason Cubbies.

Durocher, ever the curmudgeon, didn't play his regulars in the first game. "He was really angry about the condition of the field," recalls Grobstein, "so he played the reserves, using the regulars as pinch hitters late in the game. The Sox won 2-1."

Indeed, the Windy City had long belonged to the Sox, but now the times were changing. "It started in 1951," according to Bill Gleason, "when Paul Richards came in and the Sox took over the city. They held it and there was not much the Cubs could do about it. By 1968, however, the fans were in Wrigley Field in great numbers.

"You never hear White Sox fans say, 'Oh, the Sox really blew it in 1967,'" says Bill Gleason, "but they really did. It was one of the great races in baseball history. Five clubs in mid-September all had a chance to win and I have yet to find a player on one of those other four teams who did not expect the White Sox to win it. Coming out of spring training," says Gleason, "1968 was the first year since about 1940 that both the Cubs and the White Sox were given a chance of winning the pennant."

Billy Williams could see the momentum of expectancy building. "From 1966 to 1968, fan support started to pick up," he says. "By 1968 we had good young pitchers with Fergie, Bill Hands, and Ken Holtzman, a good infield with Kessinger, Beckert, and Santo, and Ernie was still hitting."

"There were big expectations." recalls Rich Nye. "We had a young staff in 1967, with everyone ready to go in 1968. We had all of our guns back, and added a few." The major addition to the Cub lineup was veteran Lou Johnson, obtained from the Dodgers in exchange for infielder Paul Popovich. Johnson, 33, had been a sometime regular for LA over the previous three years. Though hardly a star, he figured to be an upgrade from handy but light-hitting Ted Savage who had hit only .218 in 1967, managing but five home runs and 33 RBIs in his 225 at bats.

The season opened shortly after the shocking assassination of Martin Luther King Jr. in Memphis, an event that brought about the cancellation of the final exhibition game against the Sox in Wrigley Field. Rioting was a considerable concern in many major-league cities. The Cubs began the campaign in Cincinnati. Only five regulars—Ernie Banks, Ron Santo, Billy Williams, Don Kessinger, and Glenn Beckert—were present before Durocher took over the Northside fortunes.

Joe Niekro, 10-7, with a 3.48 ERA in 1967, drew the Opening Day assignment. Despite Johnson's low on base percentage and relat d disinclination to walk, Durocher led him off as the rightfielder, with Don Kessinger hitting in Beckert's customary number 2 spot. The injured second baseman was replaced in the lineup by Jose Arcia, a 24-year-old rookie from Cuba. Centerfield now belonged to Adolfo Phillips, along with elevated expectations. Phillips had evidenced great untapped talent the previous season, appearing to make a huge difference in 1968 if he broke through. Lefty Kenny Holtzman, who foresaw a banner season, tabbed the potential-laden Phillips "the key to the pennant."

The team made no strides toward pennant-contention in the opener. Niekro yielded nothing of substance through 3 innings, but then a lengthy rain delay ensued. Despite his denial, the hiatus must have hurt as the Reds chased him with 1 out in the 5th. Pete Mikkelsen and 38-year-old Bob Tiefenauer finished as the Reds rolled to a comfortable 9-4 triumph in Crosley Field.

Cub power arrived the next day as the team squared its record at one apiece on the strength of a 10-3 victory. Ferguson Jenkins notched the complete game win, as Billy Williams blasted two round trippers while Ron Santo, Aldolfo Phillips, and Fergie delivered one each in the triumph.

The Cubs sputtered badly in the early going, winning but two of their next eight. With the offense not delivering as it had in 1967 and the bullpen worse than suspect, there appeared reason for concern. Was 1967 (like 1963) merely a mirage, with the Cubs still in the wilderness? Some couldn't help but wonder.

Then came April 23.

The Cubs announced a trade. They had sent backup outfielder Ted Savage and minor league pitcher Jim Ellis to the Los Angeles Dodgers for utility outfielder Jim Hickman and relief pitcher Phil Regan.

The Cubs had acquired the "Vulture." The 31-year-old Regan had gone 14-1 with a league-leading 21 saves and a microscopic 1.62 ERA in 65 appearances for the pennant-winning Dodgers just two years earlier. Though 6-9 in 1967, he had turned in a 2.99 ERA over 55 appearances and 96 innings. He became available in 1968 because of a bizarre series of events.

As the 1968 season opened, Regan began experiencing disturbing physical symptoms. His hands, knees, and legs were swelling. One day he was unable to pick up a coffee cup. The Dodgers then sent him to baseball's medical guru Dr. Robert Kerlan for a diagnosis. Kerlan said Regan had rheumatoid arthritis. "So he gave me a shot of cortisone and a bunch of tiny pills and told me to take six each day," Regan told writer Rick Talley.

"Well, it got worse, I could hardly get out of bed in the mornings, and my leg hurt terribly."

A concerned Regan began researching rheumatoid arthritis and read of a reportedly temporary form that lasted only 30 days, about the length of time during which he had been afflicted. Immediately, he experienced relief. "We got into New York for a road trip," he explained, "and for the first time in a while, I didn't have any soreness. I think I pitched in three of the four games, including both games of a winning doubleheader. That was on Sunday. On Monday I got traded to the Cubs."

With the steal of Regan being the talk of the league, the team got a shot of energy, winning five of their next six April outings. Not surprisingly, Durocher, ever the player of the hot hand, pressed the ace into duty quickly. On April 28, for example, Regan relieved twice in Wrigley Field as the Cubs took two from the Houston Astros, 8-4 and 5-2.

A three-run Pirate 9th inning, highlighted by a two-bagger that shot past a skidding Adolfo Phillips in a rain-slicked outfield, robbed the Cubs of a .500 April. They finished the opening month in a seventh-place tie with Atlanta at 8-10. The defending champion Cardinals were already five games ahead at 13-5, followed by the 10-7 Giants.

Despite the painful finish to April, the *Tribune* was bullish on the Cubs now that the Bruins had Regan. "If Regan's assertion that he feels as sound as he did in 1966 is true, the Cubs must be accepted now as a solid contender," the *Tribune* reported. "With the relief pitching that began the season, only the wishful thinkers could have classed the Cubs as much better than a .500 club."

Nicknamed the Vulture for his propensity in 1966 to come in and pick up a quick win after a starter had gone deep into the game only to leave it tied, Regan was one of a kind. He had an awkward diving delivery, and his out pitch was a moist one that went with a tough slider. Because Regan threw what might be called a clean spitter, allowing the perspiration to run down his arms onto the ball, umpires were never able to bust him, despite their certainties that the ball coming in was less than arid.

With the Vulture anchoring the pen, the Cubs roared through the first three weeks of May, winning 15 and losing 6. Concerns about a return to the wilderness were long forgotten with the team now 23-16 for the season. The euphoria was not to last, however, as the Cubs went into a tailspin, ending the month with seven straight defeats—the last one a 3-1 setback at the hands of Larry Dierker in the hated Astrodome, a venue in which the team had never seemed able to play well.

After two months the Cubs were a .500 ballclub, 23-23. With St.

Louis also struggling in the month of flowers, going just 11-16, San Francisco grabbed the league lead with a 26-21 mark, just 2½ games ahead of the little bears, who were tied with Cincinnati for fifth. The team was fortunate to have won even half their games because the 170 runs their hitters generated were actually 8 fewer than the number of earned runs their pitchers had permitted.

The 1968 season was called The Year of the Pitcher. It was the year Denny McLain rang up 31 wins for Detroit and Bob Gibson registered an incredible 1.12 ERA, while Don Drysdale pitched six straight shutouts in hurling 58 record consecutive scoreless innings. So severe was the pitching tilt, the owners voted to lower the mound for the following season to correct the imbalance.

After 46 games it was clear the Cubs were feeling the effects of baseball's pitching dominance. They were averaging just 3.7 runs a game, well down from their 4.36 mark in 1967. The team was hitting a puny .243, eight points below 1967, with nary a hitter at .300. Their 30 home runs projected to just 106 for the season, 22 below the previous year's total. Santo's 26 RBIs led the club, but he was on pace for just 92 on the year, while the key to the season, Adolfo Phillips, was hitting a meager .180 with three homers and a dozen RBIs.

Curiously, the pitching was also in disarray. After Bill Hands (2.15) and Ferguson Jenkins (2.54), only one Cub pitcher had an ERA below 4.00, Phil Regan at 3.92. The team's overall ERA of 3.90 was close to a run higher than the league average for the season (2.99). Moreover, only Bill Hands (5-2) and Kenny Holtzman (4-3) had winning records, and the latter's ERA was a ghastly 4.59. Jenkins was a tough luck 5-5. Furthermore, both Joe Niekro and Rich Nye were parting with more than a hit per inning pitched and recording ERAs of 4.86 and 4.35, respectively.

Nye was not the only one who suffered from Durocher's lack of patience with young pitchers. "Leo told Niekro to take his knuckleball and shove it and threatened Hundley never to give the sign for it," says Nye. That knuckleball would later be the right-hander's meal ticket to a solid career containing 221 major league wins.

Leo liked conventional, meat-and-potatoes pitching. His directive to Niekro betrayed his dislike for trick pitches and unorthodox styles of any kind. In 1966 he exiled reliever Ted Abernathy after a rough start, likely in part because the veteran threw with a highly unusual submarine (near underhanded) motion similar to that of the late, great Dan Quisenberry of the 1980s Royals.

There was also the case of a rather unusual chap from the Detroit

Tigers, one William Alvan Faul. Picked up in 1965, Bill Faul claimed to be a hynotist, preacher, and karate practitioner, but it was his pitching antics that truly set him apart. Proudly wearing #13, he would turn his back to the hitters, rotate back to face them, and wave his hand in front of his face several times before throwing the sphere. In 1965 Faul divided 12 decisions for the 72-90 North-siders, turning in a respectable 3.54 ERA in the process.

Then he met Durocher. Going into the 1966 season, Leo praised him, saying the young right-hander could really fire the ball, and if he won consistently, he would allow Faul to hypnotize him. By mid-July, however, after going 1-4 in 17 outings, with a hefty 5.08 ERA, Durocher backed up the truck on Faul, sending him to their minor league affiliate in Tacoma to make room for a cameo, career-ending visit from 39-year-old Robin Roberts.

The Bill Faul story, however, doesn't quite end there. The youngster termed his demotion "spiteful and unfair." Feeling he had been dispatched in part for throwing a gopher ball to the Pirates' Bob Skinner the previous day on a pitch he had already shaken off, Faul called Durocher's credibility into question. He wondered publicly whether the inexperienced young catcher John Boccabella or Leo had called for the hanging curve he had reluctantly thrown to Skinner.

Bill Faul did not return to the bigs until 1970 with the San Francisco Giants, when he threw only 10 more innings, closing his major career. As such, it would suggest that Leo was correct in deporting the then 26-year-old. Nonetheless, Faul's charges raise the question as to whether some of Leo's angst might have been due to the right-hander's unorthodox style and upstaging personality.

As for the 1968 Windy City contingent, although Bill Hands opened June with a 3-1 victory in the Dome and closed it with a 6-2 romp over the Cardinals before 36,414 in Wrigley Field, the month of weddings proved tough for the Cubs. Their 10-18 mark made them a ninth-place team with a desultory 33-41 log for the season, fully 11 lengths behind the 46-30 St. Louis Cardinals.

The month consisted of one long offensive drought. In mid-June the team was shut out for 48 consecutive innings, tying a record for offensive futility held by the 1906 Philadelphia Athletics. Tucked into the back of the streak were three straight whitewashes against the front-running Cardinals in St. Louis. Moreover, the Bruins suffered three 1-0 losses during the 48-inning stretch. The team scored just 90 runs for the entire month, an average of just 3.2 per game. Hitting .244 as a team, the Cubs connected for just 15 home runs over the 28 contests.

Former catcher Randy Hundley has repressed the hitting meltdown out of consciousness. "I don't remember that period at all, I guess I don't want to remember it," he now says, laughing.

Billy Williams cites the quality of the hurlers at the time. "You look at the '50s, '60s, and '70s, and you see those pitchers being inducted into the Hall of Fame now," referring to the likes of Don Sutton, Jim Bunning, Gaylord Perry, and Phil Niekro in addition to Tom Seaver, Juan Marichal, and Bob Gibson. "It was the Golden Era of baseball," states the sweet swinger. "The pitchers today have that cutter, but the guys in that era had a fastball, curve, slider, and change—four pitches. And there was no letup. You faced guys like Gibson, Marichal, and Seaver for nine innings."

Cub pitching showed some improvement with a 3.51 ERA for June, but Holtzman and Nye were still over the 4.00 mark, and Niekro was at 5.27. Jenkins was the definition of the tough luck hurler. His 2.78 ERA for June got him one win against four losses. Phil Regan, though going just 2-2 for the month, permitted only five earned runs in 29 innings, translating to a 1.55 ERA.

Nye, noting a change in Durocher's style, was struggling mentally. "Early in the season I was without a win and couldn't get out of the 4th inning. We'd get down by a couple of runs early and I'd be lifted for a pinch hitter. I was losing my confidence because unless you were an established regular, once you were out of a game, you didn't know when you'd get back in again.

"Leo gave Fergie the ball every four days. There was no real rotation, just Fergie every fourth day. If you were the fourth pitcher and there was an off day in there, you missed your turn."

During his tenure with the Cubs, Nye experienced firsthand the negative impact from this uncertainty of role. "After being pushed to the pen, I remember I had a rather strong relief performance, and Leo told me I'd be starting in the second game of a doubleheader a few days later. The next day I was in the bullpen, just having a good time, when in the seventh, the phone rings. 'Get Nye loose,' Durocher said.

"I think I got in ten or twelve pitches before I was called into the game, with the score 1 to 1. I can tell you the score was not 1 to 1 when I left. With almost no warning, I was on the mound physically, but mentally, I wasn't in the game."

In late June Durocher had had enough. He fined Adolfo Phillips (who would hit .323 for the month) for loafing on the bases, while an embittered Lou Johnson, with his lone home run, 14 RBI, .244 average, and .289 on base percentage, was quietly dispatched to Cleveland in exchange for outfielder Willie Smith.

Johnson had been a mistake in more ways than one. "Johnson was boisterous," wrote Jenkins. "He didn't mind using belligerent and obscene language to get a point across, which put off a lot of fellows on the ball club, including Hundley and Kessinger, who never swore. Johnson did not seem to fit on the team, and the breaking point came when we were at Evansville, Indiana, to play a preseason game with the White Sox.

"The night that Martin Luther King Jr. was assassinated, Hundley was in a hotel elevator as Johnson and Williams got on it. Hundley, knowing that Johnson was involved in the movement, said with the best of intentions, 'Say, I heard your man got shot.' Johnson flew into a rage, cussing at Randy and yelling, 'Stop this elevator. I'm not riding with you.'

"From then on, Hundley and Johnson were at odds with each other. Whenever Johnson walked into the locker room and saw Hundley, he would turn his back on him or stare him down. It got to the point where Johnson was not getting along with more than one or two players. He was disrupting the whole team, and in June he was traded to Cleveland for Willie Smith.

"Not much later, Johnson attacked the Cubs bitterly in a newspaper interview. He accused some of the Cubs of being racists and charged that Durocher played favorites, that he used his pets rather than the men who were best for the job. Johnson charged that Santo was the big cheese on the club and that we would never win while he was playing for us. It was a lot of sour grapes."

Johnson was also angry at Durocher for icing him, something Leo would do to those who fell out of his favor. Jenkins noticed the manager's propensity for this, using Holtzman as an example: "They [Durocher and Holtzman] were always playing cards in the clubhouse. Leo did that with a lot of players. You always knew that if Leo played gin rummy with you, he was on your side. Then all of a sudden Durocher stopped playing cards with Kenny. He did the same thing with a lot of other guys. They would play cards for weeks, months, and all of a sudden, that was it. Durocher would ignore them without seeing them. . . . It was Leo's way of showing his displeasure."

Asked about Leo's tendency to suddenly ice a player, Randy Hundley, a Durocher favorite, says somewhat defensively, "He did that. He was the manager and that was his prerogative."

In 1967 the less than warmly communicative Durocher had his own way of icing the media. Leo indulged in some particularly interesting exchanges with monotonic straight-man host Lou Boudreau on his daily "Durocher in the Dugout" pregame program. After one galling loss in 1967, the conversation went something like this.

BOUDREAU: This is "Durocher in the Dugout," with Cub manager Leo Durocher. Leo, how about today's pitcher?

DUROCHER: Culp is pitching today.

BOUDREAU: Could you tell us what happened in last night's game, Leo?

DUROCHER: No.

BOUDREAU: Well, how about the moves out of the bullpen?

DUROCHER: No.

BOUDREAU: Are there any things we should look for today?

DUROCHER: No.

BOUDREAU: Anything you could tell us about the rotation ahead?

DUROCHER: No.

BOUDREAU: This has been "Durocher in the Dugout," with Cub manager Leo Durocher.

Leo did not limit his confrontations to mere words. Grobstein tells of an incident on the team plane, involving venerable baseball scribe Jerome Holtzman. Durocher reportedly ambled up to Holtzman and began reading an article Holtzman was working on. "I don't like that story," growled Leo, yanking the paper out of the typewriter in that precomputer era. "Write another one." With that, Durocher headed for the restroom and unceremoniously flushed Holtzman's literary product down the toilet.

In any case, without Lou Johnson it was now rightfield-by-committee for the Cubbies, with Jim Hickman, veteran Al Spangler, and Smith patrolling the soil. The latter could not have been more different from Johnson. He proved an absolute joy to have in the clubhouse, singing, playing his tapes, and chattering "I'm Willie Smith. I'm good. I'm wonderful Willie."

The Cubs started turning things around in early July, going 6-4 in their ten pre–all-star game outings. Moreover, they went into the break on the heels of a 5-4, 4-3 sweep of the Pirates before 32,444 cheering fans at Wrigley. Game One, which included a grand slam by Banks, was dramatic, rolling back and forth. Pittsburgh brought in ace fireballer Bob Veale in the 9th. Matters were settled when a .186 hitting Jose Arcia, who had taken over Popovich's utility role, unexpectedly homered.

"Jack Brickhouse was more stunned than anyone," recalls Grobstein. "'Look at this happy Cuban! Woo-boy!' he shrieked with dubious cultural sensitivity, while Arcia circled the bases." Don Kessinger's single gave the Bruins the sweep in the nightcap, as Phil Regan picked up both wins.

The team pushed over 48 runs in that 10-game span, with Jenkins and Regan each going 2-0. Together they parted with but two runs in 22⅔ innings. Nevertheless, all-stars Kessinger, Santo, and Williams were representing a 39-45 team whose top batsman (Beckert) was hitting just .279. Still in 9th place, the North-siders were now 15½ games down to the 55-30 St. Louis Cardinals.

The second half of the season opened with a pair in New York. It was same 'ol, same 'ol in game 1, as Dick Selma bested Ferguson Jenkins 1-0. It was Fergie's fourth 1-0 setback of the campaign, and the sixth time he had been shut out. The Cubs salvaged a split behind Bill Hands when Ernie Banks doubled in the 9th of the second tilt.

The following evening, Friday, July 12, the Cubs suffered their 16th whitewash of the season—10 more than in all of 1967—as Jerry Koosman did them in 4-0. They were now 40-47 and 15½ out. The Cubs were by no means the only team experiencing an offensive brownout in 1968. Incredibly, their .242 team batting average was good for fifth in the 10-team league, and their 308 runs (just 3.54 over the 87 games) was an even more amazing third, behind only Cincinnati and St. Louis.

On July 13 things changed.

Phil Regan picked up his seventh win against two setbacks hurling 3⅔ innings of shutout ball in relief of rookie Gary Ross, as Al Spangler's pinch single lifted the Cubs over New York 3-2 in 11. Former Cub Cal Koonce, another sudden Durocher rejectee, took the loss in relief of Tom Seaver.

A 6-2 win in Pittsburgh on the strength of a complete game effort by Joe Niekro and Billy Williams' fifth career grand slam followed. The Cubs had now allowed only seven earned runs in the five games since the break and were 42-47.

Two more wins lifted the club into fifth at 44-47, but the hard-charging Cardinals continued to win as well and were 59-31. Regan was now 8-2 out of the pen.

The winning streak reached 5 with the Cubs pounding out 16 hits in the opener of a two-for-one against the Phillies, only to suffer yet another shutout in nightcap, 8-0, at the hands of rookie Jeff James. James's case was typical because only 8 of the 15 different pitchers to throw zeroes against the Cubs in 1968 had winning records.

The team rebounded from the defeat, winning 9 of their remaining 13 July contests. Ernie Banks swatted his 18th homer in the final game of the month as Ferguson Jenkins continued his crawl over the .500 line with a 6-1 dusting of the Astros in Wrigley Field. "I'm pitching a lot better than

I did last year when I won twenty," said the right-handed ace, now just 12-10, "I have better command of my pitches primarily."

July was a turnaround month for the 1968 Cubs, as they went 21-11, 14-5 from July 13 on. Though hitting only .245 for the month, the Cubs blasted 23 homers and averaged 4.0 runs per outing. Billy Williams connected eight times, followed by Banks with six. Together, they knocked in over 40 runs. The big story, however, was the pitching. The team ERA for July was just 2.52, with Jenkins and Regan leading the way. Fergie rolled up six wins against a single 1-0 defeat, turning in a mind-boggling 1.30 ERA in the process. The virtually unhittable Vulture pitched 20 innings in July without allowing a single earned run. Two other starters, Hands and Niekro, were 4-2 and 4-0, respectively.

In brief, the good news was that the Cubs were now 54-52. The bad news was that they remained in 5th, fully 16 lengths behind the 70-36 Cardinals.

The Cubs made a minirun at the Cardinals as August opened with a series in St. Louis. After sweeping the first two, on Sunday, August 4 the Cubs faced off against the estimable Bob Gibson. Fully 47,445 swamped Busch Stadium to celebrate the unveiling of a Stan Musial statue outside the park. "The Man" was there of course, as were a number of his former teammates for the pregame festivities.

The game was high drama. Down 4-3 in the top of the 9th, light-hitting Al Spangler stunned the Redbirds with a round-tripper to open the frame. Nonetheless, the Cardinals and Gibson pressed on. In the 11th, the Cubs pushed over a run, claiming a 5-4 advantage. It was not to last, as the Cards evened it up in the bottom of the inning.

With Gibby gone after 11, the game was in the bullpen for each team. No one tallied in the 12th. In the 13th, however, the Cubs struck for the winning run on a clutch two-out pinch single off the bat of none other than future Bruin skipper Lee Elia.

Despite the three-game brooming of the Cardinals, the team remained 13 lengths away. Moreover, a week and a half later, the Cards came to Chicago and effectively knocked the Cubs out of the race permanently.

That was the season.

"Deflated" and "disappointed" at the time, George Castle puts it well. "There was a tremendous surge going into that last big Cardinal series—hoopla abounded. Right there, however, it just ended."

"I was very disappointed after the slow start," says Craig Lynch. "They had picked up Lou Johnson and I felt he would be the difference, but it didn't work out. The hitting just never came around."

"It was an up-and-down year," says Grobstein, who raced to Wrigley Field after summer school at a nearby facility. "The Cards and the Giants were just too tough."

There was, however, other drama during the month of dog days. On August 8, Regan's overactive sweat glands got him in trouble. Seemingly all but untouchable, suspicions of spitters reached intense proportions, as umpire Chris Pelekoudas went to the mound. A crowd of 30,942 Wrigley patrons booed voluminously as Pelekoudas examined the Vulture's hat and glove. When the game resumed, the umpire—who later claimed to have felt vaseline in Regan's cap—whistled the reliever for three illegal pitches. One wiped out a fly ball, another a strikeout, and still another transformed a strike into a ball. The now unfriendly hometown rooters hooted loudly and heaved trash onto the grounds of the Friendly Confines.

Durocher, Hundley, and Spangler were all shown the door by the umpiring crew. "Durocher put on a real show when Regan got checked," says Lynch, who witnessed the ruckus. "When he got ejected, the fans went crazy with rage."

Durocher was incensed. In an interview, he stated, "I guarantee Pelekoudas will never do that again." Is that a threat?" Leo was asked. "I guarantee Pelekoudas will never do that again," the skipper repeated defiantly.

The Cubs did prevail on two fronts—winning the game and later convincing NL President Warren Giles to rule that better evidence should be necessary before pitches are ruled illegal.

Jenkins, however, astutely discerned the genesis of a problem that would haunt the team in days to come. "With opposing managers urging umpires to search him, Regan became angry and frustrated. He did not know how to counter this attack. We began to lose close ball games that Regan previously would have saved. The continual harassment disrupted Regan's concentration, affected his control and rhythm, and reduced his effectiveness. He was never again the relief pitcher he had been," wrote the Cub ace.

The offense kicked in during August, as the team scored nearly 4½ runs a game, moving them into second behind Cincinnati in runs scored. With Glenn Beckert their top hitter for the month at .294 (and the season, .285), it was the long ball that drove the offense. Their 34 August jacks put them atop the NL, with 102 for the campaign. Banks and Williams each slammed eight round-trippers, while Williams and Santo each knocked in more than 20 runs for the month. Randy Hundley emerged from his hitting doldrums, cracking four homers and sending home 17 runs, while batting a respectable .271.

Jenkins, though posting a 4.40 August ERA, won four of his six decisions, as did Bill Hands, now an established starter at 14-9 and 2.98 on the season. Phil Regan was now a sparkling 10-4 and 2.19 on the campaign, having yielded a measly 99 hits over 115 frames. After these three, the pitching was suspect. Holtzman was still under .500, while Niekro and Nye had plus-4.00 ERAs.

The ballpark was no safe haven from the political unrest of 1968. Grobstein remembers well a warm August evening in Los Angeles, watching his favorites do battle at Dodger Stadium. "The Cubs scored heavily early and won easily. On the scoreboard was the message, 'In Chicago it's Humphrey on the first ballot.' The fans booed."

The Cubs closed the month with a 6-2 defeat at the hands of the Astros in Wrigley Field. Joe Niekro, now 13-9, took the loss, giving the Cubs a 17-15 mark for the month. It put them in 4th place at 71-67 for the season, 15½ behind the 86-51 Cardinals.

During the first three weeks of September, the Cubs lurched back and forth. On September 9 and 10, Billy Williams cracked five circuit blasts in two games. On the 11th, however, Ferguson Jenkins suffered his fifth 1-0 setback against the Mets. The five 1-zip losses tied a major league record.

Having gone a disappointing 8-11 thus far in the final month, with but five games remaining, the Cubs were just a single game in advance of .500 at 79-78. The team needed to win three of their final five to lock up a winning 82-80 year.

On September 24 they got the first one, 3-2 over the Dodgers in Wrigley Field. Ferguson Jenkins pitched a strong game, winning his 19th as Adolfo Phillips hammered his 12th homer.

The next day the Cubs clinched a .500 record in dramatic fashion. Right-hander Bill Singer went to the 9th up 1-0. Facing another whitewash, the Cubs managed to load the bases with one out. Up stepped the embattled Ron Santo, whom Singer fanned his previous time at bat. Fans hoped for the best, but feared the worst—a twin killing or another strikeout. They needn't have worried, as the third baseman lifted a Singer slant over the wall for a grand slam and a rousing 4-1 victory.

Phil Regan (11-5), who pitched the 9th for Bill Hands, was the beneficiary of Santo's blast. "I've been missing my pitch an awful lot this year," said the batting hero. "The time before I hit the homer, I was trying to hit a home run and I struck out. I came to the bench and I just couldn't understand how I missed those pitches—all three good fastballs. Then when

I went up with the bases loaded in the ninth, I knew all we needed was a base hit so I just tried to meet the ball."

Durocher called the win "the biggest game we've had in our last four or five. It gives the club a lift and a little momentum."

September 26 was an off day, with the Pirates coming in the following day for a weekend series.

Ken Holtzman (11-14) whipped the Bucs 4-1 in the series opener on Al Spangler's pinch hit two-bagger in the 7th. It was Spangler's eighth pinch hit of the season. Regan worked the last two frames, saving Holtzman's triumph.

The Cubs then won their 82nd game (and 4th straight) on the strength of a complete game effort by now 20-game winner Ferguson Jenkins 4-3, despite the ace yielding 11 Pirate hits. Phillips (13), newly acquired Willie Smith (5), and Ron Santo (25) smacked homers.

According to the *Tribune,* it was a stirring win. "The electric excitement, which has been so much a part of the daily Wrigley Field scene this summer, did not miss a pulsating beat even on the eve of its closing yesterday, thanks in great measure to determined Ferguson Jenkins and a 'liberated' Ron Santo," the newspaper reported.

For Jenkins, it was his 40th start, 20 of which were route-going performances. He worked 308 innings for the team, and his 260 strikeouts were a new team high.

The final game of the season was another Wrigley Field thriller. The Cubs managed just three hits against the Bucs, but still triumphed 5-4. Fittingly, Phil Regan (12-5) got the win in relief of Bill Hands, as the bullpen ace turned in three innings, yielding a lone run.

Although the Cardinals sprinted home with a 97-65 mark, followed by the Giants at 88-74, the win gave the Cubs an 84-78 log and a second straight sole occupancy of third place, a game ahead of the Reds in NL chase. "It was a nice win, I'm pleased and grateful," said a happy Durocher.

The mood among more than 16,000 Cub rooters was positively festive in Wrigley. They had witnessed a rollicking close to an up-and-down season, with the finale going to their heroes in the face of severe hitting woes.

"It was a most improbable finish yesterday in Wrigley Field to the Chicago Cubs' 93rd season of baseball," reported the morning *Tribune.* "From the remarkable assembly of 16,860 fans who turned out to celebrate as if a pennant had been won, to the five runs scored by the Cubs with only three hits to beat Pittsburgh 5 to 4, it was truly a memorable afternoon."

The passionate Cub disciples lingered in the Friendly Confines in the aftermath of a game in which the Pirates committed six errors, the last of which gave the Bruins the game and their third-place finish.

"What a finish!" exclaimed Ron Santo after the game. His robust final week, during which he all but carried the Cubs through a five-game winning streak, redeemed what had been a difficult season, one in which he had been "a brooding and disenchanted slugger."

A closer look at the Cubs' performance in 1968 indicates they were very, very fortunate to finish six over .500 for the year. The team scored exactly 1 run more than it gave up (612-611), making them a .500 operation, using the reseach formula that predicts a team's win-loss record.

Indeed, pitching dominated baseball and the National League in 1968, as fully 641 fewer runs crossed the plate for the 10 teams in the senior circuit as compared with the previous year. Hence the Cubs, who scored 90 fewer tallies than in league-leading 1967, still ranked second in scoring. In reality, their offense was hardly average, considering their home address, as they scored four runs fewer than expected when factoring in the offensive effect of Wrigley Field.

Again, scoring was adversely affected by Durocher's continued decision to make his chief table-setter Don Kessinger. The shortstop hit .240 and posted an on base percentage of only .283, a stunning 17 points under the league average. Glenn Beckert was of limited help in loading the sacks, as his OBP was just 34 points above his solid .294 batting average, owing to his seeming unwillingness to work a base on balls, as his 31 walks indicate.

Strong second-half power numbers, enabling the team to finish with a .366 slugging percentage (25 points over the league average), brought in the runs. That Beckert led the league in runs scored with 98 is testimony to the hard-hitting of Williams, Santo, and Banks. In fact, Williams, who led the league in total bases with 321, was third in slugging at .500, fourth in homers (30), and tied with Santo for runner-up in RBI at 98. Banks, hitting fifth, backed the other two with 32 home runs, third in the league, with his highest total since 1962. The Big Three hit 68% of the team's home runs and drove in 45% of the club's runs, with the embattled Santo still managing to place fifth in the league in TBR (Total Baseball Ranking).

Of valid concern, however, was the absence of any real running game. Their 41 stolen bases were the fewest in the league. In addition, they were thrown out 30 times. Because of the potentially rally-killing effect of having a player gunned down on the bases, a team has to steal successfully at least two-thirds of the time to derive any benefit at all. Not only did the team not steal often, it stole self-destructively.

Although the Cubs again led the NL infielding with a .981 mark, committing a league-low 119 errors, the pitching was spotty. The team ERA of 3.41 was 42 points over the league mean. Even adjusting for the effects of Wrigley Field, the staff yielded 40 more runs than expected.

Performancewise, the staff could be cut in thirds. Clearly, the top 3—Jenkins, Regan, and Hands—carried the load. As good as Fergie's 20-15 record and 2.63 ERA were, Bill Hands may have been even more effective. The 28-year-old had now arrived as a starter going 16-10 with a 2.49 ERA. The two combined for 31 complete games. Regan, of course, was incredible, winning 10 against 5 losses and leading the league with 25 saves after being traded to the Windy City, and registering a 2.20 ERA.

Baseball people often consider the strikeout:walk ratio to be among the best measures of a pitcher's success. The Cub triumvirate far outperformed the league average of about 2:1 favoring strikeouts, with Jenkins at better than 4:1 (260-65), Regan nearly 3:1 (60-24) and Hands well above 2:1 (181-73).

The next three consisted of Holtzman, Nye, and Niekro. Dick Dozer's preseason cautions concerning Kenny Holtzman, unfairly tabbed by many as fellow Jewish lefty Sandy Koufax's successor in the category of southpaw dominance, were well placed. After going 9-0 with a 2.53 ERA in part-time duty in 1967, the lefty fell to 11-14 and 3.35 in 1968. The other southpaw Rich Nye, 13-10 a year earlier, was just 7-12 in 1968 with a 3.80 ERA. Opening Day starter Joe Niekro posted 14 victories against 10 defeats but had a bulging 4.32 ERA to go with it.

The previously noted six hurlers accounted for 155 of the team's starts and over 83% of the innings worked. Although the rest of the staff started but seven games and worked only 235 innings, the following table, which compares the three groups, indicates how badly they performed.

	W-L	SV	GS-CG	IP-HITS	SO-W	ERA
Jenkins/Hands/Regan	46-30	25	74-31	694-585	501-162	2.49
Holtzman/Nye/Niekro	35-36	4	81-14	525-550	290-169	3.79
Others	3-12	3	7-1	235-264	103-61	5.25
TOTAL	84-78	32	162-46	1454-1399	894-392	3.41

Some of this performance differential may be attributable to how well the various pitchers had adjusted to Wrigley Field. A point Fergie

Jenkins makes to this day about Wrigley Field provides grist for thought. "That park," says Jenkins, "is unforgivable. You need pitchers who know what they're doing."

One could make the argument that the upper tier in the table, consisting of more veteran hurlers, had made a better and fuller adjustment to this Windy City horsehide cauldron than the second group and were infinitely more acclimated than the bottom group, which had little experience launching their missiles on Chicago's North Side.

On one hand, 1968 did not prove nearly as successful as the Cub organization had hoped. In fact, one could say the team underachieved, coming in 3.5 games behind the high-energy renaissance year of 1967. On the other hand, no one figured on catching the Cardinals, who again looked bulletproof once the season got into full swing. As such, the Cubs—who split their 18 games with the Redbirds—were a year away, but likely no more.

Despite the lackluster start and never really competing, fully 1,043,409 fans attended festivities in Wrigley. It was the first time in 16 years that the team had cleared the million mark. After the rousing close to the season, I looked forward to 1969. George Castle was also optimistic. "It was the first time since '46 that the Cubs had two straight winners," he says.

Despite falling short, Grobstein—who still remains an object of South Side tormentors as a sports talk-show host—was satisfied. "They managed to stay above .500 and remain in the first division. Besides, that was the year the Sox started something like oh and ten and were dead meat out of the gate, so my Sox friends were off my back."

With back-to-back winning seasons and a solid nucleus at bat and on the mound, one could indeed sense the team was now ready to make a run. There was clearly a wait-'til-next-year feeling permeating the off-season Chicago air. Durocher was back to his old predictive self, stating for the *Chicago American*, "The Cubs are now ready to go for all the marbles. We have sound hitting, the best defense in the league, and pitching that is constantly improving."

Chicago Sun-Times scribe Jerome Holtzman, wasn't buying. Calculating that only Jenkins, Hands, and Holtzman were certain for the rotation, he argued that the team needed another starter. Moreover, with Adolfo Phillips still not fully proven in the picket, hence only Billy Williams a certain offensive force in the outfield, Holtzman felt the team needed another solid addition in center or leftfield.

Durocher, however, gave no quarter to the outfield matter. He cited 18-year-old Oscar Gamble, Jim McMath, and Jim Dunegan as "three of the hardest hitting prospects you will ever see." Moreover, there was always Phillips.

Until spring training.

Adolfo changed the climate by breaking a bone in his right hand. Despite the injury, Durocher was undaunted. "Gamble's my centerfielder," Leo proclaimed. "Whatsa matter? Did 'ya ever hear of Ott and Frisch?" Durocher answered the skeptics. "They didn't need any experience. They started right off in the big leagues." As it turned out, Gamble was unable to gain the manager's confidence and was sent to the minors. McMath and Dunegan weren't hard-hitting enough to get into the lineup, either.

The resourceful skipper, always looking for young players to develop, then turned his eyes toward a 22-year-old unknown in centerfield, Don Young. Young already had the good glove label, so Leo offered this preseason analysis: "He could have a great future, but it's up to him. I don't care what he hits. I want to see more enthusiasm from him. He's got to be more aggressive."

Despite the cynics, and who could blame them with the Cub organization now 0 for 23 as far as championships are concerned, Durocher believed. The fans believed. And when I intercepted Brickhouse to ask him a question one winter night in Milwaukee, as he was hustling out of the arena after having broadcast a Chicago Bulls/Milwaukee Bucks basketball game, I know I believed.

"What happened to Holtzman in '68?" I queried the ever-optimistic Brickhouse.

"Kenny was just gathering a little wool out there on the mound," said Brick, fond of a colloquial turn of phrase. "He should be fine."

It seemed the door to the champagne room was ajar. A championship of some sort seemed more in reach, owing to the restructuring brought about by expansion. With 12 teams in each loop beginning in 1969, each league was divided into two 6-team divisions.

In the Cubs' domain—the National League East—the Cardinals seemed to have completed their dominance after being upset by the Motor City Tigers in the 1968 World Series. Pittsburgh, readying themselves for a run, was not quite there. The Phillies had run their circuit in the mid-1960s and were heading downward. Montreal was a brand-new expansion entry, destined for 110 losses. That left the Mets, who were, well, the Mets. After going a ghastly 40-120 in their maiden voyage of 1962, they had yet to have anything close to even a single winning season. The laughable entry from the nation's largest city had won but 73 in 1968, dropping 89.

Most important, the players believed. The nucleus had been there for three years and had gone a total of 19 games over .500 the previous two. Durocher was now a baseball giant in the Windy City, the man who could turn defeatist water into winning wine.

"Leo Durocher has been a tonic for this ball club. Leo is tough, he's real tough. He'll do anything to win, but he told us we were good and we believe him. He's one in a million," exulted Ron Santo during spring training.

In preparation for the championship chase, catcher Randy Hundley spent the off-season lifting weights and ingesting a high-protein diet. "The last couple of years, I spent more time working on my catching, and my hitting fell off. But this spring, I've spent a lot of extra time in the batting cage . . . and I feel my bat is much quicker," said the iron-man receiver.

Santo slimmed down to 198 pounds. Using the pronoun *we,* the captain seemed to capture the spirit of the team. "With five games to play last year, we were in position to finish anywhere from third to sixth. Leo called a meeting. It was one of his great meetings. We got the message. Look it up. We won the last five games and finished third."

The Cubs were lovable losers no more. Santo uttered the foregoing to make his point: The Chicago Cubs were now battle tested. They were tough like Leo. Those five straight victories "showed us what we can do under pressure."

"We were an enthusiastic team going into the 1969 season," wrote Jenkins, "a team with absolute faith in Durocher's leadership."

"We won 84 games [in 1968], fewer than the year before, but strangely I felt more satisfied with our progress after that year," noted Santo. "I knew something special was around the corner. I just KNEW that 1969 would be our year."

The table was set. The Cubs were now an established winner, ready to claim it all in 1969. Despite an air of confidence, Leo did indicate one area of weakness. "The only thing I'm concerned about is our lack of depth," said the skipper.

Seven

1969

The Cubs are now ready to go for all the marbles.
Leo Durocher, on the prospects for 1969

The title of this chapter, a simple number, need not be embellished.
The season was the agony and ecstasy of the second half of the twentieth
century for the Chicago Cubs. The memory of that year seems scorched
eternally into the psyches of Cub fans and those who played during that
fateful season. Ken Holtzman, a pitching cornerstone of the three-time
world champion Oakland A's and later of the champion New York Yankees,
captured the impact of that year in telling Rick Talley, "I must admit that
from start to finish, that season had more excitement than did any of my
seasons in Oakland or New York."

No year in the second half of the Cub century has received even remotely as much attention as 1969. Not 1984, not 1989, not 1998's wild
card playoff campaign. Not one comes within light years of the attention
the 1969 near championship run receives. The *Chicago Tribune* dedicated
a near total sports section to it a decade later (June 8, 1979), a former
Chicago sportswriter wrote a delightful then-and-now book on the 1969
team, and myriad baseball fans continue to discuss and debate 1969.

It was the summer of the Woodstock Music and Art Festival, where
400,000 camped out near White Lake, New York. It was also the summer
of Chappaquiddick and of Charles Manson. People were just getting used
to calling Richard Nixon "President Nixon." Riots had given way to rock

festivals, and Chicago's near north area, called Old Town, reminded tourists and city residents of parts of San Francisco, with its nightly throngs of youth walking the streets, eating in the restaurants, attending lectures in the coffeehouses, and listening to music in the lively bistros.

For those among the largest Opening Day crowd since 1929, a standing-room-only throng of 40,796, it was clear 1969 was the year of destiny for the Cubs. On that brisk April 8, I was one of the standing. The electricity of the moment was fed by the presence of fabled funnyman Jimmy Durante, popular Governor Richard Ogilvie, famed sportswriter Edgar Munzel, and 38-year-old Mr. Cub's 73-year-old father, who received a standing ovation when introduced. The pregame festivities were stimulating but also suspenseful. It was time to play ball.

After the Phillies plated a single run in the top of the 1st, it was the beloved Cubs' turn to flex their muscles and deliver a taste of Cub power. And flex them they did. With two Cubs aboard, the #5 hitter, Ernie Banks, stepped to the plate. Banks eyed Phillie ace left-hander Chris Short, then picked out the pitch he wanted, and drove it over the ivy-covered left-field wall for a three-run circuit shot. It was Cubs 3, Phillies 1, and pandemonium.

Cub fans settled in, excited and relieved. They were thrilled to witness a dramatic Cub homer and were comforted that their aging hero Ernie Banks had demonstrated he still had it in 1969. Now it was up to two-time 20-game winner Ferguson Jenkins to do what they were all certain he would do, tame the Philadelphia bats. In the 3rd inning, however, there was bonus excitement. With a teammate aboard, a Cub rocketed another Chris Short-offering over the left-field barrier to make it 5-1. That Cub was Ernie Banks.

With that, the scoring abated for the next 3 innings. With a single Phillie tally in the 7th, Jenkins took the mound in the 9th, up 5-2, and with certain victory in hand. Then disaster hit. Jenkins allowed two base runners, then threw the home-run ball to Phillie shortstop Don Money, his second of the game.

With the score now tied, Durocher summoned ace fireman Phil Regan. The Vulture mowed down the enemy in the 9th and 10th. The Cubs, shut out for 7 straight innings, took the field in the 11th, hoping this would be the winning frame.

It was. With Johnny Callison aboard, nemesis Don Money reached Regan for a two-bagger, sending the visitors ahead 6-5. The mood was one of shocking disbelief. Not only had Banks's two-homer, five-RBI game not been enough, but no less a personage than complete-game ace Ferguson Jenkins had yielded a three-run lead in the 9th. Furthermore, the Phillies had even gotten to Phil Regan, pinning him with now undeniable defeat, with the lower half of the order due up in the Cub 11th.

With one out, Randy Hundley managed to get aboard. With that, Durocher—needing a left-handed bat—instructed former boxer, sometime singer, and utility outfielder, Willie Smith, to hit for the 0 for 4 rightfielder Jim Hickman. Barry Lersch, having shackled the Cubs for 4⅓ innings, readied to dispose of the crooning batsman. For Cub fans, no song of Smith's would ever be as sweet as the sight of his swing, one that sent Lersch's slant flying over the right-field wall for a 7-6 Cub triumph.

It was absolute bedlam. The ultimate Opening Day. The players mobbed Smith and the fans rejoiced deliriously. The final three lines of the Cubs' much-played unofficial theme song, which rocked out of the juke-boxes of Windy City watering holes all summer long, said it best.

Hey, hey, holy mackerel,
No doubt about it,
The Cubs are on their way.

Anyone who didn't believe, believed now. According to Ron Santo, "I confess that I never had the feeling that we were certain to win every game in 1967 or 1968," he relates. "When the Dodgers or Giants would come in to Wrigley Field, there was a sense they had the guns to beat us every time. That all changed in 1969. Every time I went out there, I thought we would win. Every game."

Early in the season, realizing that the world champion Detroit Tigers would be following them into Philadelphia for an exhibition game, an unknown Cub wrote on the visiting clubhouse's blackboard, "See you in the World Series if you can make it."

The victorious opener led to triumphs in the next three games. A loss to the expansion Expos in game five, was a mere interruption. The Bruins then reeled off seven more wins in succession. The season barely started, the Cubs were 11 and 1. And on top.

And it was fun. Ernie Banks, echoing Holtzman's sentiments said, "It was the most joyous time of my life. For five hours a day—clubhouse, field, back in the clubhouse—we were like a bunch of brothers. Billy and Randy and Nate cut that record 'Hey, Hey, Holy Mackerel' [actually Smith, Nate and Gene Oliver]. Willie Smith would sing it on the bus or plane, and we'd all join in. I never in my life experienced that kind of fun."

A fresh epidemic of Cub fever engulfed Chicago. Cub-glorifying bumper stickers again adorned legions of vehicles, while similarly labeled

T-shirts sold wildly. The popularity of autographed drinking mugs and baseballs, along with pictures and posters, gained momentum throughout the summer. Any event featuring a personal appearance by a Cub player was a certain hit. A self-styled marketeer, Jack Childers, drove the memorabilia and personal-appearance machine. In this preagent, pre–free agent era, income from this marketing bonanza was distributed across the roster, not unlike postseason shares, all of which was overseen by player rep Phil Regan.

After bagging 11 of their first dozen outings, the Cubs embarked on a four-game losing snag. When the Cardinals handed the Cubs their fourth straight downer, 3-2 in Wrigley on April 24, Redbird skipper Red Schoendienst laid down the gauntlet. "The next time we leave Chicago, we'll be in first place," he challenged. The Cubs answered Schoendienst with five wins in their next seven games. Chicago closed the books on April at 16-7, two in front of Pittsburgh, the only other divisional foe with a winning log.

The hysteria was palpable. A huge throng greeted the team at the airport upon their return from their first lengthy road trip. Independent "good 'ol Channel 9" was now a ratings winner amid network competition. Ernie became a Sunday sports reporter and later a *Tribune* columnist. Though still spring, October was around the corner in the fans' minds, as 2,000 letters and 600 daily phone calls requesting World Series tickets, deluged Wrigley Field offices. Fans lined up in the early morning every day to purchase one of those precious 23,000 unreserved seats on sale each game day. A substantial number of those ticket buyers were part of a now nationally famous group—the Bleacher Bums. Clad in yellow hardhats, the boisterous throng cheered and celebrated gamelong.

Columnist Bill Gleason remembers them well. "The yellow construction helmets were real at first. This caught on in the bleachers, such that everybody started to buy these yellow helmets. The guys who wore them at the beginning were part of the original Bleacher Bums, and they were construction workers. These were big, brawny, profane people who would insult the other team's outfielders and threaten them. 'You want to come back of the stands after the game? I'll meet you.' They were originals. *Sun-Times* columnist Jack Griffin really made the Bleacher Bums. He ran with them, going over to Murphy's after games. He wrote many columns and immortalized a few of those nuts."

Soon the Bleacher Bums were in full fashionable boom. "They were 17–25-year-olds in the left-field bleachers," explains Craig Lynch. "I remember being there in 1969. There was nonstop cheering—not because the Cubs were winning, but like a college atmosphere."

And they had an impact, according to Santo. "They were rabid and loud: They actually became our tenth man on the field. I truly believe they were a catalyst for success from Opening Day," he claims. Dick Selma, acquired in late April to provide the team with that much-needed fourth starter, became the Bums official cheerleader, as he waved a bullpen towel to incite their vocal passions.

Relations between the bleacher denizens and the Cub players were truly cordial. Author George Castle relates a memorable example: "I saw a drunken fan fall out of the bleachers onto the warning track, and Willie Smith actually hoisted him back up over the wall—this was before the basket existed—and back into the bleachers before the security officers got to him."

"People falling out of the stands in the heyday of the Bums was why they put up the basket," claims Gleason, with good humor. "The net was not for baseballs, it was to keep those idiots from killing themselves."

WSCR talk-show host, Mike Murphy, who became famous for tooting his call-to-action bugle, eliciting a mighty "Charge!" loves to tell of a Bums' excursion to St. Louis.

"We stayed at the team hotel, the Chase Park Plaza, downtown," says the former hornblower. "It was an expensive, first-class hotel, pretty steep for a bunch of students and Vietnam vets. We all chipped in, staying 20 to a room. In the lounge we'd try to make a twenty-five-cent beer last as long as possible. One night Durocher laid down a twenty-dollar bill and declared the drinks were on him for the night. The players partied along with us. Santo, Beckert, Jenkins—guys our age—would take us with them to the racetrack."

Les Grobstein's charity softball experience illustrates the bond the fans had with the players. "In July of 1969 I was involved in a softball benefit at Thillens Stadium, a local park in the city. We got Ernie Banks and Fergie Jenkins to come and sign autographs before the game. Ernie left after the session, but Fergie stayed around for our game. Then he offered to pitch on my team and did for two or three innings. He started the next day in Wrigley Field against the Mets.

"Fergie Jenkins and Billy Williams were my favorites," says Grobstein. "Fergie had the whole package, he was the classiest guy on the planet."

Opposing players found the Bums less winsome. "They drove Willie Davis to distraction," recalls Lynch. And for good reason. The fans had unearthed the name of Dodger outfielder Davis's Chicago girlfriend and proceeded to chant "Ruthie" at him throughout the contest. The usual non-power-hitting Davis responded with two opposite field jacks over the left-field wall.

Fox broadcaster and former Giant catcher during the 1980s, Bob Brenly, refers to Wrigley Field denizens as "very knowledgeable." "In some parks the fans will rag on you, they'll call you by your number and tell you that you stink," he says. "These fans do their homework. 'Hey, you hit into 18 double plays last year, for crying out loud, how slow are you?' They don't just tell you that you stink. They'll tell you why you stink."

Though he enjoyed coming to Wrigley as a visiting player, Brenly can relate well to the Davis experience. "Chicago's a great nightlife town and a lot of the fans are out on the streets," he explains. "If they run into you there, they may remind you the next day as you do your work in the outfield before the game. 'Hey, I saw you at the Lodge last night. You think you'll get any hits today?' they'll yell."

Writer Castle, in his well-researched book *The I-55 Series*, describes the pregame guerrilla warfare in which Cardinal pitcher Jim "Mudcat" Grant engaged during a midseason series with the Redbirds. Mike Murphy, standing above the 368-foot sign in left center tooted his attention-getting bugle, evoking a voluminous "Charge!" from the throng.

That, and some good-natured barbs, hit the right-hander's threshold point. "Grant snapped," noted Ned Colletti, who later served in the Bruins' front office. Young Mr. Murphy found himself at a disadvantage.

According to Murphy, "Mudcat walked to the warning track and looked up at me. He was standing no more than 12 feet away from me. He had a back pocket full of baseballs. I was wearing the open-toed sandals that were popular at the time. He took the first ball and cocked his arm. I thought he was just going to fake a throw. But he fired a 90-mile-an-hour fastball, and it hit the top inch of the wall, just below my toe. The ball ricocheted halfway back to second base. The next ball, he did the same thing, hitting the wall one inch below my sandals. He had perfect aim." With that, Murphy took off like a broken-field runner, weaving his way through the masses. Grant didn't give up, rifling four more throws in his direction, three of which hit innocent fans.

The Bums weren't through. The following day Ron Grousi purchased seven white mice with the intention of scaring Cub nemesis—outfielder Lou Brock. When the fans hurled the rodents fieldward while the game was in progress, a cool Brock remained unfazed. Cub outfielder Willie Smith, however, was so unnerved when he took his position that he ran to the dugout, halting the game while the grounds crew rounded up the unwelcome guests.

The team roared through the first half of May, going 8-4 with a five-game winning skein. Despite losing Beckert, when the second baseman was hit in the cheek with a pitch in a May 13 19-0 shellacking of the San Diego Padres, the club didn't slow down. Nate Oliver stepped in and immediately contributed offensively. They closed the month with machine-like consistency, posting eight wins in their remaining 13 contests. May was pitching month for the Cubs, with the team hurling nine shutouts, three by Ken Holtzman. Dick Selma, who won the May 13 19-0 rout, came back 10 days later with a 6-0 whitewash of the Padres in San Diego.

The Cubs had won 16 games in April and 16 more in May. For the book, their two-month log was now 32-16, lengthening their lead to seven and a half games over the 1-over-.500 Pittsburgh Pirates.

• • •

The Lip was feeling his Cheerios like never before. Impatient with the slow-recovering Adolfo Phillips, in early May the lion roared that the centerfielder was ready "but doesn't want to play." When questioned about ripping one of his charges publicly, Durocher, never wanting for an answer, said, "In three years, I've tried everything else. I'll do everything I can to wake him up." More troubled than awakened, Phillips appeared in just 28 games, hitting just .224 in 49 at bats.

By early June Phillips was gone, having left the Cubs in a deal with Montreal for utility infielder Paul Popovich. Durocher had effectively cut Phillips off, reportedly scarcely speaking to him during his final month with the club. "One day Leo said, 'He's out of here,'" relates Randy Hundley, looking back. "We used to play Crazy 8's on the plane, Adolfo, Leo, and myself. One day Leo said, 'Get him out of here. Back up the truck.'"

Phillips, once a regular and Durocher favorite, refused to shake the manager's hand upon his departure. The once budding star left the Cubs a broken young man. He was never the same, batting only 430 more times in the major leagues and out of baseball at 30 years old.

Clearly, Durocher's impatience and impulsivity were costly in the case of Phillips. By failing to establish any rapport with the sensitive Phillips, Leo mishandled him badly, squandering the ability of a player that teammates thought was exploding with potential. "Adolfo could have been a great player," states Hundley. "I don't know exactly what happened to him."

Fergie Jenkins did. "Adolfo, a hawk-nosed, slenderly built Panamanian, was an overly gifted ballplayer," wrote Fergie. "He had great talent and did things easily, without struggling or strenuous effort. He had a strong arm, he could run, and he hit for both power and average. One-handed, he could hit the ball out of the park. He was only twenty-three [when he came over from Philadelphia with Jenkins], and it seemed as if he would become a great ballplayer.

"Unfortunately, Adolfo was not in good health. Few people were aware of it, but Adolfo had a kidney problem. When he caught a cold, it would settle in his kidney, and he had a lot of blood in his urine. His back also ached because of the kidney ailment.

"Adolfo got the reputation of not wanting to play and was accused of 'jaking.' I got to know Adolfo well, rooming with him for a while, and he always wanted to play. He just couldn't because of his health, and it was unfair of people to accuse him of being a quitter.

"People did not find out what was the matter with Adolfo until after he had been traded from the Cubs to Montreal in 1969. The following year he had to undergo an operation for a stomach tumor. He also had an ulcer caused by worry, pressure that had been put on him by his teammates and Durocher. Adolfo was extremely sensitive. He had to take tranquilizers to settle his nerves."

While many players did not take well to the banishment of their popular teammate, Popovich would prove to be a contributor. Moreover, games were being won, and an air of ongoing celebration permeated the city.

Still but a nose in front of the on-charging Cardinals in June, Santo noted a pivotal game. "Trailing 3-1 to the expansion Expos, I was giving in to negative thoughts. Then Jim Hickman, the oldest starter on the club other than Ernie, came up in the bottom of the ninth with two outs and two on. Hickman never received big attention for his hitting, particularly for the way he could hit the long ball—maybe that's because he played on the same team as a Billy Williams or an Ernie Banks. But on this day, Hickman was Babe Ruth. He hit a towering home run to leftfield, giving us a 4-3 victory and allowing us to stay in first place.

"There may have been another time in my career when I was more excited, but if so, I can't remember it. When Hickman arrived at home plate, there was the usual mob scene congratulating him. But I was leading the pack, and pounding on his helmet, hugging, slugging, yelling, and screaming like a Little Leaguer. Hickman later told me he had a migraine headache from the pounding he took from me. . . . I don't know what was going through my mind at the time, I ran down the left-field line, listening to the cheers from the fans, and for no particular reason, I jumped in the air—and clicked my heels," explained the third baseman.

Santo was apprehensive about Durocher's reaction to the heel-clicking, realizing Leo didn't approve of actions that would show up opponents and give them an angry incentive. Surprisingly, however, Leo loved it. He approached Santo and said, "Golly, Ron, this has been an exciting year, hasn't it? I've got an idea, Ron. Why don't you make this little clicking bit our victory symbol. Just at home. I think it would be dynamite."

The manager had his own rituals, according to Jenkins. "Leo had certain habits or superstitions, as most ballplayers do. For instance, the same player had to pick up the infield ball and start throwing it around every day while we were winning. Nobody else could touch it. After a victory, the next day Leo made sure the same bats were sitting in front of him in the bat rack in Wrigley Field. If a certain player had been sitting next to him on the bench when we won, that player had to be sitting there the next day."

June 29 was Billy Williams Day at Wrigley Field. Over 10,000 would-be witnesses were turned away as 41,060 packed the yard to honor Billy, and not coincidentally to observe a twin bill against the defending champion Cardinals.

Billy and the Bruins rose to the occasion in the opener as the Northsiders beat Gibson 3-1 behind Fergie's pitching and a big two-bagger by Williams. Jenkins dispensed of the Cardinals in just 126 minutes. Five days later, in 95-degree July 4 St. Louis heat, he would beat Gibby again 3-1, this time in a 10-inning tilt lasting just 2 hours and 32 minutes.

"I want to thank the Almighty God for the ability to play major league baseball. I want to thank God for protecting me over all the games I played," the humble ironman said to the appreciative fans between contests. He then went on to bang out four hits in game 2, helping the Cubs to a 12-1 drubbing of their hated rivals. When he struck out in his last plate appearance in the 8th, he walked to the dugout amid the deafening roars of a goosebump–generating standing ovation.

I remember the husky-voiced Harry Caray, then still the "King of the Ozarks" Cardinal announcer, regaling the Cubs for their consistency after Jenkins throttled the Redbirds in the opener. The Cubbies had won 16 in April, 16 in May, and now 16 more in June, he intoned. Moreover, they were now nearly 15 games ahead of the defending National League champions.

After one more June triumph, the team was 49-27 and running away from the pack. They were seven games in advance of the upstart Mets, who were a surprising 40-32 through the first three months. Things were well in hand with the perpetual failures from New York, the only team in the division within 11 games of the hard-charging Cubs.

It was becoming a season of signal individual achievements. In early June, seemingly ageless Ernie Banks was on a 31-home run, 153-RBI pace. By the end of May, Kenny Holtzman was already 10-1. On June 15 Don Kessinger played a record 54 consecutive games at shortstop with nary an error. On June 29 Billy Williams became the National League ironman, having played in 846 consecutive games.

The Cubs were now firmly ensconced as the darlings of all major league baseball. Their all-afternoon home schedule and national charisma made them a near weekly feature of Saturday NBC Game of the Week. There were few more popular interviews than that of Leo Durocher. Derisively referred to as "the dandy little manager" by Cub announcer Lou Boudreau, Leo played hard to the big-time national press while snubbing the Chicago print and electronic media. Moreover, few could appreciate the joy in Wrigley Field better than NBC play-by-play announcer Curt Gowdy, having served a long tenure behind the mike for the similarly championship-starved Boston Red Sox.

The all-star game figured to be a virtual coronation for the divisional leaders. In late May a highly impressed Walter Alston had said, "If they left it up to me, I'd pick the entire Cub infield and their catcher for the all-star team." In fact, those five players—slick-fielding keystone combo Kessinger and Beckert along with sluggers Banks and Santo, plus catcher Randy Hundley—were named to the senior circuit's squad.

Ron Santo was leaping up and clicking his heels after each Cub victory. With the Bleacher Bums, Santo's theatrics, and the novel experience of watching the team run away with the Eastern Division championship, Wrigley Field contests were now becoming events rather than mere games.

July opened with three straight wins after a surprise defeat at the hands of the woeful Expos, elevating the team's record to 52-28. Now in the middle of an 11-game road trip, the team went down three consecutive times, once in a twin bill in St. Louis. Though both Hands and Holtzman were beaten by the Cardinals, the Cubs had ace Fergie Jenkins ready to open against the Mets in New York.

Crazily enough, the employees of Shea, left for dead in May, entered the game just five games behind the indomitable Cubs. The game moved to the 9th with Chicago in front 3-1. A bizarre set of events then took place. Journeyman Ken Boswell opened the final frame with a seeing-eye two-bagger to right center, falling among Kessinger, Beckert, and seemingly frozen centerfielder Don Young. The estimable Jenkins, who entered the game at 11-5 and en route to another 20-win campaign, shook off the misfortune, retiring Tommie Agee on a foul fly to Banks.

With that, Gil Hodges sent Donn Clendenon up to pinch-hit. A right-handed slugger, Clendenon, hammered a shot deep to left center where Young grabbed it, only to let go of the ball as he slammed into the wall. With runners now on second and third, New York's top hitter Cleon Jones laced a double to tie the game. Still tied, Jenkins bore down with even greater intensity. He intentionally walked Art Shamsky to set up a possible inning-ending double play for his next would-be victim, Wayne Garrett. Garrett did ground out, but managed to move both runners into scoring position in the process.

It was now Jenkins against the lone original Met on the roster, Ed Kranepool. Bamboozled by a low-and-away pitch, Kranepool threw his bat at the offering, only to have it connect with the sphere and send it floating over Don Kessinger's head to drive home the winning run. Unreal. Incredulous. The weak-hitting Mets had pushed over three 9th-inning runs against Jenkins.

Frustrated, humiliated, and enraged, the Cubs headed for the clubhouse. Durocher, once described by baseball Olympus Branch Rickey as having the unique capacity "to make an already bad situation immediately worse," lived up to Rickey's tag. He openly blamed the inscrutable Don Young for the loss, claiming that it was "tough to win when your centerfielder can't catch a blankety-blank fly ball. He stands there watching one and then gives up on the other, it's a disgrace," lamented Durocher, only to continue within earshot of the devastated outfielder. "My three-year-old could have caught those balls."

With Durocher unhinged, Jerome Holtzman of the *Sun-Times* approached Santo, asking whether he had heard Leo's exclamations. Santo remembered that earlier in the game the usually quiet Jim Hickman had told the captain to settle down a riled Don Young, who had thrown his bat and helmet in the dugout after an unsuccessful plate appearance. Santo, who had then grabbed Young and told him to do his job, felt Young had tucked his hitting frustrations in his glove, contributing mightily to the loss.

Young's frustrations had already been in evidence as he positioned himself in the outfield. When Clendenon stepped to the plate, Jenkins motioned him over to the left center alley, but Young didn't budge. "Fergie called me over from third," according to Santo. "'What's with this guy? Why isn't Young moving?'" Fergie wondered aloud.

From the mound, Santo waved Young over. As Santo was motioning, an agitated Durocher headed to the mound and asked what was going on. Once aware of the matter, the manager was rankled. "Get his butt over there," Leo barked angrily and headed for the dugout. But the problem wasn't solved. Young moved only a few strides, and the now distracted Jenkins wanted more. "I waved, and again he was stationary," recalled Santo. "Finally, Young took a few more steps, and at last we're set to face Clendenon."

Young fed his teammates' ire by dressing swiftly and abandoning the clubhouse. Mistaking his instant exit for apathy rather than utter humiliation, Santo stated, "He was just thinking of himself, not the team. He had a bad day at the plate, so he's got his head down. He's worrying about his batting average and not the team. All right, he can keep his head down, and he can keep right on going out of sight for all I care. We don't need that kind of thing."

A firestorm ensued. Santo was awakened in his Waldorf Astoria room at 3 A.M. by a friend, informing him that the *Sun-Times* had boldly stated that he had crossed the unwritten line of publicly criticizing a teammate for losing the game. To Santo's credit, he called a press conference in his tenth-floor room that afternoon and publicly apologized to Young, a player he had conscientiously taken under his professional wing throughout the season. Reiterating his conviction that Young had let his hitting woes rule his glove, Santo spoke empathically. "I know this is true because it has happened to me. I have fought myself when I wasn't hitting and, as a result, messed up in the field. But I know I was wrong. . . . I want everyone to know my complete sincerity in this apology."

No apology, however, ever came from the lips of Durocher.

Back in the hotel the night of the defeat, Young was in no better condition than Adolfo Phillips was earlier in the campaign. Referring to Clendenon's projectile, a distraught Young took total responsibility stating, "I didn't run into the wall on Clendenon's double until I had dropped it. I should have had that ball, but I dropped it. It hit my glove, and I dropped it. I just lost the game for us, that's all I did." That game apparently broke the sensitive youth emotionally. It more than marked Young's career. It effectively ended it.

The next night the on-charging Mets sent their best to the mound, Tom Seaver. More than 59,000 fans watched the right-hander throw a perfect game for 8⅓ innings. It was broken by .243 hitting Jimmy Qualls, who delivered a clean single to left center. Qualls' position? Centerfield.

Banks was impressed with the Mets' poise. "Look at them. They're calm for such a young team. That's pretty strange," he said before the final game of the three-game set. In that one, Bill Hands reached the halfway mark to a 20-win season, besting an error-ridden Met bunch 6-2. A re-energized Santo departed the Big Apple feeling unchallenged by the Mets. "Wait'll we get them in Wrigley Field," were his sentiments.

The team seemed unaffected by the misadventures in Shea. After losing the opening game of the home stand to the Phillies, they reeled off three straight wins in preparation for a three-game set with New York, commencing on July 14. They entered the Mets' series having split their first 14 games in July.

The fans sensed the threat of the Mets and were arriving as early as 6 A.M. to cheer their heroes. By 9:30, a half-hour before the park opened, 215 Andy Frain ushers were at Wrigley for crowd-control purposes. For the game itself, the Chicago police added 28 extra patrolmen and 3 sergeants to the usual contingent. Bill Hands, now emerging as the ace of the staff, beat Seaver 1-0 in a heart-stopping series opener. With the triumph, Santo danced a jig and the Bleacher Bums roared, "ABEEBEE! UNGOWA! CUB POWUH!" mimicking a cheer of the Black Panthers.

"Yes, sir, that was a World Series game," chortled Durocher, subtly suggesting which team had handled the pressure victoriously, as the Bruins moved a more comfortable 5½ games in front of the Eastern Division pack. The Mets seemed less troubled by the loss than by Santo's Fred Astaire–like antics. When Coach Joe Pignatano hollered "Bush," at Santo before the following afternoon's game, Santo responded nonverbally with a middle finger thrust skyward. When exchanging lineups at home plate, Santo, sensitive chap as he is, had a request for manager Gil Hodges. "Tell Piggy that the only reason I click my heels is because the fans will boo me if I don't."

"You remind me of Tug McGraw," Hodges responded, matter-of-factly. "When he was young and immature and nervous, he used to jump up and down, too. He doesn't do it anymore," said Hodges to the 29-year-old, 10-year veteran. Santo had nothing to say.

Santo paid dearly for his heel-clicking. "The rest of the league wasn't so enthralled," he writes. "Once they started catching on to my act, the fastballs seemed to get a lot closer to my head. The brushback pitches seemed to come a lot closer to my chin."

Long before the Mets series, Santo had been informed of opponents' displeasure. Before a game with St. Louis, Tim McCarver told Santo "a lot of guys around the league know what you're doing and they don't like it." During that game, a messenger in the form of a fastball zipped past his chin.

Another rabbit emerged from the New York hat in the game when backup infielder, Al Weis, hit only his second home run in two years off Dick Selma, with two mates on. The dinger accounted for the lion's share of the New York runs in a 5-4 Met win. The Mets then pulled within 3½ spaces the following day when Cub reject Cal Koonce availed himself of the opportunity to stick the spear into Leo, topping Ferguson Jenkins 9-5. Jenkins, whose record fell to 12-7, was in the shower room before the close of the 2nd inning. After the game, Tom Seaver crossed the first-base line, did a dance, leaped, and clicked his heels. For Santo, it was a humiliating afternoon. "They beat us, you have to give them credit for that. Two out of three in our park. I still don't believe it," confessed the humbled third baseman.

When the Cubs packed their bags for their impending trip to Philadelphia, they left their memories of the embarrassment by the Mets behind, taking three of four in Philly. They finished out July with eight home games, four with the Dodgers and four more with the Giants. The Cubs split the two sets to close the month with a mediocre 15-14 mark. At 64-41, Chicago was averaging 16 wins a month and back in front of the Mets by six games overall, three on the loss side.

The soap opera that was July included one more life-on-the-edge caper involving Durocher. Claiming a stomach disorder, Durocher surreptitiously left a nationally televised game in the 3rd inning on Saturday, the 26, sneaking off to Camp Ojibwa in Eagle River, Wisconsin, to attend Parents' Weekend in honor of his new bride's 10-year-old son.

Columnist Bill Gleason recalls with amusement how the one-in-a-million story of Leo's AWOL behavior came to be reported by a Durocher adversary, *Chicago Today* sportswriter James Enright. "One of Enright's pals had a kid up there and he was visiting the youngster," Gleason explains, laughing. "He then called Jim and said, 'Jim, what the blazes is Durocher doing up here?' Jim said, 'What!' That's one of the great baseball stories of all time—the audacity of this guy that he could just sneak away and nobody would know the difference."

P. K. Wrigley was not similarly amused. He was so angry that he was close to waxing Leo. A profusely apologetic Leo returned to manage a victory over the Giants on July 28. The players seemed unaffected by their manager's unapproved sabbatical, but likely enjoyed seeing their fearless field leader publicly humbled.

The Cubs simply tore through early August with six straight triumphs, burying their concerns of the erstwhile contending Mets. By the morning of August 14, the Chicago Cubs—now 9-2 for the month—were 9½ games ahead of flagging New York. The team returned to Chicago after dividing a twin bill at San Francisco with the Giants on the night of August 17. They had a date the following day with the White Sox to play their annual charity game. Though wanting to rest Banks, Beckert, Kessinger, Santo, Williams, and Hundley, Durocher relented and let them play—for the most part, briefly—before a largest-of-the-season 33,333 Comiskey Park crowd. The Cubs won 2-0 on home runs by Banks and Williams.

Up to this point, the team's Big Six had scarcely been rested. Moreover, most were living off the adrenaline of the season and didn't want to sit. In any case, the 75-45 team was now home, where they were a whopping 40-17 and would play 24 of their remaining 42 outings.

Lingering doubts as to whether 1969 was the Year of Destiny for the Cubs were pretty well expunged on August 19 when Ken Holtzman threw a no-hitter against the eventual Western Division champion, Atlanta Braves. The most memorable event in the game occurred in the Atlanta 7th when the great Henry Aaron banged one over the left-field wall, or what seemed like over. Billy Williams stood looking up, with his right arm against the ivy as the sphere headed for Waveland Avenue. Amazingly, at that instant the ball appeared to stop, hang in the wind, and then simply drop into Williams's glove just inside the park.

Holtzman's recollections of the game are sharp. "When we got to the ballpark that morning, people were lined up all the way around the block trying to get tickets for a game with the Braves. It took a great play by Beckert in the first inning to save it. And the wind blew back a hit by Hank Aaron that normally would have been a homer. Billy Williams caught it with his back to the vines." So certain was Hammer that his wallop would enable him to touch them all, he went into his home run trot. He was nearly at second base before Williams grabbed it. "I'll never forget the look Hammer gave me," says Holtzman.

The celebration in Chicago had all the effects of a high school homecoming. "The fans knew the players used a side street—Berteau Avenue—as a secret shortcut to drive home," relates Castle. "After Kenny Holtzman's no-hitter, they were lined up all along Berteau to cheer Holtzman and the rest of the players. It was like a motorcade." "That day seemed to summarize everything that had been going good for us that year," said the victorious pitcher.

The Cubs, though dropping three straight and seven of the next nine after Holtzman's history-maker, closed August with four consecutive victories. Now 82-52, the squad had won 18 and dropped just 11 in the heat of August, the winningest month of their season. On the 26th, they were given the nod to print playoff tickets.

The Mets, however, having triumphed in 21 of their 31 August encounters, now trailed Chicago by four games. They were not going away. In fact, they were gaining. From May 1 through the end of August, the New Yorkers had actually outplayed the Cubs, going 67-43 while the Chicagoans registered a game and a half weaker 66-45.

On September 2, Leo's squad hung two on Cincinnati, one the

completion of a suspended game from June. The Mets, having split their first two games of the month were now five back. Met mentor Gil Hodges talked as though the curtain was falling on his gamers. "We're just playing average ball, and hardly that at times," lamented the former Dodger great, quoted in the *Chicago Tribune*. Concerned about their glovework, Hodges pressed on, "We've come this far because of pitching and defense, but we haven't been playing well defensively of late and our pitching staff has a lot of tired arms."

Met lefty Jerry Koosman reportedly had a tender arm, changing his approach from one emphasizing velocity to control. In addition, hard-hitting Cleon Jones had to sit out several games, owing to a painful hand injury. All was not bleak. Don Clendenon had picked up the offense of late and was verbally challenging the Cubs. "The pressure is still all on the Cubs. This club has learned winning ways and will stay close to Chicago," stated the first baseman. "They know if they fall, we will be right there."

On September 3, fireballing Jim Maloney beat Bill Hands 2-0 in the Queen City. No matter. The road trip was over and the Mets had been taken in LA 5–4. Now 44-24 at Wrigley, the team would be sending Holtzman, Jenkins, and a 10-5 Dick Selma against the visiting Pirates.

Bewilderingly, the first two games were 9-2 and 13-4 Pittsburgh blowouts. Meanwhile the Mets, by winning on the sixth, were just 3½ games away. After the second loss to Pittsburgh, the *Chicago Tribune*, surveying Cub fans, ran an article entitled, "They're Not Going to Fold; Cub Fans Confident."

The series finale, however, was the one that unhinged Durocher. On the strength of a Hickman homer in the 8th, Phil Regan needed just three outs to ice the game. He got two outs and two strikes. Then future Hall-of-Famer Willie Stargell hammered a shot into the teeth of what seemed to Hundley a 35 mph lake wind, over the right-field wall and on to Sheffield Avenue. Game tied, 5-5.

There was plenty of player discontent over Durocher's strategy of leaving Regan in to face the left-handed Stargell. Hank Aguirre, unscored upon in 9 innings by Pittsburgh, was ready. Leo, who apparently could not imagine that Stargell could belt one out against that stiff wind, stayed with his 12-game–winning relief pitcher. Then, after blowing a scoring opportunity in the 10th, in part because Willie Smith failed to sacrifice runners into scoring position, the game went to the 11th. When Don Kessinger committed a critical error in the top of the frame, leading to two Pirate runs, the Cubs' fate was sealed 7-5. With the relentless Mets easily disposing of the Phillies in Shea, 9-3, the Bruins lead had melted to just two and a half.

"To me, that was the pivotal game of the 1969 season," wrote Santo. "You could hear a pin drop as we walked into the clubhouse. Everyone's head was down. Nobody said a word. Our usual routine of staying around and talking about the game was abandoned; we got out of there as quickly as possible."

Durocher, however, was incensed, and aired his charges soon after. The manager seemed to imply that Jenkins—shelled just two days previous—was a "quitter." Players varied in their interpretations. Some felt Leo had aimed his tirade at Fergie, others felt the meeting was "for all of us." Still others felt the heated speech was "constructive criticism," hardly a likely possibility for the acidic Durocher. Jenkins acknowledged that Durocher "got all over me" for not challenging the Bucs' hitters after a defensive lapse in the outfield, involving Williams and (you guessed it!) Don Young.

Players wondered aloud what impact the skipper's lacing would have on their 19-game winner. Remaining quiet during the outburst, Jenkins seemed to shake it off, later pointing out that, as usual, "the slate was clean the next day" with Durocher. Nonetheless, Jenkins flatly denied the quitter charge, saying, "I definitely did not quit Saturday. I lost a little concentration, but I never quit on this club."

There could not be a more inopportune time for the Cubs to head for New York for a two-game set than right then, September 8 and 9. But that is what the schedule mandated.

The series opener, before 43,274 howling New Yorkers, could not have been more cruel. Now with a 16-12 record to go with a 2.55 ERA, Bill Hands was ready to face Jerry Koosman, having been held back for just this game. The score was 2-2 in the 6th. Then in a pivotal play in this critical contest, one that Randy Hundley flatly calls the biggest play of the year, Wayne Garrett singled to right with Tommie Agee—having delivered a two-bagger—on second. Jim Hickman fired an arrow to the plate as Agee tried to score. Hundley, with a sweeping motion, tagged Agee out, and then, knowing he had nailed Agee, reflexively positioned himself to throw Garrett out at second, should he try to advance.

The score, however, was no longer 2-2. Home plate umpire Satch Davidson called Agee safe, making the score 3-2. It was to be the winning run. Hundley executed an incredible shock and rage-driven high jump. Still agitated 20 years later, when recounting the play to Rick Talley, the forthright Hundley asserts, "I tagged him so hard I almost dropped the ball."

The game had another key subplot. Hands had a less than harmonious relationship with the Mets, due to some knockdown exchanges throughout the season. Hands drew a line in the sand when on the first pitch of the game, he sent Agee sprawling. It was not a prudent pitching decision, because Koosman hit Santo on the forearm to open the second frame. The forearm stiffened and the third baseman's power was gone.

Worse, however, in the minds of a number of Cubs was that the team did nothing about Koosman's smack. No emptying of the bench, no charging the mound, no shouting. Nothing. The late Hank Aguirre recalled it distinctly, telling Talley, "That's when we should have gotten into a fight. It hurt me deeply that Santo just walked to first base, and nobody did anything. That's when I knew we were hurting. Leo or Santo or somebody from the dugout should have started a fight. I wish I hadn't been stuck out in the bullpen or I would have started it."

"We were easily intimidated. It was a degrading incident . . . the club just folded," agreed Rich Nye.

The lead was now one and a half games, and a date with Tom Seaver was in the offing for the following evening.

Partly because of a need to juggle the rotation, owing to Holtzman's unavailability on upcoming Rosh Hashanah as well as his having been knocked out so early in his previous start, Durocher sent the chastised Jenkins to the mound on two days' rest. It was all Seaver, 7-1, as 58,436 screaming fans watched in joy. The spread was now half a game, as Mets owner Joan Payson exclaimed, "Oh, this is wonderful," after having witnessed her charges' conquest.

A sullen Durocher, humiliated with choruses of "Goodbye, Leo," to the tune of "Goodbye, Ladies," sung by the fans in New York—the city of his greatest triumphs—had nothing to say. Dispirited, the team couldn't get to Philadelphia soon enough. There was to be no solace in the City of Brotherly Love, where a Phillie team, heading for 99 losses, defeated the Cubs and Holtzman 6-2 on the strength of Rick Wise's right arm.

The Mets swept the Expos 3-2 and 7-1 at Shea that same night to take the Eastern Division lead from the Cubs by one game. It was the first time in 156 days that the Cubs were not a first-place team. The doors remained closed for 15 minutes after the Cub loss. When they were opened, Durocher had nothing to say, although Santo offered a less than convincing, "I'm optimistic, very optimistic."

Yet another defeat followed the next night, as Rick James, just up from the minors, pinned a 4-3 loss on Dick Selma. Another Met victory over Montreal drove the Cubs two games back. Moreover, another misadventure marked this loss. With the Bruins up 1-0, Philadelphia's Richie Allen had a 3-2 count with two on and two out in the 3rd. Knowing the runners would be moving, Selma lifted his leg off the rubber and whipped the ball to third for what he thought would be an easy pickoff out.

Except that Santo was not there. Tony Taylor scored the tying run as the ball skittered into left-field foul territory. Durocher hit his head on the dugout roof as he leaped in disbelief at the gaffe. The play was simply the result of a missed sign on a designed play. The pickoff sign for Santo was for Selma to yell, "It's two out, knock the ball down." It was a too well disguised signal. Santo failed to register it as a signal, inasmuch as that particular planned pickoff maneuver had yet to be attempted in 1969. He simply took Selma's words at face value and hollered "Yeah," in response—amazingly the exact verbal signal confirming the play was on.

"Durocher went nuts," recalled Santo. "Selma was so afraid of what Leo might do, he wouldn't go into the clubhouse after the game." Years later, Leo concluded his own explanation of the skull session in his book by saying, "And that's how it goes when everything is collapsing around you."

Gleason remembers a poignant scene after the game. "We couldn't find Selma in the clubhouse, so we thought he was giving an exclusive to TV," says writer Gleason. "There were about twenty-five people in the dressing room, so the New York guys came to me and said, 'What's going on? Is there anything you can do?'

"'I'm as hot as you are about this,' I said. Phil Regan was the Cub player rep and I called him aside. 'I'm not blaming you for this, Phil,' I said, 'but if you don't get Selma down here to talk to us, you are really going to get ripped in the papers.'

"Connie Mack Stadium had an alcove—a miniattic. As it turned out, Selma had hid there. Ultimately, he did come down. He had been up there weeping."

And things were collapsing. The Cubs had lost eight straight. Moreover, each of their Big Three hurlers had been beaten twice. Those eight consecutive defeats had cost them seven games (from five up to two down) in the standings, as the Mets went 8-2 in the same nine-day span.

Although the spell was broken the following night in St. Louis when Hands won his 17th game at the hands of the Cardinals, 5-1, the scribes in Chicago were ready to serve Leo his literary lunch. Robert Markus suggested that if the Cubs were in fact to come up short, "Leo Durocher is in for a savage roasting in the local press. A better loser than he is a winner, Durocher has made nothing but enemies on his way back to the top. And every one of them is going to be ready with a verbal knife to stick in Leo's ribs on the agonizing plunge back down."

Surcease from defeat was short-lived, however, as the Redbirds broke a 4-4 tie in the 8th inning en route to a 7-4 win at Jenkins's expense the next night. This was the third time the right-hander came up short in an attempt to get win number 20. Winning hurler, reliever Jim Grant, said of the Cubs, "The monkey's tail ain't long now, and it's not as short as it's gonna be."

This set up the series finale, a Bob Gibson/Ken Holtzman confrontation. After nine complete, the score was 1-1. With the Mets having lost, the Cubs could climb within two and a half with a win. Although the Cubs failed against Gibby in the top of the 10th, Cub fans took comfort in knowing that Gibson (or perhaps better, a pinch hitter) would open the St. Louis half of the frame. It was Gibson who grounded out. The next hitter, however, hammered the sphere over the right-field fence, ending the conflict. His name? Lou Brock. Who else?

St. Louis Globe-Democrat writer Harry Mitauer captured the back-breaking nature of the loss. "A disconsolate group of Cubs . . . looked downhearted as they slowly walked off the field to their gloomy clubhouse," wrote Mitauer. Now three and one-half out, the Bruins took comfort knowing they were heading to Montreal certain to make up ground against the expansion dead enders.

Durocher opted to go with Selma to start the Montreal series and then likely have his Jenkins-Hands-Holtzman triumvirate go the rest of the way. A bizarre defensive breakdown in the 1st inning started the Cubs on the path to a 8-2 defeat. The locker room was funereal after the game, which pushed the Cubs four and one-half games behind. Banks, Williams, Beckert and Santo sat lifelessly 30 minutes after the carnage had ended. The brave personas were gone. There were no "we'll get 'em tomorrow" or "we'll be all right" bromides.

The Cubs had been certain that they would reverse their fortunes, once having snapped their earlier eight-game losing skein. Instead they had dropped three of four. Put the two losing runs together and it was 11 of 12, while the Mets went a sizzling 12-3.

Montreal mentor Gene Mauch, who had presided over the legendary 1964 Phillie collapse, drew a parallel or two. "It's no fun," he said. "We were a highly emotional bunch just like the Cubs and with a real emotional team, let me tell you, from high to low emotional is a big, big gap." He saw a specific symptom that reminded him of his doomed Philadelphians of five years previous. "One thing I saw was that there was a concentrated effort on the part of everybody on the team to relax. Let me ask you something. How can you work at relaxing?" the skipper offered.

Kessinger acknowledged the team was tight. "Sure, we're pressing," admitted the shortstop. "We wouldn't be human if we weren't."

The Cubs left Canada for home the following evening on the heels of Bill Hands's 18th win, 5-4. Interestingly, Durocher made a bold lineup change that evening, playing Willie Smith at first and Paul Popovich at short.

There were no Bleacher Bums when the Cubs returned to the Friendly Confines to defeat the Phillies 9-7, giving Fergie his 20th win before only 6,062 fans. Banks hit the century mark in RBIs. Leo started a rookie the next day, but Joe Decker got no decision. Regan did, a loss, 5-3. The Cubs were five down with just 11 games left. The club split a pair with St. Louis on the 19th, while the Mets dropped two to the tough Pirates.

Bill Hands then lost his 14th the following day, as Steve Carlton handcuffed the Chicagoans 4-1. The Mets, in turn, were no-hit by Bob Moose. Still four back, Jenkins won his 21st in the series finale, 4-3. New York snapped their three-game losing streak, however, sweeping two from the Pirates. The Cubs dropped five back when Seaver won his 24th game at the expense of the Cardinals while the Cubs were idle.

There were just seven games left.

Montreal then came to town and defeated the Cubs and Holtzman 7-3. The victory was particularly sweet for Durocher-reject Bill Stoneman. "I don't talk to anyone named Leo," stated winning pitcher Stoneman.

His reaction was similar to another Durocher castoff, "There goes garbage" Cal Koonce, after the latter threw 5 shutout innings for the Mets in a key game earlier against Chicago. Koonce claimed he "wanted to send a little love to Leo." He stated, "It's the longest I've pitched this season, but the incentive was there. Look around the clubhouse—everybody is enjoying this because they know that big-shot Leo will be unhappy."

In any case, the loss to the Expos was all but lethal because the Mets clinched a tie for the divisional title with a 3-2 win over St. Louis. Just 2,217 watched as Bill Hands notched number 19 the following day with a 6-3 defeat of the Expos, but that evening Gary Gentry shut the Cardinals out 6-0.

It was over.

On September 25, *Tribune* writer George Langford wrote a Cub obituary entitled "Those were the days, my friend," recounting the summer's glories past. "The Cubs were it. They were the 'in thing.' They were thrilling the Second City as no one had since who can remember. First place. The Cubs were there, man," he wrote. Langford described more than the weather when he followed with, "Now the cold autumn wind hits you in the face. . . ."

The Cubs won just two of their remaining five games, splitting a two-game set with the Mets as the season mercifully ended. The Mets—100-62 for the year—went a stunning 24-8 for September/October. Moreover, the men of Shea had won 38 of their final 49 games. The Cubs won but 10 of their 28 September/October tilts. Their 92 wins (against 70 losses) gave the Bruins more wins by far than any season had yielded since 1945.

Plugging in the research formula, the 1969 squad actually projects as a 94-68 contingent. Again, bullpen failings (only 27 saves, almost 9 less than the league average), bringing about close defeats, did much to pull the team back.

Though ranking third in runs scored (720), the Cubs actually scored 53 fewer runs than could be statistically expected when one adjusts for the Wrigley factor. They were only slightly above the league in hitting and OBP, and 15 points over in slugging. Although Kessinger was fourth in the league in runs (109), one wonders just how many more the leadoff might have tallied had his OBP been substantially higher than .335 (just 14 points above the NL norm). Number two man Beckert's OBP was just .328.

Other than Santo's runner-up placement in RBIs (123), no Cub hitter finished in the top five of any major offensive category. Williams, Santo, and Banks's 324 RBIs accounted for 45% of the team's total. The running game was all but nonexistent—30 steals in 62 attempts.

Pitching, particularly starting pitching, was the foundation of the team. The team's ERA was just 3.34, twenty-five points under the league average. Moreover, factoring in the Wrigley Field adjustment, the staff yielded an incredible 110 fewer runs than might be expected.

Jenkins (21-15) and Hands (20-14) combined for 41 wins against 29 losses, with ERAs of 3.21 and 2.49, respectively. Holtzman added 17 wins (against 13 defeats) and a 3.59 ERA. The Big Three's total of 58 wins was the best of any threesome in all of baseball. Hands's year was so outstanding he was fifth in the league in TBR.

Moreover, the 1969 season generated an attendance of 1,664,857, the organization's largest gate ever.

It also yielded more memories.

Ken Holtzman summed up the season as well as any. "It seems that the 1969 season was the ultimate Cub season," he told Talley. "Baseball is always portrayed as a serene, pastoral game with hopes high in the spring, leading to eventual heartbreak in August and September, and what team better personifies that image over the history of baseball than the Chicago Cubs? It's the story of the Cubs franchise. The ultimate lovable losers."

Eight

WHY

They were the Cinderella team. We went to Pittsburgh, St. Louis, and Chicago, thinking this was the year. Then it was not the year.
Greg Yoder, lifelong Cub fan from Michigan

The fans were shell shocked, the city in mourning. Jenkins, who wore a tattoo with the motto Trust in God on his left arm, wrote, "That was how I felt after the 1969 season—trust in God and do your best."

For some, any analysis of the reasons that the Cubs crumbled in 1969 is of no value. It merely recalls the pain. For many, however, the ache remains, perhaps because of the suddenness and the surreal sensation. A conclusive autopsy may be needed. Closure has value, and an examination of the events of the reversal can serve that purpose.

You could say that the Cubs didn't lose it but that the Mets won it. You could reason that the New Yorkers won 38 of their last 49 and 24 of their final September/October 32 outings when the pressure was hottest. You could also consider that the Mets were really only a 93-69 team by the predictive formula and hence had won a hundred games by squeaking out the close ones (9-1 in one-run games from September forward, for example) and by generally playing way over their heads.

You could say that, but you would be wrong.

With players openly acknowledging their tendency to scoreboard watch, winning and losing become interactive. As the Cubs began melting under the pennant heat, the Mets gained more confidence; as the Mets started coming on, the Cubs felt pressure never felt before.

The Cubs faced September 3 with five games up, 14 of their remaining 26 games in the Friendly Confines. The Mets faced 30 foes, 17 at Shea. By October 2, however, there was a 13-game shift in the Games Behind column, the Cubs going from five up to eight down. Had the Cubs won 16 of those last 26, roughly the pace they had been on and a very reasonable expectation with over half the games at Wrigley, New York could—as they did—win 23 of the final 30 and gotten only a tie.

But it is highly unlikely that the men of Gotham could have gone on such a surge without the Cubs opening the divisional gate for them, shoring up the Mets with hope and confidence as they, themselves, stumbled. Moreover, the unvarnished reality is that it did not take the Mets a month to catch Chicago.

It took one week.

Simply by winning six of their first eight from September 3 on while the Cubs rolled over seven straight times (twice to the Mets), New York owned the division and never looked back. In addition, the Cubs did nothing to apply hot compresses to the backs of the entry from the Big Apple once the lead switched hands. They went on to lose four of the next five, all but vanishing from view.

No matter the Mets. The Cubs lost it.

From September 3 through the end of the season, the Cubs were 8-18. A brownout like that has to show up in the numbers, and it does.

First, look at the offense. One often hears that baseball is 70% or even 80% pitching. That, of course, is nonsense. The grand game is 50% offense (scoring runs) and 50% defense (preventing runs). As for that first 50%—scoring—the Cubs tallied only 80 runs in those 26 outings, an average of just 2.5 a game. Prior to the September 3 slide, they had already registered 640 runs, 4.7 a game. That's a 2.2 per game skid, which will show itself in the won/lost column.

Moreover, the Cubs scored only 41 runs in their 18 losses, just 2 fewer than the 39 they pushed over during their 8 victories. The team registered a puny 2.3 runs per defeat, less than half of the 4.9 they tallied per win. Furthermore, the 2.3 falls nearly 2 runs per game short of the National League mean (4.05).

A team's score that falls off so severely usually means it has simply stopped hitting. The Cubs batted just .220 over the 26-game span and just .195 in those 18 losses. Contrast that with their premeltdown average of .259, in a league that hit .250.

Among baseball scholars, however, the most important offensive statistic is not batting average, but on base percentage (OBP). (Unless otherwise indicated, we will use a simplified version of only walks and hits, omitting hit batsmen.) The league OBP for the season was .317. Heading into September 3, the Cubs were at .329. From then on, however, they were an unbelievable .282, fully 47 markers down. No team in the league had a simplified OBP under .300, not even the lowly Expos who lost 110 games.

Single out the 18 losses, and the OBP plummets to .264. That's slightly better than one base runner per inning. Not one hit, but just one base runner—about what an ace pitcher would allow.

Right behind OBP comes slugging percentage, which is derived by taking a batter's total bases gained on hits (4 for a homer, 3 for a triple) and dividing it by the number of at bats. It is a well-named power statistic. Through September 2, the team slugged at .395. The slugging number plunged 70 points for the last 26 games.

The following table sets out the offensive collapse in stark form. Reading from the left, the first column reflects the National League average for 1969, the second column show the worst NL team performance in the category, the next three depict the Cubs' performance through September 2, September 3 on (the last 26 games), and then, for runs, batting and OBP, the last 18 losses.

	NL	Worst	Thru 9/2	Last 26	18 Losses
RUNS/GM	4.05	2.89	4.71	2.50	2.28
B AVG	.250	.225	.259	.220	.195
OBP	.317	.281	.329	.282	.264
SLUG	.369	.329	.395	.325	

The Cubs were well ahead of the league in all five offensive categories prior to the skid. After that they performed light years below the average league performance. In fact, their LAST 26 performance in all but OBP was worse than that of the worst offensive team in the league—the expansion San Diego Padres, also losers of 110 outings. Moreover, they were but 1 point ahead of those sorry Californians in the OBP department and fell way under them in those 18 losses. Comparing the team to itself, one could safely argue that—using particularly runs scored as a measure—

their offensive performance dropped by nearly 50% in the last 26 games, and more than that in the 18 defeats.

Who broke down? The answer can be found in the following table in which the performances of the seven key regulars are represented. The first column presents batting averages and home run and RBI totals through September 2; the next column provides those numbers from September 3 through the end of the season (last 26); the last column presents batting averages only during a particularly ghastly period—those 19 games (after the off day on September 4), beginning with their home stand with the Pirates on September 5 and running through September 23—an absolutely killer stretch during which the team went 5-14.

	Thru 9/2	Last 26	9/5–9/23
	(AVG)(HR)(RBI)	(AVG)(HR)(RBI)	(AVG)
Kessinger	.287 4-53	.171 0-0	.148
Beckert	.293 1-33	.200 0-4	.203
Williams	.293 15-81	.294 6-14	.329
Santo	.293 27-110	.262 2-13	.262
Banks	.262 21-92	.209 2-14	.156
Hundley	.273 16-60	.157 2-4	.188
Hickman	.240 17-47	.226 4-7	.246

Comparing the first 136 to the last 26, Kessinger's average dropped 116 points. This as a leadoff man, a rally-starter! In addition, he failed to knock in a single run after September 2. Beckert's average crashed 93 points while an overused and exhausted Hundley's also fell 116. Each drove in exactly 4 runs during the period. Banks and Santo, though suffering power outages (each with but a pair of jacks) did not completely disappear. Hickman, despite his low average, supplied some power. Only Sweet Billy Williams came through. Note, however, that although hitting .294 with 6 homers, Williams was able to generate but 14 RBIs, a clear indication that the #3 hitter was stepping in without Kessinger and Beckert on the sacks.

In baseball, defense consists of both pitching (about 80% of the defensive half of the game) and fielding (the other 20%). Just as at the plate, the Cubs played like a tired, tight team in the field and on the mound.

Fielding stats are rarely interesting or understandable. Nonetheless, the table following shows that the fielding fell apart dramatically once the reversal was on. Through the first 136 contests, the Cubs allowed 485 runs, only 53 of which were unearned. Their unearned runs per game rate (0.39) was substantially better than the league average of 0.49. In fact, only the Mets (0.33) were clearly better.

Things changed mightily after September 2. Of the 126 runs yielded in the last 26 games, 18 were unearned. That is a per game pace of 0.69—a 75% jump, worse than the yearlong 0.65 turned in by the bumbling expansionites from Montreal. Moreover, fully 13 of them occurred during their 18 defeats. The unearned runs per game rate in those outings moved up to 0.72 a tilt, nearly twice their 0.39 number over the first 136 games.

NL Avg.	Worst Team	Thru 9/2	Last 26	Losses
UE/GM	UE/GM	UE-UE/GM	UE-UE/GM	UE-UE/GM
0.49	0.65	53/0.39	18/0.69	13/0.72

Looking at errors through September 2, the team committed just 94 miscues in their first 136 games, about 0.69 per tilt, better than the league average of 0.90. They blew 28 chances during that 8-18 meltdown—better than an error a game pace (1.08), an over 50% greater error frequency, and nearly as bad as the Expos, losers of 110 contests.

NL Avg.	Worst Team	Thru 9/2	Last 26
ERROR/GM	E/GM	E/GM	E/GM
0.90	1.14	94/0.69	28/1.08

Over half of those 28 errors, 15, were the responsibility of the Cubs' keystone combination. Shortstop Don Kessinger committed just 13 errors in the first 136 games—less than 1 for every 10 games. He bobbled 7 in the final 26, better than 1 in every 4. Considering that he sat out four contests,

Kessinger was booting more than three times as many balls during the fold as before. Second sacker Glenn Beckert blew eight chances in those post-September 3 games, a miscue rate about twice his earlier pace.

"Our team was making tons of errors at the end," said Ken Holtzman to writer Rick Talley. "It's tough to measure what defense can do to a pitcher. Ask Fergie. Good as we were during the first five months, that's how bad we were in September."

•   •   •

Beyond the errors are the uncountable baseballs that leaked through the infield past fatigued glove men. "Often, after you threw a ground-ball pitch, confident it would be an out, you'd turn around and watch an outfielder picking it up," says Nye. Again there is no way to tabulate the number of seemingly routine outs that became base hits.

Except for clutch right-hander Bill Hands, the pitching staff as well also wilted after September 2. Hands was outstanding with a 4-3 mark to go with a 2.29 ERA, actually better than his first five months of the campaign. The other four all struggled, compiling an aggregate 3-14 log. In fact, Holtzman, Selma, and Regan were a combined 1-10. Each of the quartet watched his ERA leap—Jenkins's doubled, Regan's hopped almost 3 per 9 innings, and Selma's just exploded, although Durocher used him sparingly, despite having tossed a pair of shutouts earlier in the campaign.

	Thru 9/2			Last 36		
	W-L	IP-HITS	ERA	W-L	IP-HITS	ERA
Team	84-52	1234-1134	3.18	8-18	220-232	4.25
Jenkins	19-11	270-229	2.83	2-4	41-55	5.71
Hands	16-11	237-208	2.54	4-3	63-60	2.29
Holtzman	16-8	213-201	3.42	1-5	48-47	4.31
Selma	10-4	166-126	3.47	0-4	3-11	12.00
Regan	12-5	99-102	3.36	0-1	13-18	6.23

"The collapse," as Durocher noted, "was total." It jumps out at you in the post-September 2 hitting, fielding, and pitching numbers. If, however, you want to know which side—offense or defense—declined the most, the table below will help. Using runs scored and then runs allowed, the table compares the first 136 games with the last 26, and then the final 18 losses.

	Thru 9/2	Last 26	DIFFCE	Losses	DIFFCE
RUNS/GM	4.71	2.50	2.21	2.28	2.43
OPP R/GM	3.57	4.85	1.28	5.72	2.16

On offense, the Cubs watched their runs per game fall from 4.71 tallies per contest for the bulk of the season to just 2.5 in the last 26—a drop of 2.21 runs per game. In the 18 downers, they pushed an average of just 2.28 men across the plate, a 2.43 falloff from their first 136 games.

As far as allowing runs is concerned, the team gave up just 3.57 an outing through the first 136. After September 2 the rate swelled to 4.85, up 1.28 runs per tilt. Things really came undone in those devastating 18, however, with the Bruins permitting 5.72 a game, a corpulent 2.16 runs per game jump.

If we look at the entire 26 games, the offense appears the greater culprit, skidding 2.21 per outing, while defensively the differential is 1.28. Nonetheless, when we zero in on only those September/October defeats, things even out a bit. At bat the slide is at 2.43 runs a contest, in the field it is 2.16.

In reality, a Cub fan can pick his or her poison, depending on which number is looked at. The brownout was indeed total—at the plate and on the field.

Now that we know statistically what happened, we need to turn to why.

Leo's Role

If you had asked the Chicago media at the time, they would have sung as one in charging Durocher with prime responsibility for the team's swoon. In fact, celebrated author William Barry Furlong wrote a hostile article in then nationally famous *Look* magazine, citing 1969 as the year Leo Durocher blew the pennant. In it, Furlong quoted Jack Brickhouse as calling Leo "the most unprincipled man in sports." Brick himself wrote, "I would like to be able to lay the full blame [for 1969] on Manager Leo Durocher, but realistically that would be unfair." He does say, "That Leo did more than his share to help lose the pennant goes without question. He lost control of the Cubs in '69."

Brickhouse put his finger on a major issue, Durocher's endless feuds. "[Durocher] added fuel to the fire with the tensions he created by nit-picking controversies with certain of his players and certain members of the media." His acrimony with the latter is legendary. He called Brickhouse a "mental midget," George Langford of the *Tribune* "stupid," and referred to sportswriter Jim Enright (who broke the Camp Ojibwa story) as a truant officer masquerading as a sportswriter, while others were derisively termed pen pals, jackals, and the Unholy Six. Once when radio play-by-play man Vince Lloyd lit a pipe in Leo's presence, the manager yanked it out of his mouth and tossed it in the toilet.

Moreover, at one point the Lip was so angry at *Sun-Times* writer Jerome Holtzman, he would lie about his pitching rotation.

"This was in 1969," explained Holtzman, "and Leo never came out of his hotel room on the road. I asked him if [Ken] Holtzman was going to pitch and he said, 'No, Hands is pitching.' I was ready to write that, but the other writers tipped me off that it would be Holtzman. I waited till we got to the ballpark and I watched Holtzman warming up. I said, 'Leo'—and I said this in front of the players—'you told me Hands,' and he said no, he told me Holtzman."

The two nearly came to blows over the dispute, having to be separated by Santo. For his part, Ken fired a six-hitter for a Cub win, and Jerome fired an eight-word witticism later, "It was a great night for the Holtzmans," remarked the wry writer. Holtzman's statement that Leo "was a pathological liar" was recorded by Durocher biographer Gerald Eskenazi after Leo's death.

"Leo was all bluster," points out Bill Gleason, "he hollered at people and would cower them. If you hollered back at him, though, using the same language, he would back off."

After the game in Philadelphia involving the misthrow by Selma, Gleason went on to follow the Mets while Edgar Munzel, who covered the Cubs for the *Sun-Times,* flew with them to St. Louis.

Gleason relates, "I got a call from Edgar in St. Louis about seven the next morning. He apologized and said, 'I'll bet you're wondering why I'm calling you at this time in the morning, but Durocher wants to talk to you and I'm calling to see if you want to talk with him.' 'What's that old buck doing up at six A.M. in the Midwest?' I said. Munzel said, 'He's very upset. He said you threatened his players last night.'"

It turned out to be Gleason's statement to Regan that he would be roasted in the press if he didn't try to get Selma into the clubhouse to talk with the writers. "That was the basis of it," says Gleason, chuckling, "that I had threatened his players physically.

" 'I'm forty-seven years old,' I said to Leo. 'Do you think I'm going to punch out some guys who are 30. What is wrong with you?' 'Well, Bill, I misunderstood,' Leo said, backpedaling. 'I got all upset and flew off the handle.' He really had believed I had threatened to punch somebody on his ball club. He didn't get that from Regan, I'm sure, he just jumped from one point to the other."

It went beyond the media. During one game, Durocher danced around umpire Shag Crawford calling him "Dummy! Dummy!" It so infuriated the arbiter he challenged Durocher to a fight right there on the field. Late in the season when the Cubs were victimized by a number of clearly outrageous calls, observers wondered aloud as to whether Durocher was reaping an ugly harvest for his umpire baiting.

As early as May, an unnamed regular stated, "This club will never win the pennant as long as Leo is manager. He just doesn't know how to handle players." A teammate who liked Leo agreed, claiming, "He keeps the tension too high." *Sport Magazine,* doing a feature on Durocher and the then exciting, winning Cubs, cited Leo's psychological effect on his players. After reporting various Durocher anecdotes, a repetitive literary staccato would follow: "Durocher. Tension." Leo's enmity for the media raised the anxiety level among the players. Late in the season, when Durocher uttered nothing but "No bleeping comment" to beat writers, players realized they risked the manager's wrath if they cooperated with his hated adversaries.

Santo wrote, "Leo did have a short fuse, and it was that trait that caused numerous problems in the clubhouse. Kenny Holtzman . . . never got along with Leo. He resented Leo, never had any respect for him or his theatrics." For his part, Durocher called Holtzman a gutless Jew. "Leo didn't think Holtzman had enough aggressiveness to be a winner in the major leagues," said Santo. Though the two often played superficially friendly gin card games in the clubhouse "they were angry gin games," noted Santo. Holtzman made his statement nonverbally by not attending Durocher's wedding.

According to Jenkins, from 1969 on, Durocher picked away at Holtzman. "Kenny, why don't you forget that dinky change-up and start throwing hard. You were like an old woman out there tonight," Leo would rasp, indicating his preference for conventional fastball pitching. The manager would go on, telling the young lefty to throw steamers like Jenkins and

Hands, enraging the young Holtzman who was trying to establish his own pitching identity.

When revisiting the 1969 players for his wonderfully nostalgic where-are-they-now? retrospective, *The Cubs of '69*, Rick Talley asked each player's thoughts of 1969. Many of the comments cited here come from his interviews with the players. "I guess what I remember most about the 1969 season," said Rich Bladt to Talley, a utility outfielder who spent some time with the team, "was Leo Durocher calling Kenny Holtzman a 'gutless Jew' in front of other players. Then when I went back to Tacoma, I remember my teammates saying, 'The Cubs are going to make it.' And I said, 'No way, not after the things I saw.'" Jim Colborn, admitting he was young and sensitive at the time, said he "could see the dissension growing in the club."

Of course another sensitive soul was that of Adolfo Phillips, the nervous young outfielder. Hating brushback pitches, Phillips didn't want to bat leadoff and didn't like running in practice. When the once Durocher pet with the troubled stomach struggled in 1969, Durocher of course iced him, and wanting no more to do with him, banished him to Montreal. "The Cubs needed me," stated Adolfo, "no trade me, no lose. But I was glad to see that man suffer. He was no my friend."

Captain Ron Santo was often caught in the crosshairs. Players would approach him to ask Leo why they weren't playing. According to Santo, "Leo's answer was usually that the guy wasn't good enough to play. Then Leo would turn around and yell at the guy, 'You'll be in Podunk before you'll play here.'"

Santo put a good cap on the issue of Leo's fractious impact. "He brought us closer to a pennant than anyone else had in a generation. But he also brought disruption and chaos."

Apparently having had his fill of 1969 and its calamities, longtime Durocher assistant Pete Reiser quit.

Despite the bad reviews, there were players who backed Durocher. Jenkins wrote, "He was up-front, especially back there in 1969. . . . He was a man who would tell you what he thought to your face. He didn't talk behind your back." Phil Regan felt Leo showed restraint at times when it would be reasonable to expect the skipper to veer out of control. "Playing for Leo was different than playing for anyone else I ever played under. He was totally different from how I thought he'd be. You picture him as fiery, and he could be at times, but he was only like that when we were winning. Then he would be on everybody. But when we were losing, he was very quiet. He wouldn't say anything when we were losing."

A true Leo backer, Henning, Tennessee's Jim Hickman, whom Durocher affectionately called Farm Boy, also noted the manager's self-control, telling writer Jeff Guinn, "I played for some guys who, when their teams lost a big game, came back into the clubhouse yelling. Leo never did that. He was, in my opinion, first class all the way through '69." Santo, in his book, also credited Durocher, "During the 1969 near miss, Leo kept an even keel, even during the stretch drive when the Mets overtook us."

Durocher himself wrote, "You can only bear down so hard on them, and they can only bear down so hard on the field. It's too late to plead with them or blame them."

As for a fatigue factor, Ron Santo went on record, claiming it was illusory. "It has also become fashionable to say we were tired down the stretch. That isn't true. The adrenaline alone of being in a pennant race kept us going; I know it did for me," he protested.

Randy Hundley, who had to be as tired as any Cub, defended Leo's staying with his main men. "It's real easy to have hindsight, retrospect, and all of that stuff. But if Leo had taken me out of that lineup in those days, he would have heard from me. You do what you have to do as a manager. You put your best guys out there." Interestingly, Don Kessinger, who openly acknowledged his exhaustion, refused to blame Durocher for staying with his nucleus. "I just can't blame Leo," he said. "First, we were on a roll all summer. Sure, it's easy to say now that we should have been rested. But if he had come to me in August and asked, 'Do you want a day off?' I would have said no . . . I was playing great and felt good."

Curiously, however, Hundley did confess that he was exhausted. "The heat. I'm sure it took a toll. It does every year in August. I lost so much weight I couldn't reach the warning track."

"But let's face it," wrote Brickhouse, who felt Durocher-induced fatigue was a critical variable in the Bruins' collapse, "the Cubs were a rag-tag team in the stretch, wandering aimlessly, with assorted regulars physically exhausted as the result of failure to get a day off here and there when their lead was commanding. That had to be Leo's responsibility."

Don Kessinger was emphatic about the issue of drained energy. "What I remember most is that we were a tired ball club. A lot of it had to do with playing day baseball in Wrigley Field. It's the sun that does it. I just feel when you play eight guys in the hot sun most every day, you had to be a lot better than anybody else to win. We may have been better, but unfortunately, we weren't a lot better." Spending parts of the summer in the military reserves rather than resting may have sapped the shortstop even more.

It was Jenkins's contention that Durocher drove his troops excessively. "The real cause of our collapse was that some of our regulars were exhausted by September. We said we weren't tired, but we were. We had good bench strength with Paul Popovich, Nate Oliver, Willie Smith, Jimmy Qualls, Jim Hickman, Bill Heath, and Gene Oliver, but Leo did not use the bench enough. He did not want to play anyone but the regulars unless he was forced to by injuries.

"Whenever someone was hurt, Leo would put in an extra man who would perform just as well as the regular had. That made no difference to Leo. The moment the regular was well and said he wanted to get back into the lineup, Leo put him back in. It made no difference to him how well the substitute was playing. Nate Oliver did a great job of filling in for Glenn Beckert early in the season, but when Beckert thought he was well enough to play, Oliver was out of there. I think that took something out of Nate. The same thing happened to Paul Popovich later. Leo did not care if the substitute hit 1.000 while he was filling in.

"If a man had a slight injury or was just plain tired, Leo didn't want to hear about it. He just rubbed the man's nose in the dirt and sent him back out there. He would not take the pressure off the regulars. He backed them into a corner and kept them there. Durocher was from the old school and did things as they had been done thirty years ago. You played until you dropped."

Leo's pitching coach Joe Becker was also emotionally intense and clearly old school, according to Fergie. "What's wrong with you," Becker would holler if there was any hesitance about pitching after only two days' rest. "Haven't you got any guts? Where's your heart? If you were a big league pitcher, you wouldn't even have to think about it."

"By September the constant pressure had worn down the club," Jenkins claimed, who saw it from the mound. "Don Kessinger could hardly get into the hole behind second base. Don blew plays that he had easily made earlier in the year. The last month of the season shattered our infield because the fellows had not gotten enough rest. Beckert was faltering; so was Santo. Like Kessinger, they were not making the plays they had made earlier in the season. They were dropping balls and throwing them away. We had the best infield in baseball, but in one stretch of nine games, we made seventeen errors.

"Leo would not go to our bench. Only after we were five games behind the Mets did he start using the extra men. By then it was too late."

Oscar Gamble, then a teenage outfielder, stated his opinion succinctly, "No way those old guys could play in that heat that long."

Reserve outfielder Jimmy Qualls, best known for breaking up a would-be July no-hitter by Tom Seaver in Shea, had this to say. "I hate to second-guess, because I've seen the same thing happen to other teams, but our boys were so dad-gummed tired they couldn't walk in September. Bruno (Beckert) couldn't catch a grounder, and the boys on the bench who could have helped just sat there."

Ken Rudolph, stopgap backup catcher, attributed the brownout to exhaustion. "Physical fatigue," he said. "Our guys just couldn't get it up in September. Leo had all-stars at most positions, but they got tired. Heck, Randy lost so much weight he had to start wearing suspenders. I'm a firm believer that twenty-five men are on a team for a purpose. But we didn't serve that purpose with the Cubs. We just sat there and watched everything happen."

Paul Popovich, ace utility infielder, liked Leo and put a softer touch on the matter. Nevertheless, Popo did say, "It wouldn't have hurt him to give some of the guys a few days off, but he didn't. That wasn't Leo's way." Even Durocher apologist Jim Hickman allowed, "We possibly were a little tired. Leo believed in playing the same guys every day."

Many feel Durocher's bias against using young players contributed heavily to the team's demise. Backup catcher Bill Heath alluded to the inactivity, saying, "Sometimes I think it was tougher on those of us on the bench who had to watch."

For young pitchers, it was even worse. "All the young pitchers were afraid of him," according to Regan. No youngster had a harder time with Durocher then Jim Colborn, who later developed into a 20-game winner after being traded to Milwaukee. "Leo tried to bury me. . . . It's hard enough playing baseball, but when you have to overcome another obstacle, a man on your own team trying to run down your confidence and ego, it's really hard."

Colborn, who once called Leo a viper during a clubhouse meeting, shared another anecdote citing Durocher's cruelty. "Once I was standing near the end of the dugout cheering for the guys on the field, and Leo came down and stood in front of me. So I moved two feet and he moved two feet. Finally he bumped me, acted like it was an accident, and said to somebody, 'Get this kid hurt.' He was mad because I was cheering."

Southpaw Dave Lemonds, who pitched only five frames for the 1969 Cubs, had this to say. "I always thought I had something to offer that they didn't accept. My minor league pitching instructor, Fred Martin, told them I could throw harder than Kenny Holtzman, but Leo had no tolerance for young pitchers. He only trusted experience."

Gary Ross, a young right-hander who was granted one start in 1969, related, "Leo always seemed mad at me, I never understood why. I'll never forget one game in 1968 when I was pitching against the Giants, and he was so mad because I wasn't hiding the ball in my glove. So he kept yelling to the Giants what I was throwing—but they still couldn't hit me."

Archie Reynolds, who got in just two starts and 7 innings for the Cubs, spent five challenging postbaseball years in Saudi Arabia testing oil and gas wells, which he said "was nothin' after tryin' to pitch for Leo. I could never get a straight answer from him. We all compared him to George Allen of football because he'd rather go with a forty-year-old veteran than a kid with potential."

"In retrospect, Leo probably should have used [veteran] Ted Abernathy more than he did," stated Regan. "Aguirre, too, in spot situations. But Durocher never had any confidence in our kid pitchers. He was always backing up the truck."

This aversion for youth was a clear and dramatic reversal of the Lip's stance from 1966 through 1968 when Durocher deployed not only Kessinger, Hundley, and Hands but Phillips, Nye, and Niekro as well. For many, it suggested that Leo's energy for developing young talent may have been ebbing and that he may have been losing his daring edge.

As determinants of the slide, Dick Selma cited not only fatigue but also Leo's erratic use of the pitching staff. "I could throw harder than Nolan Ryan or Tom Seaver. We didn't have speed guns then, but that's what Johnny Stephenson said after he caught all of us with the Mets. I got off to a great start after coming to the Cubs in 1969. I think when Fergie and Holtzy had eleven wins, both Hands and I had ten. Then two things happened. After the all-star break, Leo looked at the schedule and decided he could use a three-man rotation some of the time. Well, then I would go ten days without a start. Then we went into September, and he pitched me two days in a row. I got KO'd in the fourth inning of one game, and he brought me back the next day when Fergie's arm was sore. Then he did it again. I got knocked out in the first inning of one game, and he used me the next day. I lost every time."

Veteran reliever Don Nottebart sounded a similar note. "I won a game in relief for the Cubs on May 14 against San Diego and lost one in Houston on May 17, and that's all I pitched, baby. Leo forgot me. He had some guys he would use and that was all. He forgot Aguirre, Nye, Abernathy, Colborn, and me. He tried to win the pennant with six guys. I just sat there and watched it go down the tubes. I wasted my entire last year of baseball on the Cubs' bench."

The late Hank Aguirre bristled for a long time over the home-run ball that right-hander Phil Regan threw to Willie Stargell. "There was no left-handed hitter alive that I couldn't get out. That's why I was always sorry I wasn't pitching to Willie Stargell that day he hit the home run to beat us. I thought Leo did a great job of using me and Ted Abernathy until the last month of the season. That's when he just forgot about us and kept going to Regan."

"It got to be a joke the way Leo would telephone the bullpen and tell Rube Walker, 'Get Regan up,' " says lefty Rich Nye. "He had forgotten everybody else."

Reliever Phil Regan is a prime example. After hurling 127 innings in the previous year, Durocher used him over another 101 frames 62 times prior to September. Registering his 12th win on August 24, the Vulture did not win a single game the rest of the season. He gave up seven earned runs in just 11 innings after September 1. Baseball people were remarking about the possible overuse of Regan as early as May. "Durocher has a lot of faith in him," Boudreau would state. That faith would abate by late August, leaving Durocher with no one to slam the door in the late go.

Veteran reliever Ted Abernathy had familiar words for Talley. ". . . in those days, the players had no say in anything. Everything had to be Leo's way, and he just wore poor ol' Phil Regan out. He plum forgot Hank Aguirre and me in the second half of the season. I pitched my best when my arm was real tired—that's when the submarine sinker worked best, and I also had mastered the rising fastball—my arm sure didn't get tired that year."

Asked about Regan's fade, Hundley concurs with Abernathy. "We had to go to him an awful lot in 1969 and it just wore Regan out. There's no question about it."

"Once we got by Regan," Hundley says today, "we had a tough time with pitchers getting hitters out. That's one of the reasons we lost it. We just didn't have that stopper in the last six or eight weeks of the season."

Though Hundley's point is well taken, had Durocher crafted some semblance of roles for his other veteran relievers, it is likely that the whole pitching breakdown could have been avoided. The problem, however, is that Leo deployed his 25 charges, particularly his bullpen, erratically, leaving observers—including players—scratching their heads. By utilizing his bullpen in a wholly unpatterned, impulsive fashion, Durocher all but assured that they would be ineffective when they were pressed into duty.

Don Nottebart sounded a similar note. "I liked Durocher, I really did. He just didn't have a clue about handling the bullpen. Joe Becker was a good pitching coach, but Leo wouldn't listen to him."

Rich Nye also indicated that by turning almost exclusively to Phil Regan, Durocher had no intelligent distribution of roles on the staff. "The way Leo handled his pitchers in 1969 was chaotic. He simply did not know his personnel. Regan must have gotten up 400 times."

Nye cites the erratic experience of those who pitched for Leo. "I remember this insane road trip in June. I hadn't been in a game in three weeks, but Hands got knocked out early in Atlanta and I ended up pitching the last 7⅔ innings, giving up one hit. Well, after that, I pitched in almost every game on the trip."

Randy Hundley agrees with Nye. "Leo would ride the white horse as long as he possibly could," he points out.

Often players were either in or out. "That was Leo's way. You didn't pitch at all or you pitched every day," said Rich Nye to Talley. Dick Selma, after winning 10 games, with 4 complete games and two shutouts over 5 months, pitched less than 4 full innings after September 2.

For his part, Leo hardly acknowledged his overuse of his players. Late in the season when Lou Boudreau questioned Leo on his pregame show about resting tired players, the manager said, "These are the best men I've got, Lou."

"Shouldn't I have rested them?" Durocher queries in his memoir. "Well, if I had known what was going to happen, I'd have given everybody a rest for three days and played nine pitchers. The way we were getting beat, it wouldn't have made any difference if I had played nine girls. You can only play what you've got, though. You've got the same twenty-five men you've had all year."

"Durocher abused his players' physical abilities," summarizes writer George Castle. Citing Hundley's resistance to rest, he adds, "He should have forced Randy Hundley to the bench. Hundley was a bear on the bench, but Durocher should have taken control."

On September 13, *Tribune* writer Robert Markus delivered some solid blows. "Slicing up Durocher would be nothing more than a meaningless exercise in vitriol. . . . What could be easier, for instance, than to point out that . . . of all the managers in the game, he may be the worst tactician."

From there, Markus cited several blunders, focusing mainly on the skipper's reluctance to make pitching changes when a starter was either exhausted or in duress. There had been myriad other mistakes, "too many to recount," according to Markus. Fortunately, the various strategic deficiencies did not always result in defeat, claimed the writer, because the team had been strong enough to "overcome their leader's ineptitude" on a number of occasions.

As if he had not plunged the knife liberally, himself, Markus concluded by saying he would "leave it to others to carve their initials in Leo Durocher's anatomy," the task being "far too easy and distasteful."

Inept strategy and a refusal to make gutsy moves gave rise to the notion that the reputedly bold and daring Leo froze during the losing snag. Regan, of course, indicated surprise that Durocher said nothing to his charges when they were losing. Aguirre summarized a common sentiment, telling Talley, "There became a lot of disappointment around the team that as we continued to lose, Leo didn't do something, anything. We were all waiting for him to just close the door and raise all kinds of Cain, but he didn't. It's a second guess now, but we really needed shaking up."

During a lopsided September loss to the Expos, announcing adversary Lou Boudreau was overheard saying in the booth, "He [Durocher] wants to win, but he isn't taking any drastic action."

Reserve catcher Bill Heath related his observations. "I watched the whole gory thing. It wasn't sad, it was stupid. You could see what was happening, everybody getting tighter and tighter and nobody doing anything about it. Leo Durocher went into a trance." Durocher, appearing distracted, kept a distance from players and would often play cards until 10 minutes before game time.

The common barb of Durocher being too old and out of touch was becoming a chorus. Before he managed his first Bruin contest, Buzzy Bavasi had already uttered his remark "The game has passed him by." The *Tribune*'s Markus claimed it obvious that "Durocher has let the game pass him by." Jack Brickhouse felt that Durocher had gone from a keen-minded mentor, who could sense when a pitcher was tired, to an old man losing his grip. He weighed in in his book with, "I was to learn later [than 1966] the game had passed him by."

The Players' Role

One other psychological scenario has merit. Because of their 24-year championship drought, the Cubs and their adherents were so elated from the opening game on by an apparent winner that they did not wait until October to celebrate. Not at all. From bumper stickers to bleacher bums, from posters to personal appearances, 1969 was one long celebration from April through August; a veritable five-month Octoberfest.

The fans weren't the only ones who indulged. Players openly cashed in on every opportunity for turning their celebrity into a buck. They demanded money to talk on radio or television for more than 90 seconds, asked (but didn't receive) a hefty cut for a 30-minute local special on the team, and wanted money for a book toward which they had contributed nothing. "The greed in that clubhouse was unbelievable," said one TV man. Durocher, regrettably, was the role model. He exploited every speaking date and commercial for the maximum dollar by setting up this economic sideline for himself before a player pool had been established. Therefore, he could pocket all the loot himself.

Owner P. K. Wrigley was unhappy about the off-the-field ventures. "I think that outside activities had a lot to do with it," he asserted, in retrospect. "I know if a ballplayer has a business and gets wrapped up in it, it takes his mind off baseball. I've had a lot of that kind of player in forty years. I think that all the TV appearances, the speaking engagements, the columns the ballplayers wrote in the newspapers, and the autograph-signing parties took the players' minds off the game."

The words of the aristocratic gum magnate—ever referred to by Leo and players alike as Mr. Wrigley—seem terribly dated amid the near omnipresent huckstering among star athletes today. This, however, was a premedia-intense era, one in which players commonly had to seek gainful employment in the off-season and pursue second careers at the conclusion of their playing days, largely because sports marketing was yet to be invented.

Wrigley may well have put his finger on the key issue by observing, "They were all young, and our Chicago players weren't used to being celebrities. They didn't know how to handle it. They got overconfident, and that had a lot to do with the way they played."

One who stayed focused was Billy Williams. Aware of the grind of pennant contention, he told a teammate that he had to be in bed by 9:00 at night to keep up his strength. Not all the players practiced Williams's formula. Bill Gleason recalls a conversation with Don Kessinger about the 1969 season. " 'They were always talking about playing all those day games and how that took the energy out,' he told me, 'but nobody ever asked how many of our guys were home in bed at 10:00 after a day game.' That made a tremendous difference," stated Gleason. "During times when all the teams played day games, the carousers on every team were out, but when the Cubs were the only team in a given week playing all day games, there's no question that the 3:00 in the morning guys were hurting their team."

Adored nationwide, the Cubs joined in the merriment associated with an apparent impending championship. Banks talked openly of the fun of the 1969 season, while Holtzman rated the excitement of the odyssey above the championship years in both Oakland and New York. "Sure, they fooled around a lot and cut a record and did some other off-the-field ventures," wrote Brickhouse.

Pitching coach Becker felt partying was the team's undoing. "I still say we celebrated too soon that year," he asserted. Reserve infielder Nate Oliver agreed. "The truth is that we ran the flag up the pole too soon. No doubt about it. We celebrated too soon. The entire season was a blast, but when I think about 1969, I think about the agony of defeat."

In addition, there was a me-first air evident among some of the players during the season. "There were some egos in that clubhouse," stated Becker.

"There were individuals on that team," echoes Nye today, "while the Mets were really together. Al Weis still talks about the family atmosphere they had."

Santo affirmed the celebrity of the Bruins. "People weren't talking politics, war, or economics the summer of 1969 in Chicago," he related. "They were talking about the Chicago Cubs. We were treated like rock stars; we would have to fight through the crowds just to get to our cars three hours after the game, [and the players] ate it up," according to the third baseman. Durocher wrote of his disappointment with the players' nonbaseball activities. "I was on a pregame call-in show . . . and in answering a question about our collapse, I intimated that the players had run out of gas. The players knew exactly what I was referring to, and it had nothing to do with their play on the field."

On September 15 in Montreal, 4½ games back, with a day game following a night game, a concerned and curious coach Pete Reiser decided to do a bed check on the little bears. "Know how many of them had been out?" asked Leo, rhetorically. "Thirteen. And a couple of them were young kids we had just brought up. I don't think I have ever been more discouraged in my life."

Though Brickhouse did feel such reverie "didn't hurt the club," he may have been too dismissing. As noted by Wrigley, this collection of players was clearly in uncharted territory. Far from just another team, they became, seemingly overnight, baseball America's darlings—the in people of sports in 1969—playing the season amid a fairlike atmosphere. Celebrating is fun. It is also exhausting. Hence, when you spend months celebrating a seeming success, which at the last minute becomes jeopardized, there is likely little emotional, let alone physical, gas left in the tank to reclaim what may be lost. In brief, the players may well have been too busy enjoying and celebrating their championship season to be sufficiently focused and preserved to be certain that that championship was, in fact, won.

The word players assiduously avoid using when explaining collapses is *choke*. It is politically incorrect. Frequently one hears a player say, "We are professionals, and we are accustomed to performing in the spotlight. We may not always be successful, but we don't choke."

Bricklayers choke. Attorneys choke. Ministers choke. Physicians choke—Players choke.

Choking then is neither disgraceful nor uncommon. Moreover, in my years in sports psychology, more than one player has told me point-blank that they have choked.

Scoreboard watching is often an initial hint that the players' collars are tightening. "Don't let anybody tell you ballplayers don't look at the scoreboard," said Billy Williams. Santo came clean, describing the latter days of August. "And then suddenly, we started to tail off at home where we had been so dominant all year. . . . I'll admit we were starting to watch the scoreboard; even though we were playing decent baseball, every time I looked up at the scoreboard the Mets were somehow winning," he acknowledged.

By September, after the Pirates downed Chicago in Wrigley, the third baseman felt it. "I was starting to get alarmed; the Mets were red hot, and I felt like we couldn't afford to lose any games." But they did. Nine of the next 10.

By September 9, after the team dropped a pair at Shea, the noose really tightened. "Our mood was never worse; even though we had the lead, we knew we would have to at least split the next series with the Phillies to keep the momentum and stay in first," noted Santo. But then two more losses followed, the second of which involved the Selma pickoff gaffe.

The late veteran Aguirre was direct. "I think all the time about 1969 and how we self-destructed. . . . We lost that pennant in 1969. I know the Mets were terrific, but we lost it. No doubt about that. I kept saying, 'It ain't over, boys,' but everybody was dead."

Moreover, the old lefty felt the Cubs lacked a feisty edge. "Did we choke?" he asked rhetorically to writer Guinn. "Well, this is the way I looked at it. I'd been with the Tigers, and in the '60s the Tigers were a very rambunctious bunch. I swear every season we got into fights with every other team in the American League. As soon as I joined the Cubs, I knew that wasn't the case with them. The Cubs were sort of mild-mannered. And that's what happened in '69. The team was too nice. I kept on tryin' to excite 'em, get something going, because in that last thirty or forty-five day stretch when we lost our lead, it didn't have to be inevitable."

Aguirre harkened back to the night in which Bill Hands opened in Shea by plunking Tommie Agee, only to have Jerry Koosman nail Ron Santo the next inning, injuring his arm. "Ronnie grabbed his arm and thought about going after Koosman, I think, but then he just went on to first base. In Detroit, I guarantee our hitter would have charged the mound. I was hoping Ronnie would start something. Maybe that would have done it, would have given us that kick we needed."

According to Nye, "We should have won. We had the horses." Reserve infielder Nate Oliver pointed out that the team lacked late-season pennant pressure experience. "We had one of the great teams to be assembled in that era, but our problem was that nobody knew what to expect. Phil Regan and I were the only ones with any postseason experience."

Also citing inexperience, Williams pointed out, "None of us had been there. Most of the time there is somebody on the club who can tell you how to feel. We had nobody. Just a bunch of guys who made it so far and couldn't get over the hurdle. I remember wondering to myself, 'How are we going to regain our momentum?'"

Glenn Beckert, hardly as physically tired as others because he missed 31 games, closely echoed Nate Oliver and Billy Williams's observation. "Tired? I don't know, we just came up short. More than anything, I think we were emotionally drained. None of us were accustomed to the crowds and the intensity. An awful lot of what happened was mental. The whole thing was a sobering experience, but we were young. I still believe that if we had won in 1969, we would have won again and again."

Ernie Banks offered a similar view. "It was fear. When you haven't won, it's scary, and that's life. Dealing with uncertainties, the unknown. And that's what I think happened to us in 1969."

Banks apparently saw it coming. According to Ken Holtzman, well before the collapse, Banks had a few drinks with the young southpaw after a game in Pittsburgh. "Kenny," he said, "we have a nine-game lead, and we're not going to win it because we've got a manager and three or four players who are out there waiting to get beat."

For the then 23-year-old hurler, the conversation with Banks was chilling. "He told me right to my face, I'll never forget it. It was the most serious and sober statement I'd ever heard from Ernie Banks—and he was right." Holtzman's take was similar to that of Mr. Cub. "I think that team simply wasn't ready to win. I'm telling you, there is a feeling about winning. There's a certain amount of intimidation. It existed between the [three-time World Series champion] A's and the rest of the league."

Touching on Aguirre's theme, Holtzman offered, "The Cubs didn't have that—the overall intimidation never existed with the Cubs. I've told the other guys that had we won in 1969, I would have bet my life savings we would have come back to win at least two more. In Oakland, when we took the field, we knew we would find a way to win. The Cubs never found that way.

"In 1969 I was just a kid. I was too young to understand how to handle the stress. I started the season weighing 185, and by September I was down to 162. What we went through was overwhelming. By the end of the year, I was physically and psychologically drained, back and forth to the National Guard, the whole thing. I had just had it. I think my record in September was 1 and 5."

Though an adversary of Durocher, Holtzman gave the skipper a waiver. "It wasn't managerial tactics that lost that pennant; nobody can blame Leo. But it is my contention that during that summer—even when we were ahead in July and August—we had guys on the team waiting to get beat."

Ron Santo affirmed Banks' and Holtzman's perceptions. "For much of that 1969 season, we couldn't lose. Then things started to happen, and I'll have to admit there came a time after the losing started that we were *waiting* for something to happen."

Outfielder Jim Hickman felt the negative momentum, citing the losses in New York as the turning point. "We couldn't bounce back. It's hard to understand why you can't win once you start backward. That's the bad thing about it. We could all see what was happening, but nobody could do anything about it."

Don Kessinger, though citing fatigue as the team's primary undoing, pushed the pressure door open as well by saying, "We lost momentum. We went bad at the wrong time. Then it became a mental thing. Every day we'd go out and look at the scoreboard, and those suckers [the Mets] had won again."

A bitter Don Nottebart felt betrayed. "We should have won it," he said. "I saw some gutless players who couldn't handle the pressure, that's what I saw. Banks and Williams were terrific. So were Hundley, Hickman, and Hands. Regan held up too, but you know the guys who folded. It's something those guys have to live with. They weren't winners."

Reserve receiver Bill Heath also touched the choke issue. "It was really sad to see somebody like Kessinger missing those groundballs; Beckert too. It's not that they didn't want to win, but the harder we tried, the worse it got."

Bill Hands, who stepped up as a prime-time pressure performer, minced no words. "I don't want to hear all the stuff about day games and the guys being tired. I don't buy that. I thought it was such an advantage to play in Chicago, it wasn't even funny. Biggest home field advantage in baseball, no question about it. Here we were, home with our families getting normal meals and a normal night's sleep, and here are these other guys down on Rush Street beatin' their brains out with three hours sleep." For Hands, then, the punch line was obvious. "We had so much pressure on us that we folded. It's that simple. We folded."

For Billy Williams, the lone clutch hitter down the stretch, it was all just disappointing. "We could have been recognized as one of the great teams of the half-century. That's how close we were, but we never got over the hump . . . [We] didn't know how to get past it. We just couldn't cope, and if we had, I know we would have won two or three more times. We were that good."

Using soap as a writing implement, Williams went so far as to scrawl on the clubhouse mirror the dollar amount involved in the World Series, but the incentive failed.

On the outside, there were many who saw it at the time. Jackie Robinson—the virtual definition of greatness under pressure— touched on it. In Chicago for a September speaking engagement, he left little to the imagination in stating, "I think the Cubs have blown it, I think they've given up on themselves."

The fans definitely thought so. Late on September 19, during a 7-2 drubbing in the second of a twin bill against the Cardinals, a number of fans let loose on the very players most often cited as the ones who broke down. According to the *Tribune,* "The wind was sour with the smell of spilled beer, and a highly vocal minority of patrons in the box seats were venting their stored frustrations built over the last three weeks on a down and beaten team."

The fans set their sites on Ron Santo, Glenn Beckert, and Don Kessinger (three players that Nottebart did not exempt when he talked of folding).

"It was brutal, the most brutal I've ever heard," said a veteran member of the Cubs at the time.

A mellowed Leo Durocher was gracious when later assessing his Cubs of 1969. "It was a great bunch because of their attitude. After I came to Chicago, their attitude changed, and they became an exciting team. They gave me 100 percent and tried to give 115 percent, but they couldn't. They played their hearts out, but the Mets, well, they ran over everyone, including us."

What Really Happened

There seems little doubt that all the reasons cited above contributed to the decline. For Durocher's part, his feuds, his attempts at intimidating young players, particularly pitchers, and the general tension he generated must have worn on the players.

And the wear was more severe because of his unwillingness to rest his players and to use his entire roster more wisely. Despite the occasional protestations to the contrary, the team was tired. One need only look at the statistical crumbling, evident in the records of individual players, to draw that conclusion. Only Bill Hands and Billy Williams averted a season-closing freefall.

Durocher had been overusing his position players since he came to Chicago. A glance at league statistics clinches that case dramatically. For example, there were but 15 National League players who had more than 540 plate appearances each year, from 1966 through 1969. No less than six of them—Kessinger, Beckert, Williams, Santo, Banks, and Hundley—were Cubs. Only one other team had as many as three. No catcher other than Hundley made the list.

Pitchers burn out much faster than position players. There were only 13 National League hurlers who totaled at least 475 innings for 1968 and 1969. Three of them pitched for the Cubs. Jenkins was tied with Bob Gibson (behind Juan Marichal) for 2nd on the NL list, with 619 frames. Bill Hands was 7th at 559, and Holtzman 13th with 476. The Cub trio combined for 1,654 innings, tops by far among NL threesomes. Durocher was no more merciful to his top reliever Phil Regan. The Vulture appeared in more games (139) than any other NL pitcher during those two campaigns and hurled 239 innings (second only to Clay Carroll).

Durocher compounded the fatigue factor by daring his players to admit they were tired. Furlong reported that in August, when asked by a writer whether he planned to rest some of his regulars, Leo exploded. Cursing at the writer, Durocher called an impromptu team meeting to embarrass him. "Are any of you tired?" he hollered. "Anybody want to sit down for awhile? This man wants to know. Go ahead—anybody who's tired just speak up." Not wanting a quitter label and knowing the answer Leo wanted, the players were mum.

Whether Durocher had truly lost his grip by 1969 is debatable. In fairness to Leo, the team had limited offensive options, and hence, hardly invited daring strategies. Though fans questioned Leo's abandonment of the running game, one could argue that when a team attempts 62 stolen bases and is thrown out 32 times, it does not seem wise for the manager to turn the running light green. Nonetheless, a host of players indicated dismay and surprise at Leo's uncharacteristic passivity and unwillingness to experiment, if only with lineup changes and player deployment.

As for the players, they were unaccustomed to their season-long rock-star status. Days and nights of reverie, national and regional attention, as well as seemingly easy victories could hardly have sufficiently hardened their competitive edge to ward off a late-season challenge. On the contrary, the team seemed stunned at the Mets temerity, responding as if the New Yorkers had no right to try to seize the Cubs' yearlong Day in the Sun.

The undisputed fact is that statistically, the Cubs rolled over as the Mets came on. They didn't start playing even .500 ball until the Mets had all but irreversibly taken over the race. Then, with paradise lost, the Cubs seemed to relax and perform in a better, if only mediocre, fashion.

No less a personage than the immortal gridiron mentor Vince Lombardi was quoted as saying, "Fatigue makes cowards of us all."

When people perform in a tense atmosphere, are tired, are led ineffectively, and are then unprepared emotionally for a major challenge, they are likely to collapse. They are likely to choke.

To the extent that there was a choke—as with the answer to a simple multiplication problem—it was the understandable product of a variety of critical factors preceding it.

Nine

THE YEAR AFTER

This is not the time for important decisions. You think better when you let it rest for three or four weeks.
General Manager John Holland, when asked in
October of 1969 on changes for 1970

Rage remained in the nation. The Vietnam conflict, which Nixon had promised to end, continued with no certain end in sight. Campuses shut down early, in a chilling spring amid protests that found students dead at Jackson State and Kent State. With National Guard gunfire killing youth, the Nixon administration was on the defensive.

Moreover, concern about the environment and the population explosion across the earth moved to the forefront becoming political as well as humanitarian issues. The women's movement was now picking up momentum as well, making the phrase "male chauvinist pig" common in the English language.

For many Cub fans, pain was all that was left after the 1969 season of promise closed. To sharpen the hurt, the Miracle Mets rolled over Atlanta in the first ever league championship series, known more commonly as the play-offs, and then defeated the seemingly invincible Frank and Brooks Robinson-led Orioles of Earl Weaver in the fall classic.

It was now complete. What the Cubs had planned to do, their hated conquerors had done.

For Chicagoans, the football season was now time for fellow Wrigley

Field residents—the grown-up Cubbies, the Bears—to help Windy City fans move on from the summer game, with its poignant memories, to supply fresh gridiron memories.

The Chicago Bears finished 1-13.

By the spring of 1970, I was a Chicago resident. No longer confined to WGN radio broadcasts and occasional Game-of-the-Week telecasts, I anticipated watching the certain-to-contend Cubbies daily on "good ol' channel 9." Yet, like so many other Cub fans, I was afraid to hope. On the face of it, the season looked very, very promising. There were a number of sound reasons for optimism.

First, the Cubs looked as good a bet as anyone to take the Eastern Division title. Every team had soft spots. For openers, it was simply impossible to imagine the Mets repeating. Never having had a winning season in their previous eight years of existence, the New Yorkers had turned the impossible dream into a baseball reality. Catching every available bolt of lightning in their Gotham bottle, they had risen up in their final 49 games to win 38 of them and then, living off that magical force called momentum, went on to vanquish all foes en route to a world championship.

On the heels of their football counterparts, the Jets' 1969 Super Bowl III miracle, the men of Shea were simply a sports version of the Cinderella story. Midnight, not to mention reality, had figured to arrive in 1970 for this magical outfit.

As for the rest of the division, the once vaunted Cardinals were on their way down by 1969, winning 10 fewer games than in their last 97-win pennant season of 1968. Moreover, the Pirates had not won since 1960, and despite their late season success when the Cubs stumbled, still finished four games behind Chicago. As such, in spite of some quality young players and pitching strength, they hardly looked like an impending juggernaut. That left the Phillies who were in the throes of rebuilding, and the Expos who were in quest of mere respectability.

As for the Cubs, they were not only returning their nucleus of stars but had taken some concrete steps toward filling in several soft spots. Holland sent Dick Selma and Oscar Gamble to Philadelphia in exchange for star rightfielder Johnny Callison. A solid veteran, Callison had nearly won the league MVP award in 1964—the year of the Phillie fold—and was still only 30 years old. The team released star-crossed picket man Don Young two days before the season opener, but picked up outfielder Cleo James who—with the acquisition of Boots Day from the St. Louis Cardinals in exchange for lefty Rich Nye—figured to end the centerfield merry-go-round of recent seasons. This left Durocher the option of spotting hard-hitting Jim Hickman at first base without sacrificing punch, should Banks's creaky 39-year-old knees give way for a final, irreversible time. Beyond that, with Hundley out with a broken thumb for the season opener, Chicago shored up their receiving corps by adding veteran J. C. Martin.

Durocher seemed to have dropped his vendetta against young pitchers, praising prospects Jim Colborn, Archie Reynolds, and Joe Decker, all of whom had performed ably at Tacoma in 1969.

Upon assessing this bevy of young arms, Durocher was enthusiastic. "If I can't find myself two starters from among that bunch of kids, I'm not trying," he said with customary swagger. By the end of spring training, during which the North-siders put up a powerful 19-10 record, it appeared that one starter would surely be Joe Decker. The right-hander finished the preseason firing 16 straight shutout innings.

Moreover, Durocher proposed to conserve the energies of his core veterans not only by playing no intrasquad games but also by resting them liberally during spring training exhibitions. This energy conservation measure followed an earlier request from management that their key performers spend a week at a place called Buckhorn Spa, taking mineral baths.

In addition, Durocher tried to keep the pressure off the players. Not only had he shifted the blame away from them, he had voluntarily taken the rap for the 1969 fadeout, acknowledging that he had made some errors in handling his troops. "Maybe we ran out of gas," the Lip nonetheless intoned somewhat defensively, "but if the Mets had played just .500 ball, we could have hung in there. They just kept winning, winning, winning."

The players appreciated Leo's protection of them and committed themselves to a better 1970, according to Jenkins. "We told ourselves that we would be stronger this year, that we could start the season as we had in 1969, and that this time we would not fold up in the last month.

"Durocher was as optimistic as the rest of us. He had taken the blame during the winter for what had happened in 1969, but he did not let it get him down. He had a good attitude in the spring and told us, 'Forget what happened. There's nothing you can do about that. That's gone. We have a fine ball club on paper, and we can prove it on the field. If anything we're stronger than we were last year.'"

Here, perhaps, the 64-year-old Durocher demonstrated one of his greatest strengths, his capacity to persevere in the face of setbacks. Now in his 21st year of major league managing, in a career that had commenced in 1939 in the dugout, Leo had been fired twice, suspended for a year (1947), and divorced four times. Beyond that, there were the myriad fines, brawls, lawsuits, controversies, and shattered relationships. If nothing else, Durocher was resilient—able to pull down the shade on past disappointments, ever pressing forward. It is likely that, consciously or not, the irrepressible Leo modeled that inner resolve for his team, one badly in need of forging forward.

The air was indeed lighter in spring training. Not only had the team addressed some personnel weaknesses and purposed to keep their stars fresh, but Leo was cooperating with the media and so setting a pleasant tone. Logically, 1970 figured to be the Cubs' year. Logic, however, rarely seemed to govern the North-siders' fortunes. The brownout of 1969 remained fresh in the minds of Cub fans. It had been so sudden and stunning that it had taken many fans the entire off-season to move beyond shock and denial into a painful acceptance. Hence, despite all the signs of imminent diamond success for the team, an almost conditioned fear of hoping for a Cub championship gripped their followers, including this one. It was an I-hope-they-win-but-I-can't-take-another-major-disappointment feeling.

The Opening Day lineup was a familiar one. It was again "Kessinger, Beckert, and Billy Williams," as play-by-play man Vince Lloyd had intoned for now five years, followed by Santo and Banks. Newly acquired Johnny Callison hit in the 6 hole, followed by Hickman in center and J. C. Martin behind the plate. With Fergie pitching, the team had all their key people in familiar spots, save for the injured Hundley.

The result was not as encouraging as in 1969. The Cubs won but one of their first three. That one, however, was high drama. Down 1 zip with 2 gone in the bottom of the 9th against lowly Montreal, newcomer Johnny Callison delivered a two-run circuit shot to put the Bruins in the winner's circle. Despite their 1-2 log, fans were buzzing—they now had another potent clutch bat to go with their other established performers. Maybe things would turn out all right after all.

After losing the following day, the team kicked in with 11 straight triumphs, the final one coming on a 1-0 sparkler behind 22-year-old Joe Decker on April 27. Their 12-3 mark put them 2½ games ahead of the Mets. Realizing there was yet a long season ahead, fans rarely place much credence in a strong start, although baseball scholars do.

Bill James conducted a study using 18 seasons and 430 teams to determine the significance of a fast or slow start. He found that only a dozen teams in his sample (2.8%) had managed 12 or more triumphs in their first 15 outings. The average final winning percentage for the nine teams opening at exactly 12-3 was .546, or the equivalent of an 88-74 season. If one employs the rather cumbersome formula James developed to predict how well a team will do in its remaining games after any given start, the Cubs again projected to 87 or 88 wins. For those in the know, then, clearly the 1970 team did not figure to roll over because of some lingering defeatist stupor coming off 1969.

The previous season did have a residual effect, however. From the outset of the campaign, all the bums in the bleachers were not friendly. Rowdy fans engaged in fights, threw things onto the field, and occasionally leaped over the outfield walls, halting play. The attempt to rein in free-spirited rebels gave birth to the current wire basket, 2½ feet from the top the ivy-covered outfield wall, running from foul line to foul line.

In any case, the joy of the hot start was offset by a major injury to a Cub cornerstone. In the 6th inning of an April 21 7-4 victory over the Cardinals, Carl Taylor rounded third and headed home for a jarring collision with Hundley, resulting in a ligament tear in the left knee of the all-star back-stop. The Cubs were 7-3 at the time, while Hundley was hitting just .227 on just five hits in 22 trips, with no runs scored and but two knocked in.

Nonetheless, losing Hundley was telling. Ferguson Jenkins captured well the value of the ace catcher. "Having Hundley catch for you was like sitting down to a steak dinner with a steak knife. Without Hundley," said the perennial 20-game winner, "all you had was a fork." Cub pitching used only a fork from April 22 until after the all-star break, as a May 21 diagnosis of Hundley's knee revealed cartilage damage, requiring surgery.

Despite Hundley's injury, however, the baseball sky was bright on Chicago's North Side as April closed with the Cubs leading the Eastern pack at 13 and 5, which put them 2½ lengths ahead of the Pirates (11-8) and 3 in front of St. Louis (9-7), with New York and Philadelphia tied for 4th with 10-9 marks.

With Boots Day not contributing, the Cubs peddled the outfielder to Montreal on May 12 for catching help in the person of Jack Hiatt. May 12, however, brought more than Jack Hiatt to the Cubs. It was the day that Ernie Banks—hitting sixth in the order in the second inning—belted a Pat Jarvis breaking pitch over the left-field wall for his third homer of 1970 and 500th of his Hall of Fame career. Trailing 3–1 behind Kenny Holtzman to Atlanta going into the 7th inning stretch, the Bruins rallied with one in that frame and another in the 9th to set up what would be a 4–3, 11-inning win. Rainy weather kept all but 5,264 fans from witnessing the event live, but Brickhouse's "Hey, hey" echoed loudly out of Chicagoland televisions during the nightly news.

Owing to a strong April, the team's 3-9 swoon opening the following month did not cost them first place. Meanwhile, Durocher had hardly mellowed in his relations with NL umpires, garnering a day's suspension for making obscene gestures at an arbiter during one of his famous snits. The Cubs posted a sorry 12-15 mark in May, but closed the monthly books in first place. Their 25-19 mark was a game better than that of the 25-23 Mets, and 4½ paces in front of the 23-26 Pirates and 21-24 Cardinals.

Well into June, the Cubs were 35-25, and 4½ games ahead of the second-place Mets. Disaster, however, would soon visit. With Banks's knees beginning to talk back, Glenn Beckert suffering from a pulled muscle, Don Kessinger fulfilling a military obligation in the reserves, and Ferguson Jenkins off-form, winning only 3 of his first 10 decisions, the team suddenly went into reverse.

A losing streak was under way on June 23 when a blown save by closer Phil Regan resulted in a 12-10 ten-inning loss at Wrigley Field to the dreaded Mets, on a two-run bomb by backup catcher Duffy Dyer. It was already Regan's 32nd appearance in the team's 64 games. The loss left Regan's pitching line for the season at:

IP	H	R	ER	W	SO	W	L
47	46	23	21	19	16	4	4

His ERA was at 4.02, hardly a number befitting his key role as the team's door-slammer.

Though Jenkins attributed Regan's fading effectiveness to umpire harassment for his moist deliveries, which the Vulture would continue to experience, it seems likely, retrospectively, that Regan was burned out from being overused during the previous two seasons. He had appeared in a whopping 144 games and hurled 246.2 innings, tantamount to pitching roughly 2 innings every other game for two seasons. Now just 64 games into the 1970 season, he had again appeared in half the games and was averaging about an inning and a half per outing.

After two months and two days in first place, the Cubs yielded the top spot to the hated Mets on June 24, losing a twin bill by 9-5 and 6-1 margins. The twin win gave the Gothamites a 36-31 record against Chicago's 35-31. Ron Santo, heading into the action with an injured elbow and a meager .235 average to go with but 7 homers and 39 RBIs in 238 at bats, was unceremoniously benched in the two-for-one confrontation. The less than joyous third-sacker was careful to voice the company line by saying,

"Leo is a different kind of man. He doesn't walk up to you and say 'You're not playing today.' I'm just not producing and he feels some rest will help me. Maybe that's the answer."

Meanwhile Durocher was turning sour on two of his young pitchers. "I'm not happy with the way Decker and Colborn have been going lately," stated the skipper. "I'll probably give (Archie) Reynolds and (Larry) Gura an occasional start." The Cubs managed to lose their sixth straight, their fourth to the Mets, on the following day, 8-3. Ron Santo played but went 0 for 4 in the contest.

Shades of September of 1969, things got no better in Pittsburgh. After a rainout, Fergie fanned 14 Pirates only to lose 2-1 to Dock Ellis. Durocher reverted to his customary stoicism in defeat. "Leo knows we're busting our backs to win," said an unnamed regular, "but maybe if he raised a storm, it would do some good."

The next day, June 28, saw the Cubs lose a pair to the Bucs—3-2 and 4-1, in the Pirates' final outing at venerable Forbes Field. The crowd of 40,918 was the largest in 14 years, eclipsing even the throngs at the 1960 World Series final game in Forbes.

The opener got away in the 8th amid a controversy involving Phil Regan. With two men on base, Regan replaced Larry Gura. Running the count to 3 and 2, he walked Gene Alley to load the sacks. Then, with a 2-0 count on Jerry May, plate arbiter Al Barlick went after the Vulture again in search of the origin of the precipitation on the right-hander's pitches. According to the *Tribune*, "The Cubs were not happy at the harassment of Regan. Al Barlick, first-game plate umpire, plucked the ball from catcher Jack Hiatt's glove before there was a chance to wipe it off after the second delivery to Jerry May in the decisive 8th inning.

"Barlick went straight to the mound while Regan hurriedly wiped his brow dry. He told Regan the ball was moist and jerked the hurler's cap off to inspect the brim. It was ball two already, and even though Regan later threw two strikes, he finally walked the weak-hitting May (.207), and the winning run came home at half-speed."

On the 29th, with Ron Santo opening in leftfield instead of Billy Williams who later pinch-hit, Ernie Banks slugged two homers in yet another Cub loss, this time 8-6 in St. Louis. Regan was used again, and again lost it in the 8th. It was the team's 11th consecutive defeat. The nightmare stretched to a dozen on the last day of June, with a 5-4 verdict against the Cardinals. The Cubs opened strongly, hanging a three-spot on the great Bob Gibson in the first frame, but Decker was knocked out in 4th, and Gura later took the loss.

Decker likely sealed his fate with Leo in that game. When the manager strode to the mound to take him out, Leo incurred insubordination. "I told him to stand there until the relief pitcher arrived. So what did he do? He turned his back on me and walked away. Eyeball to eyeball, he defied me," growled the enraged manager. Labeling the hurler's actions defiant, Decker was fined $100 and given a box seat in Durocher's doghouse.

The Cubs closed June in an 0-12 funk, tumbling to 4th place, 4½ games behind the 40-33 Mets in the process. Pittsburgh held 2nd at 40-37, with the Cardinals at .500 (37-37) in 3rd. The Cubs were a dismal 10-18 for the month, giving them a year-to-date mark of 35-37. The 10-18 log was identical to their September/October record of the previous year. Moreover, they had played 10 games under .500 (22-32) since the end of April and were 28-34 since Hundley went down.

Durocher's preseason cocksureness in his development of a brace of starters from among the young arms auditioning before him proved hollow. In reality, by season's end the only youngster to hurl even 100 innings would be Decker, and he threw but 109 frames, only 26 of which came after the run-in in St. Louis. On June 25 the Cubs purchased the contract of a veteran right-hander from the Atlanta Braves, one who would be a mainstage performer on and off the field for the duration of Leo Durocher's tenure.

Miltiades Stergios Papastegios, otherwise known as Milt Pappas, was an interesting case. He pitched just 11 innings of minor league ball before breaking in with the Baltimore Orioles in 1957 at 18 years old. The picture of consistency, Pappas went 110-74 in his eight full years with the O's, twice posting ERAs under 3.00, while never turning in a losing season. Nonetheless, he was viewed as a bit of a disappointment. Tagged as a teenage phenom, the 6 foot 3, 190-pound right-hander was expected to mature into a truly dominant hurler. He had never, however, won more than 16 games in a single season. Moreover, only once did he throw even 250 innings in a campaign, or complete 15 games in an era of route-going outings, or strike out as many as 150 hitters in a season. "Pappas had a history of being a pitcher who worked six good innings and then wanted to get out of there," noted ironman Jenkins.

After the 1965 season, he and two teammates were dispatched to the Cincinnati Reds for the great Frank Robinson. Robinson, labeled as "an old 30" by some in Cincinnati, won the triple crown for the Orioles who won the American League pennant by nine games as the Reds slipped eight games under .500. As for Pappas, in his two full years in the Queen City, the moundsman won 28, losing 24. Again, he averaged less than 215 innings per season, fanning an average of 131 and posting a two-year ERA a shade over 3.80. Starting badly (2-5 with a 5.60 ERA) in 1968, he was dispatched to Atlanta in a multiplayer deal. Though going 10-8 for the Georgians, Pappas did little to contribute to the team's divisional title the following year. He compiled a 6-10 log, yielding better than a hit an inning and registering a 3.63 ERA against a leaguewide mark of 3.58.

After dividing four decisions in 1970 while turning in a bulging 6.06 ERA in 35⅔ innings, Atlanta decided to let him go. Pappas, still only 31, had already won 158 major games against 123 defeats. To put that in perspective, he had won about the same number of games at 31 as 324-game winner Don Sutton won at the same age.

Similar to the younger Sutton, Milt's trademark was consistency as opposed to big seasons. He had won 10 or more games 11 straight seasons (1958–1968) and had posted but one losing record (1969) in his 12 full years in the majors. Moreover, only three times did Pappas turn in an ERA over 4.00; in eight of his years, he was under 3.50, twice under 3.00. Nevertheless, given his 1969 and early 1970 performances, there was a question whether Pappas was rather prematurely at the end of the major league line.

Furthermore, Pappas's reputation as a proven major league hurler was exceeded only by his notoriety as a clubhouse lawyer. "That's why Baltimore, his original club, had let him go; it was, from everything I heard, why Cincinnati had let him go; and it was probably why he no longer felt he had a glowing future in Atlanta," Durocher claimed in his book.

Pappas was a friend of Blake Cullen, the Cubs' traveling secretary, and began lobbying him to convince GM John Holland to rescue him from Atlanta. According to Durocher, Pappas worked the skipper as well, beginning with a seemingly chance meeting in a restaurant in Acapulco, where Leo and his wife were vacationing in the winter of 1969.

From there, Leo says Pappas applied a full-court press. "The following summer he wooed me. Early in the season we played three games in Atlanta, and he came to me three different times. The first two times, he came over while I was watching batting practice to let me know Atlanta wasn't using him and he definitely could be had. The last day, I was told that he was waiting for me at the bus outside the clubhouse.

"Same thing when Atlanta came to Chicago a week later. And all the time he kept telling Blake Cullen how much he would like to be with the Cubs, and Blake would come to me and ask whether I thought Pappas could help us.

"There was no question that he could help us. We needed another starting pitcher bad, and you only had to look at the box scores to see that Pappas was right in feeling that his future did not lay in Atlanta. So I talked to John Holland about him. John wasn't crazy about the idea, but I finally was able to talk him into it."

July 1 was a boiling summer night. I was in Tiger Stadium watching Denny McLain bring an end to the suspension Commissioner Bowie Kuhn levied against him for half a season. It was so hot I witnessed a vendor, besieged by parched fans all night, throw his metal drink container, and with his face full of heat, anguish, and frustration, holler "Back off!" to the fans converging on him.

McLain was not nearly as hot as the night. Or after. Having hurled 661 innings the previous two seasons to run his career mark to a heady 114-57, the 26-year-old was now languishing in the backwater of ineffectiveness, going 17-34, finally leaving baseball before he was 29.

On that July night the Cubs team enjoyed better fortunes, but their manager did not. Although the Bruins ended their streak of futility when Ferguson Jenkins threw a 5-0 at St. Louis, the streak-breaking triumph was trumped by another story. Radio station WIND ended Leo Durocher's controversial radio show. DUROCHER BENCHED BY RADIO STATION, screamed the *Tribune* headline. Phil Nolan, the station's GM, had dispatched the following telegram to Leo in St. Louis.

> LEO: In view of the situation show tonight too tough for [Moderator] Bill [Berg], you, and those listeners who are unable to come up with new questions. Take the night off from radio. Everybody here at WIND is cheering you and the team. Good luck.

There was no plan for the resumption of the show.

Leo, as always, was quick to put his own spin on it. "I want it made clear this is my own decision. I am too busy now with the Chicago Cubs. There are too many things on my mind, I'm just not going to do the show anymore. I'm through with it completely and that's all there is to it."

During the previous off-season, Durocher had signed an eight-month pact with WIND to do a talk show. The price tag? $40,000—a tidy sum in those pre-free agency days during which precious few superstars were garnering even $100,000 for a season's work. According to the *Tribune,* much of the tumult occurred because ". . . Durocher often uses the show as a forum to make routine player announcements and reveal policy decisions while shunning the newspaper writers who travel with the team." Players also complained of Durocher's tendency to critique them openly and disclose lineup changes on his show.

Some felt P. K. Wrigley moved behind the scenes to scotch the enterprise. In any case, the owner challenged the station's stated reason for its deletion. "I can't believe they just cut Leo off the show just through compassion for the Cubs. The team is going bad, the show has dropped in ratings, and I think it's just a matter of business economics."

Nonetheless, speculation on Leo's tenure had begun, as the Cubs seemed to be repeating its 1969 collapse. Wrigley moved quickly to squash the rumors. "I am not considering a change of manager," he stated for the record. "If we can just win a few games, the boys will be back doing all right."

On July 3 the team played one of those summery Wrigley Field specials with Pittsburgh. Down 7-1 on the heels of a six-run Pirate explosion in the 2nd, the Bruins posted six tallies of their own to tie. Both teams pushed 2 over in the 4th, and by the 8th, the home town favorites held a 13-10 edge. Phil Regan came on in the 8th and "ran into a buzzsaw," as the late Jack Quinlan put it, eventually taking the loss in a 16-14 defeat. It was his sixth blot against four triumphs, the last of which had come on June 7. At this point, Regan had parted with 52 hits and 23 earned runs in 49 innings, giving him a 4.22 ERA.

There was good news, though, on Independence Day. Although gaining only a split in a twin bill with the Bucs, Milt Pappas rang up his first Cub win in the nightcap, 7-2. Moreover, Billy Williams was on a tear, blasting three circuit shots that afternoon. It gave the sweet swinger 24 for the season, to go with 75 RBIs. Jim Hickman, the other power generator, had 19 round-trippers with 56 knocked in. Santo continued to struggle with 7 and 42, respectively. The team clearly missed Ernie. He had hammered 10 over the wall, but in just 173 at bats.

Banks and his arthritic knees were getting on the Lip's nerves. Realizing that Banks's wounded wheels cut down his already limited range and his ability to run, requiring constant medical treatment and rest, Durocher sat him down. Durocher was increasingly annoyed with Mr. Cub's insistence in the media that he could play, only to have Leo accused by writers and broadcasters of idling Banks out of envy.

"He can hardly walk," Leo finally asserted on his pregame show. "People are saying I don't want to play him. But you've got to be in good condition to play, and the newspapers never say that he's not playing because he's hurting. I'm getting tired of being made to look bad, of being criticized for not playing Banks. I'm tired of being the middleman."

A loss the following day put the season mark at 37-40, with the team now having lost 15 of its last 17. Hank Aguirre's lament over the 1969 team's lack of feistiness, however, was not applicable to the Cubs in midseason 1970. The team's humbling experience in June had apparently made them more angry and frustrated than defeatist, as witness the happenings on July 5 against the Pittsburghers.

In that mean-spirited game, the Cubs' Jim Colborn and the Pirates' mercurial Dock Ellis began playing chin music with the two teams' hitters. Leo and Buc skipper Danny Murtaugh were called out of their respective dugouts and warned to stop the dusting. The combative Dock Ellis then yelled at Durocher as he was heading back to the dugout. With that, the now 65-year-old mentor turned and moved toward Ellis, and the rumble was on.

The civil disorder must have served as some kind of elixir for the struggling Chicagoans, as they swept a pair from the Expos the following day, 3-2 and 14-2. Bill Hands and the defiant Joe Decker got the victories. Though only 39-40 and 4½ behind the front-running Mets, winning two straight gave reason for hope. It was three in a row the next day as Billy Williams's 25th jack helped push the team back to .500 at 40-40.

When Ferguson Jenkins shut out the Phillies 2-0 in Wrigley Field on July 10, the club was 42-41, but still 4½ away. Also on the plus side, Hundley was activated and was declared ready for action after the all-star break. In the final game before the summer classic, Kenny Holtzman won his 9th against 7 setbacks at Wrigley Field as the Cubs pounded Philadelphia 10-2 on the strength of four Hickman RBIs before 28,270 happy patrons. The club, now 43-42 and five behind the 50-39 Pirates, had won six of its previous eight, and for Leo, things were looking up.

"I feel that we're healthy at last; now that Randy will be ready to play after the break," said the joyous skipper, "it's gonna make a big difference. I'd say we did well to be this close not having him the first half." For the record, the Cubs were 36-39 in Hundley's absence.

Durocher's optimism belied the numbers. The team had played just .481 (25-27) in their division. Moreover, their mark against the East's big 3—Pittsburgh, New York, and St. Louis—was a paltry 13-22, with an 8-15 mark against the Pirates and Mets.

Amid the mediocrity, the team did have standouts. Billy Williams was on his way to his best-ever season. Moreover, three Bruins—Kessinger, Beckert, and Jim Hickman—were named to the NL all-star team. Hickman, who had taken much of the sting out of Banks's absence, went into the break hitting .335 with 19 home runs and 60 RBIs. He was outdone by Williams with 26 home runs and 80 RBIs, to back a .317 average. Kessinger was hitting a solid .281 and Beckert .261. The offensive disappointments were Ron Santo and Johnny Callison. Santo was dragging at .246 with but 11 homers to go with 57 RBIs. Callison, from whom much was expected, was at .250, having hit just 8 circuit blows and driving in only 37.

Overall, however, the team was delivering at the plate. Hitting .252, it had scored 426 runs, an average of better than 5 per game. On the mound the team was not doing as well. Ace Ferguson Jenkins had divided his 20 decisions evenly with an uncharacteristic 4.00 ERA. Bill Hands, 10-7, had an ERA of 3.65, more than a point higher than his 1969 mark. Holtzman, 9-7, was also struggling with an ERA of 3.97. Joe Decker's 3.77 mark was actually second-best among the most used starters.

The bullpen was even worse. Phil Regan, still the dominant figure in relief, now had a luminous 4.69 ERA with but 4 wins in 10 decisions. The staff had parted with 381 runs (4.5 an outing), with an ERA of 3.98. Another mark of their ineffectiveness could be found in their hits-per-innings-pitched ratio. It stood at better than one a frame (764 hits in 757 innings).

Durocher, selected as a coach for the National League stars, was still unhappily fielding questions about his tenure in Chicago. "The thought of retiring has never crossed my mind," he stated stoutly. "Plans for the future? I have none—except to manage the Chicago Cubs. I'll manage as long as Mr. Wrigley wants me, but I've said that before. I have a contract through this year, but it really means nothing. We work on a handshake. I hope I can give him a championship."

A few weeks earlier, on the heels of the 0-12 schneid, a reactive Durocher had told *Tribune* columnist David Condon, "Resign? No way! The thought never entered my mind. I just manage the ball club and do the very best I can."

In the interview, Leo took familiar shots at the local media. "All writers have access to my office and are free to ask any questions they want. The trouble is that after I answer a question, they turn around the question—load it—and ask it out in the clubhouse. They're looking for two different versions."

Switching from his spring training tack, Leo now deflected the heat on to his charges. "The players have to win it. We score 14 runs today [in the 16-14 loss to Pittsburgh] and don't win. There's nothing I can do about it. As a manager, I have to take the blame. Of course, our bullpen wasn't very good today; that's for sure."

As for criticism in general, the manager trumpeted his popularity among the masses. "I have nothing to say about criticism. Ninety percent of my fan mail is favorable. It's nice to know how the fans feel. This sort of thing has happened to me before, and when it happened, I couldn't get to my desk because of the files of fan mail." As for the papers, Durocher chalked up their interest to economics. "So they're planning another newspaper series on me? Don't the papers always have to rehash stories about me every year? I guess it sells papers."

At the All-Star Game, Hickman, who produced the definition of *career year* in 1970, figured prominently in the outcome of the July 14 classic. With the NL trailing 4-1 in the bottom of the 9th, fans were beginning to leave Cincinnati's Riverfront Stadium, hoping to avert traffic snarls. When Dick Dietz led off the round with a home run off Oakland ace Catfish Hunter, it seemed of little consequence. But the Nationals pressed on with three singles and a sacrifice fly, tying the score at four.

Coming on in the 10th, Claude Osteen hurled three shutout innings, setting up the 12th-inning NL heroics. With two outs, hometown hero Pete Rose singled. Billy Grabarkiewitz moved Rose up a base with a hit. With that, Jim Hickman's chance at lasting fame came. The universally liked gentleman from Tennessee lashed a single, setting up one of the most famous plays in baseball history. On the hit, Rose came roaring around third, obsessed with tallying the winning run. Unfortunately for Cleveland catcher Ray Fosse, Rose and the ball arrived simultaneously, resulting in a Richter scale–like home plate collision. Rose prevailed as the ball got away from a never-the-same-after Fosse and the NL won 5-4.

Leo's "farm boy" was one of the skipper's favorites, which showed years later when the 6-foot-4 slugger lost his farm around Christmas of 1982, forcing the one-time all-star into a penniless rural existence. "Word got out on what happened, and the first call I got was from Leo, who was retired in Palm Springs," Hickman told writer Jeff Guinn. "Leo told me, 'I'm not rich, but I've got $10,000 and I'm sending it to you.' That's why when people talk about Leo and how he was supposed to be so bad, it hurts me. That generous side of him never gets told about."

Frustrations continued in July. While the starting rotation—the Big Three plus Pappas—was pitching well, the bullpen, again headed by Phil Regan, was ineffective. The pen's deficiencies were not helped by a bizarre late May deal. After posting a 2.00 ERA in 11 games, the Cubs inexplicably sent the seemingly ageless submariner Ted Abernathy—in his second tour of duty on the North Side—to St. Louis for reserve infielder Phil Gagliano. This time, Durocher's apparent dislike for unusual pitching styles would cost him dearly. Abernathy exposed the Cubs' folly by pitching 22 games for St. Louis and 36 more for Kansas City that year, winning 10 and saving 14 more, while losing only three. It was the second time the highly successful Abernathy was sent packing by Durocher. As for Gagliano, he entered only 26 games for Chicago, hitting .150 in 40 at bats.

With Banks on the disabled list and the team generally limping, the Cubs made another major personnel move. On July 29 the team purchased the contract of colorful Joe Pepitone. Pepi, 29, had spent his first eight years with the New York Yankees. Although he played on two pennant winners, was a three-time all-star (1963–1965), and hit 166 homers in those seven-plus seasons, Joe Pepitone was considered an underachiever. Seemingly blessed with near Mantle-like talent he chose to live much like the Mick and by his own admission, often drained his singular athletic energies in off-the-field capers.

On December 4, 1969, the Yankees dispatched the disappointing Pepitone to Houston for Curt Blefary. For the Astros, he banged out 14 home runs, drove in 35 runs, and hit .251 in 279 at bats. Not surprisingly, however, Pepi did not resonate well with right-wing skipper Harry "The Hat" Walker. "Harry Walker, the Astros manager, and I didn't get along," he told writer Jeff Guinn. "He's one of those baseball-is-religion guys. He told me I was gonna get shipped out.

"The day I joined the Cubs, he [Leo] took me aside and said, 'Have fun and do what you want to do. I'll show you respect if you'll show it back to me.' And I did. Of course, with my habits I knew playing so many day games would be tough, but sunlight agreed with me. I hit .307 the rest of the year, and in my first twenty-eight ballgames, I drove in thirty-two runs."

Pepitone's statement indicates that he had the same concern for facts as Leo did when telling a self-embellishing story. In reality, Pepi hit .268 the rest of the way. He cleared the .300 hurdle the following year. He did, however, go on an immediate RBI rampage upon joining the team, sending home 44 while hitting a dozen round-trippers in just 213 at bats. On his first day of wearing the blue and white, the Cubs played two with the Reds. Pepi knocked in the game winner in the opener and drove home another in the nightcap of the Bruin sweep.

Hungering for attention, Pepitone arranged for a limousine, driven by "Fabulous Howard," to squire him to and from Wrigley Field daily. Upon his arrival, the machine's horn would honk a version of "The Bridge over the River Kwai." Durocher, perhaps unconsciously jealous of Pepi's attention-getting endeavors, did not like it.

In the meantime, Durocher was tiring of the antics of fellow newcomer Milt Pappas, despite his generally solid performances. A lover of complete game efforts, Leo was becoming agitated with the hurler's tendency to keep the Innings Pitched column less than bulging. "The guy could pitch all right. But he always wanted to spit the bit out," claimed Durocher. "He'd give you a great six, seven innings, and if he had a one-run lead, he was through. If he won it, fine, he got credit for the win. If you lost, he was off the hook. If he was a run behind, it was a different story; he'd really be bearing down.

"The time that tore it, he was pitching against Cincinnati after he had been with us about a month, and he was pitching just great. [A couple of weeks earlier he had shut out the Reds, the only time they were shut out all year.] This time, I made the mistake of sending Joe Becker, my pitching coach, over to ask him how he felt, 'Aaah, I'm all in,' Milt said. 'I'd get a new pitcher in there.' I took him out. My fault.

"Cincinnati tied the game in the eighth and beat us in the ninth. If that wasn't bad enough, he threw a temper tantrum in the clubhouse when he heard the score had been tied."

Claiming to have called a team meeting, Durocher asserted that he said, "I want to apologize to the rest of the team. I screwed up today," referring to the removal of Pappas. He then addressed the pitcher directly, "You're going to start and you're staying in there until I take you out, and nobody's going to ask you. Quit looking over your shoulder at me. I blame myself because I should know better."

For the rest of Leo's sojourn in Chicago, he purports to have taken a different tack with Pappas. "From that day on, he never got to talk to me. He'd come into the dugout looking for me, and wherever he went, I'd go the other way. He'd look into the dugout from the mound, and I'd put my head down. It didn't matter what he said to the coaches. They were under instructions never to relay any of his complaints to me. I made him stay nine. Pitch, I'd say to myself. You ain't going to get out of there today; you're pitching too good. They're going to get a couple of men on, and somebody's going to get a base hit before I take you out now. Tired or not, you're pitching too good."

The numbers suggest that Durocher did decide to weld an effective Pappas to the mound. In little more than half a season in 1970, Pappas rang up 144⅔ innings. Though winning but 10 of 18 decisions, his ERA was a masterful 2.68. The following season saw him pitch a career-high 261 frames, completing 14 of his 35 starts.

Partly due to the Pappas-Pepitone reinforcements, the Cubs enjoyed a resurgence in July, going 19-12 for the month. They picked up 2½ games on the Mets who went 15-13 for the same period. As such, the club entered August with a 54-49 log, just a pair in arrears of the 55-46 New Yorkers and a game and a half away from 56-48 Pittsburgh.

"Even so, it was clear the rift between Durocher and the players was widening," noted Jenkins. An incident in Montreal on August 6 confirmed it. Santo had been struggling at the plate. On the skipper's "Durocher in the Dugout" pregame program, he stated that he was demoting Santo once again, this time to seventh in the lineup. "It may take some of the pressure off him. I'm going to take him out of the cleanup spot because he no longer earns it," explained Leo.

Santo was boiling when he saw the lineup card and confronted the manager, asking why he had been dropped. "You're not doing the job in cleanup, so I'm dropping you down in the batting order," was the Lip's reply. Santo went off and Durocher cut in. "I'm still the manager of this club. You hit where I want you to hit or you don't play."

Humiliated, the hitherto cleanup hitter let fly to the media, "He didn't say a thing to me. Not one word. He's a funny man. I don't understand him anymore."

Joey Amalfitano, close to both Santo and Durocher, attempted to be the peacemaker, but was unable to reunite the manager with the player who had once been his biggest admirer. "Amalfitano's failure to smooth things over was significant," according to Jenkins. "Durocher was not listening to his coaches and players. He did not seem to talk to anyone. A lot of us no longer understood Durocher. He became more and more withdrawn."

Though Durocher may have taken defeats quietly, he did not suffer difficulties with players passively. In early August he brought in Herman Franks (who would manage the Cubs in the late '70s) to replace ailing Joe Becker. He stirred the pot by stating the reason for Franks's presence was that the new first mate would "light a fire under those guys."

"Franks was an outspoken, hard-driving man, and he gave us a lift for a while," reported Jenkins. He made his presence known quickly in the clubhouse. "If card playing was the game, you guys would be leading the league. Get rid of 'em. Get your minds on baseball. No more cards," he bellowed.

An individual sidelight to the season was that of Billy Williams's ironman streak. Durocher never had anything but good to say about the Alabamian with the swing. "For six years I was able to walk into my office and start the day by writing his name in the number 3 slot of the lineup card," wrote Durocher. "Never had to say a word to him. He'd be out on the field early every day practicing. Like clockwork. He set his own time schedule and he never wasted a minute.

"Another double professional. He set a National League record by playing in 1,117 consecutive games, a streak that had begun two years before I got there and ended in September 1970. Actually, we had tried to end it earlier. Billy had gotten to be thirty-two years old, we were right in the middle of another pennant fight and the streak was wearing him down—emotionally as well as physically. Finally, I called him in and I said, 'Bill, what do you want to do?'

"'I want out of it,' he said. 'It's getting to be a monster.' Good. We made the announcement that the streak was coming to an end, and I told him to go home. He didn't. We fell behind early in the game, and while we had a rally going in the fifth inning, Billy came out to the dugout. In uniform. When I looked down the bench for a left-handed pinch hitter and saw him sitting there—well, who else would I want? 'Come here, pal,' I called. 'I want you to hit.' He got the hit that tied the ball game, and we went on to win it.

"A couple of weeks later he came to me on his own and said, 'Leo let's break this thing once and for all. Let's get it over with.' 'There's only one way I know,' I told him. 'Don't come to the ball park tomorrow. If I don't see you, I can't use you.'"

Durocher, displaying his rancor for Mr. Cub in a rather thinly disguised reference to what he believed had been Banks's efforts to manipulate the media against him when Ernie had to sit, commmended Williams's public statements on the close of the streak. "Billy went right to the newspapermen and told them he had asked to be taken out. Took all the pressure off me. Cream and sugar. Billy Williams is in a class all by himself," stated Durocher.

Going into their final 59 games of the season, the cast of characters representing Cub fans' interests was an intriguing one—from the emotional Santo and Pepitone to the steady Williams and Jenkins, from the reactive Pappas to the subdued Hickman.

Moreover, the veteran crew was now locked in an intense three-team sprint for the Eastern Division crown. As the Cubs headed into the dog days of August, the largely unspoken question among their fans was whether the beloved Bruins would expunge the lingering pain their followers felt from 1969 or inflict a second dose in 1970.

Ten

THE RACE

He just seems to go with one stopper until the guy wears down.
Reliever Ted Abernathy on Durocher

The bad news was that the Cubs were only 15-15 in August. The good news was that Pittsburgh went 14-15 and the Mets 13-18. As such, it was now clearly a three-team struggle involving the Mets, Pirates, and Cubs. For the record, the Pirates closed August at 70-63, with Chicago but a length back at 69-64, and New York 68-64. From the all-star break through the end of August, the Cubs had won 26 of 48 contests, picking up four games on the now front-running Pirates who went just 20-24 over the same period.

Despite the Santo/Durocher tensions within the clubhouse, the team hardly needed a plane to fly home from San Diego after their final August outing. Bill Hands ran his record to 15-12, scattering 7 hits and walking none en route to shutting out the Padres, 3-0. The victory was dramatic, with Joe Pepitone blasting a three-run dinger in the top of the 9th off rookie southpaw Dave Roberts, breaking a scoreless tie. "The kid just made a mistake," said Pepitone. "He got a curve ball a little too far out. Now we go home and we've got the Phillies and Mets and we'll see what happens."

Pepi was all the rage. It was his sixth homer since joining the club, and he had driven in 30 runs in 29 games, hitting .285 along the way. The

Tribune claimed his "growing popularity would be a threat to Mayor Daley if he ever decides to enter Chicago politics."

"Pepi is beautiful, isn't he?" enthused winning pitcher Bill Hands. "How many games has he already won for us? Four winning hits in a month."

"He has played absolutely sensational for us," exclaimed the what-have-you-done-for-me-lately Durocher. "He's some kind of ball player and some kind of guy, and he's great for this team. He keeps them loose and laughing. . . . Pepitone and Milt Pappas have turned this ball club right around. It's tough enough to find one guy you need during a season, but when you come up with two, that's really something."

A 20-year-old Les Grobstein was aboard the happy fan charter back to Chicago. His seatmate was none other than Ernie Banks, who gave the future talk-show host a never-to-be-forgotten taste of the player/fan bond of that era. "I always idolized Ernie Banks and still do to this day," states the unabashed Grobstein. "Ernie rode the fan-chartered plane rather than the team charter back. He asked to hear the play-by-play I had done on my tape recorder in the stands. 'Great! This is great!' he exclaimed when he heard it. He just poured it on. He was awesome."

Heading into September, the Cubs looked as good a bet as any to take the Eastern Division bunting. Fans, once again, dared to hope. After all, their favorites had gone 30-24 since July 7, and now with battle-tested veterans like Pappas pitching well and Pepitone driving home tallies, they were a much stronger team than the early July edition. If Phil Regan could step up and lead the bullpen, champagne would be sipped all over the Windy City in October.

Regan did not step up in the home stand opener. Suffering his eighth loss against just four triumphs in a 3-2 11-inning grinder at Wrigley against Philadelphia, the month opened ominously. Newcomer Milt Pappas, however, helped reverse the team's fortunes the next day in a 17-2 thumping of the Phillies. The Cubs followed that 20-hit explosion with a 7-2 victory in the series finale. Hickman erupted for 4 RBIs as Fergie rang up his 18th win in the game with which Billy Williams voluntarily brought his NL record ironman streak to an end at 1,117 games.

Well as the team was playing, as September 4 dawned, Cub fans were nervous. A simple two-game, early September set—at home—was generating most of the anxiety. The bedeviling Mets were coming to Chicago to call the Cubs' psychological bluff.

September. The Mets. A pennant race. Much as the players dismissed it as "just another game," everyone viewed it as an acid test for the 1970 Bruins.

Fully 39,981 adherents piled into Wrigley Field to witness the series opener. The hometown heroes entertained their delirious followers with a 7-4 victory. Durocher used five pitchers in the triumph, with reliever Roberto Rodriguez picking up his third win against a single loss in the stirring triumph. With the Pirates at 71-64, the Cubs were now at 72-65, pulling even with Pittsburgh and seemingly with the emotional wind at their backs.

The significance of a September vanquishing of the Mets was lost on no one. In a subtle admission that the 1969 Cub edition had indeed knuckled under to pennant pressure, team leader Randy Hundley described a different team psychology after the win. "I hate to bring it up, but after the disappointment of last year, we learned that losing a ball game was not the end of the world. We found out that when we went out to play a game, saying, 'We've got to win this one,' we got ourselves keyed up. We were too anxious and we wound up doing things we didn't normally do. We've matured since then. Joe Pepitone has helped by keeping us loose as well as by getting the big hits. Now we just go out relaxed, knowing if we give 100% we'll be all right."

There were, of course, continued jitters about the team's ability to break the tape on a divisional title. Despite having added several proven veterans, the 1970 club was playing fully 11 games behind the pace of the 1969 squad, which posted an 83-54 log after their first 137 outings. Nonetheless, the 1970 experience was clearly different from that of the previous campaign. The North-siders were now the pursuers. The pressure was on the Mets. Rather than trying to hang on, the Cubs were now coming on. In fact, their 33-25 mark over the past 58 games was actually a notch better than the 1969 contingent's 32-26, suggesting that momentum was indeed building.

It has often been said that "Momentum is as good as the next day's starter," and by that measure, momentum was not good for the Cubs. Despite fanning 10 New Yorkers, Kenny Holtzman picked up his 11th loss, giving up all five runs in a 5-3 defeat.

There was little time to reflect on the loss, however, as the team immediately boarded their plane for Pittsburgh, where the first-place Pirates now awaited them.

It rained on September 6, necessitating a twin bill on September 7. When Ferguson Jenkins took the mound in the nightcap, the Cubs faced the foreboding possibility of falling four games behind the Bucs, with 22 to play, after Milt Pappas had been pounded for nine hits and six runs in 4⅔ innings in an 8-3 opening game loss. But Fergie was at the top of his game, going the route and parting with but five hits and no walks in a 9-2 victory. It was his 19th win.

The Cubs would either be one or three games behind Pittsburgh after the September 8 series windup at Three Rivers. Bill Hands drew the clutch mound assignment.

The game was tight through 6 with the Cubs up 4-2. As fans sweated it out while watching or listening on WGN-TV or radio, the Cubs broke through with one tally in the 7th and five in the 8th en route to a 10-2 walloping of the Pirates.

"And their success was their 8th in the last 11 games, indicating the Cubs are beginning to create momentum for the September stretch run," crowed the *Tribune*.

The Cubs' sky was not cloudless, however, as Bill Hands acknowledged he was not the pitcher he had been in 1969, when as the team's stopper, he hung 20 skins and posted a microscopic 2.49 ERA. "I have no explanation for it; I didn't seem to be making as many mistakes last year as I am this year," confessed the right-hander. Moreover, Hands was less than enthralled with his most recent effort. "I was more of a thrower today, I'm a sinker ball pitcher and my ball was not sinking until the end of the ball game," he said.

But it did sink at the end, and the team was heading home just one game out, eager to face the divisional dead-enders, the Montreal Expos.

Few forms of revenge are enjoyed more by Durocher castoffs than that of evening the score against their former skipper. On September 9, a long-forgotten Cub expatriate entered the game in the 9th as a pinch runner in a 2-2 tie. Adolfo Phillips seized the moment with a stolen base and then scored on Bobby Wine's infield hit, giving the Expos a 3-2 lead. The Cubs' failure to score in the bottom of the 9th left them with a 74-68 mark, a game behind not only Pittsburgh but also the suddenly hard-charging Mets, both at 75-67.

Ernie Banks hammered his 509th career homer the next day as the Cubs coasted to a 9-3 victory before just 8,624 patrons. Still a game down to the Pirates and Mets, the Cubs received permission to roll the presses on World Series tickets.

After an off day on September 11, the Pirates paid a critical Wrigley Field visit the following day. Ferguson Jenkins, 10-4 since the all-star break, was ready to face the Bucs before 33,199 enthusiastic rooters. Parting with only two runs through 8, he trailed 2-1, setting up a controversial strategic decision in the Cub half of the inning. With a runner on and

Fergie due up, Durocher summoned Johnny Callison to move the runner with a bunt. He failed, sending the game to the 9th still 2-1.

Journeyman Juan Pizarro, who had tossed three shutout innings two days previous, was brought on to hold the Pirates in check. Neither he nor ex-Met Bob Miller could get it done, as the Bucs erupted for 3 in the frame, putting the tilt out of reach. The loss was particularly galling as the Cubs answered with a rally of their own in the bottom of the 9th, hanging themselves with an agonizing one-run defeat. The killer loss sent them into the series finale 2 down to the 77-67 Pirates, and 1½ away from the 77-68 Mets, with 18 to play.

Few games in Cub history are better remembered than their next game, a September 13 date with the men from the Steel City.

George Langford of the *Tribune* caught the drama brilliantly. "Only the leaden sky over Wrigley Field was as dark and bleak as the Cubs' hopes yesterday afternoon as Willie Smith's fly ball soared into the cold wind whipping in over the centerfield bleachers.

"Two were out in the ninth inning. The Cubs trailed, 2-1, and Pittsburgh ace Steve Blass had permitted only a bunt single since the second inning. Centerfielder Matty Alou waved his arms signaling all was secure, he had the ball in range. Then he jogged a few steps, preparing to make the catch, which would push the Cubs three games out of first place in the National League East, with only 17 games remaining.

"Blass could not contain himself at the sight of the certain out. He leaped with joy on the mound, resembling Zorba the Greek on the beach in the moonlight. Catcher Manny Sanguillen and second baseman Dave Cash also moved toward the pitcher to join in the celebration.

"But suddenly Alou was in trouble. His jog became a trot and then a race with the wind, which was pushing the ball away from him toward the infield. He reached for the ball and it tipped off his glove to the turf."

With that, the Cubs ripped into the Bucs. With Smith at second, Don Kessinger rifled Blass's first pitch into rightfield to tie the contest. On the very next Blass offering, Glenn Beckert shot a single to center, putting Bruins on first and second. With that, Murtaugh pulled the stunned Blass and handed the ball to southpaw George Brunet to face lefty-hitting Billy Williams. With a 1-0 count, the slugger sent a single to the opposite field and the race was on between the fleet Kessinger and the throw from leftfielder Willie Stargell. Kessinger beat the parabola by two steps, and the Cubs were back within a single game of the shell-shocked Pirates and within half a length of the Mets.

"It was the sort of victory a contender always hopes for—a springboard toward success," reported Langford. "The Cubs, an hour later, still had not settled to earth. Even Manager Leo Durocher, always calm and collected whether in victory or defeat, could not contain himself. He was as boisterous and wild-eyed as all the others, who had seemed a thoroughly beaten outfit for 8⅔ innings."

Hopes were now rising. The Cubs were following the opposite script of a year ago. Instead of wallowing in missed opportunities as they skidded into oblivion, the North-siders were giving evidence they were a never-say-die club, able to deliver in the clutch.

After a celebrative off day, the lights continued to look green, as another Wrigley Field wind came to the aid of the hometowners in a 5-3 win. A 20-mph breeze confused Cardinal rookie outfielder Luis Melendez in the 6th, as the Cubs broke a 2-2 tie and never looked back. Better yet, Ken Holtzman, who had struggled badly in September of 1969, was pitching well and had lifted his mark to 15-11. Perhaps more heartening was that Phil Regan, who had not pitched since September 4, picked up his 11th save.

At close of business on September 15, the standings in the East are shown, as follows.

	W	L	PCT.	GB
Pittsburgh	78	68	.534	—
Chicago	77	69	.527	1
New York	78	70	.527	1

There were only 16 games left.

On September 16, Cardinal ace Bob Gibson slammed the door on the Cubs' paws with a six-hitter, sending the Bruins and Milt Pappas (12-8) to an 8-1 defeat. The following day, the Redbirds jumped on struggling Bill Hands as the North-siders took a 9-2 pummeling. Tommy Davis, the erstwhile ex-Dodger star, picked up for the stretch run, making an inauspicious 0 for 4 debut.

Despite the two-game reversal, hopes remained high as the team's 77-71 record was still only two games worse than the Pirates' 79-69 mark, with the Mets just a shade better at 78-71. Regrettably, however, the Cubs were out of home games for 1970, where they drew 1,642,705 loyal observers. All 14 contests still on the books would be played on enemy soil.

A twi-nighter against the Expos awaited them on September 18. Canadian Fergie Jenkins hurried to Montreal from his mother's funeral for the opener, arriving just 90 minutes before the first pitch was thrown. The grieving right-hander answered the bell, delivering a five-hit 3-2 win and running his record to 20-15 in the process. In the nightcap, fading Phil Regan hurled three clutch frames, giving up a lone run and getting the win as the Cubs took another one-run contest, 5-4 in 10 innings. Cream and Sugar Williams homered in each game, giving him 41 for the campaign.

All but bereft of available pitchers, Durocher ingeniously employed a spring training style strategy in game 2. "Herman [Franks] and Joe [Becker] came to me with the idea a couple of days ago," Leo graciously acknowledged. The scheme had reliever Bob Miller working the first 2 innings, Larry Gura the next pair, and Jim Colborn the 2 following that. Regan worked the 7th, 8th, and 9th, and then with a precarious 5-4 lead, Leo yanked out the stops and handed the ball to starter Bill Hands who put down the Expos in the 10th for the save.

Holtzman followed the twin win by turning in his 16th victory in the next game. Phil Regan, now seemingly restored to full pitching fellowship by Leo, pitched a perfect 9th in the 8-4 victory. Winner Holtzman, however, hardly sounded confident. "We're getting closer to the Jewish holidays, and it must be that Jewish luck that's rubbing off on me. I didn't have anything today. Everybody deep down inside is really nervous. We all walk around laughing and joking and acting like we're loose, but anyone who says we're not nervous is a liar."

By that measure, Ron Santo hardly figured to pass a polygraph examination in saying, "I've never felt more loose and relaxed in my life, honestly, and I've never seen this team more relaxed."

In any case, with the hated Mets finally faded, it was now a two-team race.

	W	L	PCT.	GB
Pittsburgh	81	69	.540	—
Chicago	80	71	.530	1.5
New York	78	73	.517	3.5

And that was as good as it got. With just 11 games left, the Cubs reenacted 1969 in miniature.

Everything looked promising on September 20 in Montreal, with the Cubs leading 4-1. Disaster, however, hit when the Expos delivered a four-run 8th, giving them a 6-4 win. The surrealistic turnaround loss prompted Durocher to bring Jenkins out of the pen to stop the bleeding, but the Expos were not to be denied. The team was now two games down with just 10 left. The arithmetic was disturbing. If Pittsburgh merely split their last 10, the Cubs would have to go 7-3 just to tie. And they would have to do it on the road. Nonetheless, maybe the curse of 1969 had moved eastward and would now grip the Pirates. One could hope.

An off day was followed by another two-for-the-price-of-one on September 22 in St. Louis. Durocher played it to the edge, sending Ferguson Jenkins and Bill Hands to the hill in the twi-nighter. Jenkins drew Bob Gibson in the opener. Each pitched a complete-game sparkler, but Gibby was the better, yielding a lone Cub hit to Glenn Beckert in a 2-1 triumph. Fergie struck out a dozen Cardinals and allowed just seven safeties in this, his 16th loss.

Rookie Jerry Reuss hung another 2-1 verdict on the Cubs in the second game, saddling Bill Hands with his 14th loss against 17 victories. Bad as the two agonizing losses were, the team was still just 2½ in arrears of Pittsburgh, with 8 still to play.

A day of rain was followed by a comfortable 7-1 win over St. Louis, as Holtzman (17-11) registered another strong complete game outing.

Seven left and still down 2½, the team headed to Philadelphia, hoping to pick up ground in a three-game set against the sub-.500 Phillies.

Cub bats went dead in the series opener, as Rick Wise beat Pappas and the Chicagoans, 5-3. Now 3½ back and desperately needing a triumph, Leo announced he would bring Bill Hands back on two days rest for the next day. "He reminded the writers to remember 1951 when his New York Giants were five games behind with eight to play and won—but this is 1970," chided the *Tribune*.

The overused right-hander was promptly shelled, yielding six runs in less than 2 innings as the Phillies won a 7-1 laugher. Meanwhile, the Pirates clinched a tie for the Eastern Division crown. Employing curious logic, Hands explained his peformance thusly, "My arm wasn't tired, but it just didn't have any zip."

Neither did the Cubs, according to the *Tribune*. "The Cubs went about their work . . . as if they were condemned men without a hacksaw—a listless, punchless group apparently resigned to a fate which is now evident," the report read. "The heart, which has maintained a competitive beat throughout this long season, was missing for the first time."

The collapse was real—five losses in six outings.

The 5-3 victory the next day was hollow as the Pirates beat the Mets 2-1 to lock up the East. For the record, Jenkins won his 21st.

Now out of it, all that was left was a four-game series in Shea to determine who would claim the bridesmaid's role in the division.

With the diabetic Santo absent because of a death threat, the Cubs divided the four games, finishing a length ahead of the Mets at 84-78, but fully five games behind Pittsburgh.

The Pirates showed a gutsy resiliency, going 12-5 after that fateful blown game to the Cubs, and 7-3 in their final ten. The Cubs were 8-9, and 4-6 over the same spans. Nonetheless, it was really the last 11 contests that sealed the Bruins' fate. Though their record was 4-7 for the final run, half of that quartet of wins came in the final two rather meaningless games of the season, when nothing but second place was at stake.

Ken Holtzman may well have been nervous down the stretch, but he and particularly his starting pitching compatriots were certainly not the problem during those final dark weeks of 1970. The following table makes that obvious. It compares the team's numbers for three periods in the season—the first 85 games, the 66 games following the all-star break, and then the last 11 contests. The categories include hits per 9 innings, walks per game, strikeouts per full outing, and ERA.

	HIT/9	BB/9	K/9	ERA
All-Star Break	9.08	3.36	6.38	3.98
Sept. 19	8.51	2.53	6.16	3.53
Last 11	8.30	2.70	6.08	3.48

In general, the numbers got better as the season wore on. Considering that Randy Hundley missed 75 of the first 85 games, a strong argument could be made for the import of his calling the signals when one notes the dramatic improvement in Cub mound fortunes after the break. In fact, the numbers suggest that the club would likely have won four more games before the all-star hiatus had the staff pitched as well then as they did after Hundley returned. More on that later.

As for the final 11 confrontations, the staff actually posted its best numbers in hits per game and ERA in those tilts. With the league ERA at

4.05, Cub hurlers pitched more than a half a run better than the loop average during the 11-game snag! Moreover, their walk and strikeout numbers remained respectable as well.

Individually, it was Fergie and Kenny who were there in the clutch. Both players' numbers reflect growing effectiveness.

Jenkins	W-L	HIT/9	W/9	K/9	ERA
All-Star Break	10-10	8.61	1.67	7.94	4.00
Sept. 19	10-5	6.90	1.67	7.55	2.83
Last 11	2-1	5.15	2.40	9.27	2.40

Holtzman	W-L	HIT/9	W/9	K/9	ERA
All-Star Break	9-7	9.41	3.61	7.05	3.97
Sept. 19	7-4	7.47	2.29	5.49	2.82
Last 11	1-0	7.00	1.67	5.50	2.00

Midseason pickup Milt Pappas flourished in Chicago, though pitching in tough luck. His post-all-star numbers were excellent, while his performance in the final 11 was creditable.

Pappas	W-L	HIT/9	W/9	K/9	ERA
All-Star Break	4-3	9.92	1.68	5.64	4.42
Sept. 19	8-5	8.04	2.18	5.42	2.71
Last 11	0-2	10.9	3.48	3.98	3.48

Bill Hands clearly showed signs of deterioration after hurling 300 innings the previous year. After winning 20 with a 2.49 ERA in 1969, he never approached that season's numbers. Moreover, his performance fell off as the year wore on, particularly in the hits per game and ERA categories.

Hands	W-L	HIT/9	W/9	K/9	ERA
All-Star Break	10-7	8.76	2.98	6.08	3.65
Sept. 19	7-6	10.9	2.18	5.36	4.09
Last 11	1-2	10.5	2.62	6.28	4.19

Regan was largely a nonfactor in the last 11. Durocher apparently had lost faith in him. Despite using the veteran in critical situations immediately prior, Leo employed his services but twice for a total of one inning over the 11-game finish.

Regan	W-L	HIT/9	W/9	K/9	ERA
All-Star Break	4-6	10.1	3.78	3.96	4.68
Sept. 19	1-2	7.20	3.96	3.24	3.24
Last 11	0-1	45.0	0.00	0.00	45.0

The problems were at the plate.

• • •

The following table—focusing on runs scored per game, team batting average, and team slugging percentage—paints a foreboding picture of how complete the team's offensive breakdown was in its final 11 games. For purposes of perspective, each row first presents the league average, then the best performance in the league, and then the worst. This is followed by the Cubs' performance at three key points in the season. The first All-Star Break (ASB) refers to the team's record for the 85 games (43-42) before the all-star break. The second (Sept. 19) registers the club's efforts in the 66 games (37-29) running from the break through September 19. The final statistic (L 11) is the Cubs' number during their disastrous final 11 (4-7) games.

	NL	Best	Worst	ASB	SEPT 19	L 11
RUNS/GM	4.52	5.13	3.69	5.01	5.27	2.91
BAT AVG	.258	.270	.237	.252	.278	.194
SLUG	.392	.436	.356	.406	.446	.289

Note that in each category the team's performance improved markedly in the second phase (the 66 games following the break), only to fall through the floor in the final 11 outings. Scoring plummeted by more than two runs per game as compared with the first two measuring points; batting average dropped 84 points below the post-break .278; slugging fell 67 points under Philadelphia's league worst-team performance for 1970.

• • •

On an individual level, only Joe Pepitone (not with the team for the first four months of the season) came through. Pepi hit just .241, but slugged .655 while hitting four home runs in the process. No one else did anything.

Below are the numbers for seven key players. The categories are batting average, slugging percentage, runs scored per at bat, and runs batted in per at bat. No one hit better than .250. Four were under the Mendoza line (.200).

Kessinger	AVG	SLUG	R/AB	RBI/AB
All-Star Break	.281	.394	.174	.066
Sept. 19	.259	.318	.153	.058
Last 11	.200	.200	.075	.050

Beckert	AVG	SLUG	R/AB	RBI/AB
All-Star Break	.261	.328	.168	.075
Sept. 19	.335	.392	.169	.058
Last 11	.156	.200	.156	.000

Williams	AVG	SLUG	R/AB	RBI/AB
All-Star Break	.317	.607	.229	.235
Sept. 19	.341	.584	.216	.169
Last 11	.250	.425	.100	.150

Hickman	AVG	SLUG	R/AB	RBI/AB
All-Star Break	.335	.622	.207	.218
Sept. 19	.317	.579	.198	.262
Last 11	.162	.297	.135	.054

Santo	AVG	SLUG	R/AB	RBI/AB
All-Star Break	.246	.416	.134	.187
Sept. 19	.302	.578	.182	.249
Last 11	.200	.280	.040	.040

Callison	AVG	SLUG	R/AB	RBI/AB
All-Star Break	.250	.400	.127	.142
Sept. 19	.286	.500	.152	.148
Last 11	.143	.143	.000	.000

Hundley	AVG	SLUG	R/AB	RBI/AB
All-Star Break	.227	.227	.000	.091
Sept. 19	.255	.385	.065	.155
Last 11	.179	.179	.000	.107

Remembering that the league slugging mean was .392, after Billy Williams, no one rose above .297. Moreover, all seven players' runs and RBI per at bat numbers were the lowest in the final 11. A strong case could be made that Don Kessinger wore down again in 1970. Whereas the other six players generally performed as well or better in the 66 games after the break, the wiry shortstop's numbers fell off alarmingly. In the last 11, he again all but disappeared.

Why 1970 Was Not Their Year

As much as is made of the 1969 disappointment, 1970 should truly have been the Cubs year. Ninety wins—two fewer than they won the previous year—would have done it, but in spite of a projection of 95 triumphs using the research formula, the Cubs posted just 84 victories.

Why?

Indeed the final 11 do suggest, as Ken Holtzman indicated, that the team felt the pennant pressure acutely. To be fair, however, this team faced unique emotional tests. Not only was this collection of all-stars already renowned for being title-absent, but they played the season under the stigma of having collapsed in the late-season pennant heat of the previous season. Moreover, no matter how well the Cubs may have performed over the first five months of the campaign, fans and media nationwide would not really be watching until the heat was turned all the way up during the final month of the season. It was almost as if the first 133 games were mere exhibitions in preparation for the final 29.

Nevertheless, regardless of that end-of-the-season sag, the team did go 15-14 from September 1 on. They were 10-18 during the same period in 1969. In brief, although those last 11 were a substantial factor in this fall short year, it was neither the only nor the most important variable.

Despite tallying 44 fewer runs than their Wrigley Field occupancy would have projected, the team scored a whopping 806 runs in 1970. Again, however, they played the season without any table-setters. In a league with an average OBP of .332, the Cubs led off with a player (Kessinger) whose OBP was just six points ahead of the loop and followed him with a number 2 man (Beckert) whose number actually fell eight points under the league!

The only way that pair could combine for the 199 runs actually scored was if the hitters behind them delivered in the clutch. And deliver Billy Williams, Jim Hickman, and even Ron Santo did. The sizzling seasons of Williams and Hickman, along with the late-season clutch hitting of Santo, resulted in 358 RBI (44.4% of the team's 806 runs). In fact, the triumvirate was so dominant, no one else came within 40 RBI of Santo's 114, the lowest of the three.

Williams and Hickman carried the team offensively. Williams had a monster year, hitting .322, launching 42 home runs and sending home 129 runners in the process. He led the league in Total Bases with 373, runs scored (137), and hits (205). He was second in homers and RBI, fourth in both batting average and slugging percentage. It was the finest season in his Hall of Fame career, one in which he finished second to Johnny Bench in the MVP balloting. "I got off to a fast start," says Williams today. "I was disappointed that I didn't win the MVP vote, but I did win the *Sporting News* Player of the Year award."

Hickman, never more than a journeyman outfielder/first baseman, packed as much into a single season as any player in recent memory. An all-star for the first and only time, Leo's favorite smacked 32 home runs, drove in 115, and batted a lofty .315. In addition, after a gloomy first half, Ron Santo rebounded strongly, closing the season with 26 jacks to go with his 114 RBI.

Despite Hickman's signature season, the team missed Banks. His 12 home runs and 44 RBI in just 222 at bats tap out to 30 smacks and 110 RBI over a full 555 at bat campaign. With Ernie Banks and Randy Hundley down for much of the season, and Johnny Callison turning in a rather ordinary 19 homer/68 RBI year, the team was far too dependent on the big three mentioned earlier. Fortunately, Joe Pepitone picked up some of the slack, contributing a dozen home runs and 44 RBI in just 56 games.

In addition, the centerfield dilemma was never resolved. The Cubs used 15 different players—including the athletic Pepitone—in 1969 and 1970. A walk-getting, or at least base-stealing, performer in the picket could have made a substantial difference, especially in view of the softness at the top of the order. Had the lid of the lineup been characterized by higher on base performers, and the rest with more offensive muscle at the bottom of the order, the 1970 squad could well have scored as many as 40 more runs and turned at least five games around. In addition, there was just no speed available to counter these problems. The Cubs stole but 39 bases (in 55 attempts) all year.

It is hard to overestimate the effect of the loss of Randy Hundley. A case could well be made that Hundley's 75-game absence alone spelled the difference.

Here are some telling numbers. The team was 48-39 with him available, just 36-39 without him. Their winning percentage with Hundley present was .552, three points better than the Pirates' division-winning rate of .549.

Ferguson Jenkins's description of the difference between having and not having Hundley behind the plate as metaphorically equivalent to digging into a steak with a steak knife or merely a fork hardly seems far-fetched. Hundley, himself, explains how much Durocher depended on him. "As far as pitching was concerned, he'd say, 'What do you think about this guy? What do you think about that guy? Does he still have it?' He turned me loose. 'Randy, you're my manager on the field,' he said. So I gave him my opinion."

The following table presents the team's pitching statistics during 87 games for which the steak knife was available, and then for the 75 when it wasn't.

IP	H	H/9	ER	BB	BB/9	SO	SO/9	ERA
766	729	8.57	294	228	2.68	518	6.09	3.45
669	673	9.05	306	247	3.32	482	6.48	4.12

Sharp differences in hits and walks per innings pitched, to go with a whopping 0.67 variance in ERA. The contrast is beyond bold. It is inescapable.

Again the staff was carried by its starters. The team's ERA was 3.76, almost 30 points better than the NL norm. In addition, the staff yielded an eye-popping 118 fewer runs than would be expected by factoring in the Friendly Confines.

The Jenkins-Hands-Holtzman-Pappas quartet, which started 139 of the team's 162 games, went 67-50. Their combined .573 winning percentage translates to a 93-69 mark over 162 games, four games better than the Pirates 89-73 finish. The rest of the team—mainly, the relievers—was a meager 17-24. Moreover, the Big Four got precious little help from their mates in the pen. In a league with a team average of 34.2 saves, the Cubs had but 25—18 fewer than the champion Pirates.

Nothing stands out more sorely in assessing the team's inability to get it done in 1970 than Durocher's failure once again to put together a functional relief corps. Just as he had assured the team's beat writers of his intention to develop several young starters, Leo gave voice to spreading out the relief chores. In spring training, he told veteran submariner Ted Abernathy he had made a mistake in not using him more in 1969.

"He told me he wasn't going to let that happen again," recalled Abernathy in September (long after he had gone on to eventual American League stardom, having been traded in late May). "I was tickled to death. I felt we had a good chance to win. Here I was in my 10th year in the big leagues—finally with a chance for the World Series money. But when the season started, all of a sudden I was a once-a-week pitcher again. I've got to pitch more than that. He [Durocher] just seems to go with one stopper until the guy wears down."

After appearing in more games than any other NL hurler over the previous two campaigns, Phil Regan wore down fast. Moreover, Leo's penchant for continually going to Regan after the previous season's disappointment made utterly no sense. From the very outset of the season, the 33-year-old righty's stats reeked of ineffectiveness. As alluded to earlier, he appeared in half the team's first 64 games, registering an ERA of 4.02. In an era in which a closer was brought on as early as the 7th inning, not having several pitchers conditioned for late-game pressure duty was folly.

But that was not Leo's way. Abernathy, who worked 9 Cub innings in seven weeks, made clear it was the manager who had him peddled. According to the reliever, GM John Holland said, "I hate to see you go, but the man down there is running things." In any case, it was not until watching Regan's ERA swell to 4.69 in 50 innings by the all-star break, while walking almost as many hitters as he struck out in the process, did Durocher awaken.

Typical of the skipper's style, Leo then lurched to the other extreme. He all but abandoned the Vulture, giving him but 5 innings of work in July, 11 in August, and just 10 more from September 1 on. Because Durocher had developed no additional relievers early on, not only did the team spend much of the season scrounging around frantically for bullpen assistance—employing the likes of Roberto Rodriguez, Bob Miller, Juan Pizarro, young Larry Gura, and ancient Hoyt Wilhelm—they had no answers when relief was needed at the close of the season.

During those final 11 games, the bullpen merely poured the baseball equivalent of kerosene on opponents' offensive fires. Here are the numbers.

W	L	IP	H	R	ER	W	SO	ERA
0	2	13.2	17	11	11	6	5	7.24

Bullpen mismanagement, more than anything else, killed the 1970 Cubs. According to the research formula, the Pirates—who outscored the opposition by 65 runs for the season—should have won 89 games, exactly the number they did win.

The Cubs, having already outscored their opponents by 45 runs, should have been 47-38 at the all-star break. They were just 43-42. They went on to post an 82-run scoring edge over their opponents the rest of the way, translating to a 48-29 projection. That is fully seven games better than their actual 41-36 log.

Putting it together, had the Cubs won at the expected rate for the season, they would have taken the division by a comfortable six-game margin, with a 95-67 mark. They fell a whopping 11 games short of that projection.

With such a discrepancy often owing to an inordinate number of losses in close games, one need look no further than the bullpen. Although the team went a decent 22-7 in games in which members of the firemen corps came on with the Cubs in the lead, they posted an unimaginable 2-15 mark in outings in which relief was sought with the game tied.

Arguments will continue to rage over whether the best team won the divisional title in the bizarre campaign of 1969. Although the Cubs led the pack for more than 150 days, well into September, the Mets did manage to win 100 games.

There is no doubt about 1970. The Chicago Cubs were clearly the best team in the East. Owing largely to Durocher's failure to give shape to his bullpen, however, the Pittsburgh Pirates drank what should have been the Cubs' champagne.

Eleven

CONFRONTATION

The tension between Leo and the players kept building.
Ferguson Jenkins on Durocher, in 1971

By 1971 civil disorders and youthful protests were abating as the Nixon presidency was gaining its grip on the nation. Though the Vietnam War still raged, troops were being withdrawn. Renowned international negotiating guru Henry Kissinger was stimulating hope that he and Nixon could end the turmoil.

With Chappaquiddick now two years old, but still dimming Edward Kennedy's presidential ambitions, the Democrats turned toward Maine Senator Edmund Muskie, the lone figure to emerge untarnished from the 1968 debacle, as their hope for unseating Nixon the following year.

As for hopes pertaining to the Cubs, despite the twin disappointments of 1969 and 1970, Ron Santo remained a believer. He pleaded publicly with the Cub brass to retain the team's nucleus and give the veterans one more shot to loft a championship banner in Wrigley Field.

The sun, however, was going down on the core of Durocher's Cubs. There would not be many more opportunities, given the age of the team's key performers. In 1967 a bright, young team was now in 1971 a largely past-their-prime bunch. With the extensive and careful baseball researchers determining that the average player reaches his peak at 27, the age of the Cubs' nucleus suggested the performance arrow was pointing downward.

Ernie Banks—now in his last season—was a 40-year-old man with hopelessly arthritic knees. Santo and his roommate, Glenn Beckert, were 31, while the latter's keystone partner, shortstop Don Kessinger, would turn 29 during the 1971 campaign—the same age as catcher Randy Hundley. By midseason leftfielder Billy Williams would be 33, and first baseman/outfielder Jim Hickman, 34. Joe Pepitone was 30.

Except for ace Fergie Jenkins (27) and Kenny Holtzman (25), age was invading the heavily used pitching corps as well. By May, Bill Hands—no longer relying on his fastball—would be 31, a year younger than Milt Pappas, and three years the junior of 34-year-old reliever Phil Regan.

Leo Durocher was soon to be 66 and as contrary as ever.

Over the winter he objected to the formation of the Cub basketball team, which served to keep the players' stomachs flat and wallets fat. GM Holland initially supported the manager's resistance, but then relented after meeting with the persuasive Santo.

The Lip, himself, eventually attended some of the games but would exit once the team fell behind. "It got to be a standing joke that whenever we were losing, Leo would leave. It made it seem he was quitting on us, and that feeling carried over into the 1971 season," reported Jenkins.

The skipper also took time at the January baseball luncheon to label outfielder Johnny Callison a disappointment. Callison took the criticism badly, claiming that Leo pushed his players too hard. "It got to the point where I even worried how I looked in batting practice," the top performer of the ill-fated 1964 Phillies asserted, reflecting on his first year playing under the Lip.

Despite a few youthful bright spots in the form of outfielders Jose Ortiz and rookie Brock Davis, the spring brought bad news. Randy Hundley was injured again, this time in a rundown. Though the problem was now the right knee, it was severe enough that preliminary indications suggested he would miss the first month of the season.

Nonetheless, Santo was not the lone believer. *Tribune* scribe Bob Markus saw the Cubs sipping champagne in 1971. "When I arrived at the Cubs' spring training camp in Scottsdale, Arizona, four weeks ago, the baseball writers assigned there were so darkly depressed you'd have thought they were covering the Bataan Death March instead of a baseball club's spring rites. The passage of time has brightened their mood considerably now, but at that time the most optimistic guess about the team's ultimate destiny in the pennant race that starts this afternoon in Wrigley Field was fifth place," he wrote.

Acknowledging that these were "the same Cubs who blew it the last two years," Markus felt they had been close enough to the bunting in those campaigns that the improvements for 1971 could well put them over the top. He noted the existence of a quality four-deep starting rotation, something with which the little bears had not opened a season since pennant-winning 1935. He also cited the "strong" but "untested" young arms as potentially helpful to the team's fortunes. For the optimistic Markus, however, the strength of the team was its "day-in, day-out batting order."

Clearly, the Pirates stood in the way. They, however, were vulnerable, having dispatched slick-hitting outfielder Matty Alou to the Cardinals, and would be even more so if "their injury-plagued shortstop Gene Alley" were again to come down "with the arm miseries."

Markus handicapped the top two as follows:

"1—Chicago. Solid in every position. Starting pitching, along with Mets, best in baseball. Bullpen uncertain, bench short on quantity but with Paul Popovich and Ernie Banks long on quality.

"2—Pittsburgh. Can hit with the Cubs but infield defense not as strong. Pitching improved. Need healthy Alley all season."

Had the *Tribune* scribe studied better the principal factors in the Cubs' downfall in 1969 and 1970, he might have seen the Bruins' glass far more empty than full. The starting pitching corps was definitely stronger, but the previous years' disappointments had not been the result of pitching brownouts.

Indeed, these were essentially the same Cubs of the past several seasonal disappointments—same in the sense that they appeared to possess the same fatal flaws. The team still did not have a quality leadoff hitter, there was still a dearth of speed, a bench had not been built, and the bullpen was up for grabs. In brief, the team's fundamental problems had not been addressed.

Apparently, the fans sided with Markus, as a throng of 41,121, half-filling Wrigley Field four hours before game time, jammed the park on Opening Day. The Cubs sported an altered lineup from the ones their fans had become accustomed to. After 17 straight seasons, Banks's arthritic hinge kept him out of the opener. In addition, with Randy Hundley's knee sprain slow to heal, Ken Rudolph took over behind the plate. Banks and Hundley may have been missing, but with four-time 20-game winner Ferguson Jenkins facing off against the Cardinals' brilliant Bob Gibson, the confrontation with the rival Redbirds promised to be a tense thriller.

It was.

The contest was locked at 1-1 after 8 frames. Things looked ominous in the 9th when newly acquired Matty Alou dropped a get-on-base bunt and began legging it out. Before he hit the bag, however, the ball was there, thanks to a charging, lunging, bare-handed pickup, thrown by fielding wizard, shortstop Don Kessinger. A former slick-fielding shortstop himself, The Lip called it "the greatest play I've ever seen by a shortstop."

Neither team scored in the 9th. When the Cardinals went down in the 10th, it was shades of Willie Smith's 1969 heroics on Opening Day against Philadelphia, as 1970 hero Billy Williams stepped to the plate and promptly launched a solo shot out of the park to give the hometowners a dramatic 2-1 triumph.

Jenkins scattered just three hits over the full 10 innings, walking none and fanning seven in the process.

Unlike 1969, however, the thrilling lid-lifter did not propel the team to greater heights. Santo somewhat sarcastically rendered the lyrics of "What a Difference a Day Makes," as the Cardinals—with the help of six Cub errors and a raft of unearned runs—bombed the Cubs 14-3, with Steve Carlton going the route in the season's second outing. Bill Hands was removed with two out in the 4th, having permitted eight hits and eight runs (three earned) with but one strikeout. Bill Bonham, a 22-year-old right-hander, made an inauspicious big league debut retiring no one while walking three and yielding four runs, only one of which was earned. Phil Regan gave up two more (one earned) in the pair of innings he pitched.

The club then went 4 and 9 over the next 13 tilts, leaving them with a fifth-place, 5-10 rating after the first several weeks. The Cubs split their final six April outings, to close the month in fifth place at 8-13, five lengths behind the 12-7 New York Mets.

Prospects were gloomy as Randy Hundley's return was not imminent. On April 12 Hundley, in a pinch-hitting role, further damaged his knee. By month's end, fluid was still being drawn from the wounded limb. Moreover, backup Ken Rudolph, although throwing out 8 of 10 would-be base stealers, was hitting under .100.

With April turning into May, the hustle was just not there. There was a laconic, mechanical nature to the team's play, aggravated by its inability to make things happen on the bases, owing to age and lack of speed. Durocher tried to address the inertia several times with locker room meetings. Although a few players did speak, baseball lightning remained out of the bottle, and tensions lingered in the psyches of alienated ballplayers.

Tribune beat writer George Langford wrote, "The Cubs are flat, listless, and certainly not the most alert group of athletes who ever pulled on a Chicago uniform." During one Cub defeat, Billy Williams uncharacteristically pulled a skull that betrayed a lack of concentration. After catching a flyball for the inning's second out, he headed in thinking the inning was over while a runner scored from third.

In early May, the Cubs were shut out for 21 straight innings as Fergie lost his third straight in Pittsburgh, watching his record fall to 8-5. After a blazing start, there was now genuine concern about Jenkins's performance. In his last three starts, he had yielded an unFergielike 32 hits and 16 runs in 22⅔ innings.

Although the team rebounded through the early weeks of the month, a disastrous 2-9 finish left the Cubs mired in fourth at 21-27, putting them 10½ games behind the high-flying (32-17) Cardinals, eight in arrears of (29-19) Pittsburgh, and 7½ below (27-18) New York.

Durocher, having endured a near daily battering from Chicago columnists during the disappointing closing weeks of the 1970 campaign, entered the season an embattled field general. Now, with the team appearing corpselike early in 1971, rumors were rife that Leo's days in the dugout were numbered. After meeting with Holland and Wrigley and gaining their support, he called a clubhouse meeting, trying to reassert his authority to his uninspired troops. "I've been reassured that I'm not going to leave this team," he announced. "I'm still the manager of this club, and nobody had better get any ideas about cooking up any harebrained schemes to try to force me out."

Meanwhile, Randy Hundley continued to be dogged with injury. On May 25 his knee collapsed, and on May 30 he twisted it again, swinging at a pitch. On June 3 he would face surgery, leaving him on the shelf for six to eight additional weeks. (It turned out to be much more time, as Hundley would appear in only nine games in 1971.) Moreover, as the month closed, Joe Pepitone, hitting over .300, had to have his left elbow x-rayed to determine the condition of a bone chip that had locked his elbow occasionally in the previous few days.

With the team in a 9 of 11 swoon, owner P. K. Wrigley spoke out. "I BLAME THE PLAYERS: WRIGLEY," blared the June 2 *Tribune* headline. The owner had reportedly held a baseball summit conference with GM John Holland at Wrigley's Lake Geneva, Wisconsin, estate, from which emerged three major conclusions, according to the *Tribune*'s George Langford.

1. The Cubs have 'very good players who just aren't putting out.'
2. Leo Durocher will continue to be manager for the rest of this season and 'I think he will be around for a long, long time to come.'
3. The Cubs 'will not make a major trade. We will just have to raise [new talent] on the farm.'"

In other words, there would be no real changes. It was totally up to the players.

Though not naming names, Wrigley was clear about the lack of hustle. "It is a matter of some very good players who just aren't putting out." He, nonetheless, remained optimistic about the future. "We have nice young material coming up in the farm system and we don't want to rush their development. We just can't trade for new players, we'll just have to raise them. Unfortunately, we started our farm system a little later than other clubs."

He then clarified Durocher's status. "Leo does not have a signed contract, therefore I can't fire him from one and wouldn't. What I do have with Leo is an oral agreement, which I do not choose to break. Leo said when he came to us that when he felt he couldn't do the job, he would quit. That is good enough for me."

As for the manager himself when asked what was plaguing his club, Durocher was unresponsive. "They asked me these same questions in 1951 when my [miracle, pennant-winning] Giants lost 11 in a row," said Leo, sounding ever more ancient.

Fresh from an off day on June 1, the Cubs took two in Cincy, 6-3, and 4-1. Life was suddenly good. "Everybody came alive tonight," proclaimed Bill Hands (5-7), after struggling through the opener. "We had the best spirit we have had all year," chimed Phil Regan, who leveled his record at 1-1 by winning game 2.

The big bats boomed, as Ernie Banks hit his first round-tripper in the opener, and Billy Williams and Ron Santo hit numbers 13 and 11, respectively, in the finale. The twin bill also featured sterling defensive play by 27-year-old journeyman rookie Brock Davis. The centerfielder recorded 13 putouts in the two games (10 in game 2), with 3 sensational grabs.

On June 3 good things continued, as Ken Holtzman hurled a powerful 1–0 no-hitter, his second as a Cub. "I had trouble with my curveball because it was breaking so sharply I couldn't control it," said the southpaw. "I only threw two for strikes the last five innings and I didn't throw a change-up after the first inning . . . almost everything else was fastballs, I was quick tonight." Striking out six and walking four, the victory was only his third against six setbacks. The Cubs were now 24-27, still 8½ down to St. Louis.

On June 4, Jenkins posted his 100th career triumph at Atlanta, whitewashing the Southerners 11-0, and lifting his record to 9-5. In addition, Pepitone, feeling better after his bout with bone chips, hit his fifth homer in the win.

Nearing the one-third pole, the Cubs were a team of extremes.

Though ranked in the middle of the pack offensively, with a team batting average of .256 and scoring 3.8 runs per game, some key players were stepping forward. Glenn Beckert was on his way to a career year, placing fifth in the loop in hitting at a robust .349. Pepitone followed the second sacker at .311. Santo (.290) had 11 homers to go with 36 RBI, and Williams, close behind at .288, had 13 jacks and 32 runs driven in. Both Santo and Williams were among the league's premiere home-run and RBI performers.

Others were stepping back. Kessinger was hitting a mediocre .265, having scored just 28 runs from the leadoff position, and Jim Hickman and Johnny Callison were struggling. Hickman had but seven homers, and his .232 mark was 83 points below his 1970 season standard, while Callison had but a pair of dingers and was hitting a puny .209.

Aside from Jenkins (9-5, with a 3.19 ERA) and Pappas (6-5, 3.58), pitching was also a problem. Bill Hands's ERA was at 4.00, having won only five of a dozen decisions. Ken Holtzman (3-6) had a swollen 4.81 ERA. The Big Four, then, having logged over 80% of the team's innings, were a combined 23-23, with an ERA in excess of 3.80. The bullpen was 2-4.

The team, however, did appear to be hitting its stride. After losing an 11-inning, 6-4 grinder on June 5, in which Regan was tagged for four hits and three runs in 2⅔ innings, the Cubs reeled off 13 wins in their next 21 games, closing the month with a resounding 10–5 win over the Dodgers in Wrigley, behind Holtzman.

Going 14-9 over their final 23 June outings, the Cubs finished the month in third place at 39-36, a game and a half in front of the floundering Cardinals who had lost 19 of their previous 26. They were still, however, 8½ games down to division-leading Pittsburgh who was 49-29 and 6½ in arrears of New York (45-29).

During those final 23 games, the top of the lineup took hold. Beckert hit .345, Kessinger .340, and Williams .330. Moreover, Santo blasted four homers and knocked in 23 runs. On the hill, Hands, Holtzman, and Jenkins led the charge, winning 10 of 15 and recording a combined ERA of under 2.00.

Milt Pappas, 1-3 over those last 23, opened July on a tear. He won three straight, including a 2-0 complete game victory at San Diego in the opener of a split with the Padres, on the final day before the all-star break. The divide put the team at 47-41, exactly 10 games behind the Pirates and even with the Mets. Glenn Beckert was the Cubs lone starter in the midsummer classic, but was joined on the team by Ron Santo, Don Kessinger, and Ferguson Jenkins.

The Cubs played .500 ball after the break and closed July in third place, at 55-49. Pittsburgh was now at 67-49, 11 up on the Chicagoans, while the Cardinals—having rebounded to 58-49—were a game and a half ahead. As the month ended, the Cubs were enduring an offensive dry spell. The skipper, having used an all right-handed lineup (resting Williams and Pepitone) in hopes of striking fire in a 5-2 loss at Shea against Mets' southpaw Ray Sadecki, said, "The way we're hittin' we've got to get somebody to pitch a shutout."

The numbers were still up and down. Glenn Beckert was now hitting .356, Pepitone .321, and Callison was up to .250. Moreover, Brock Davis seemed to have settled the centerfield dilemma, hitting .302 in 209 at bats. The problem was a power outage in the middle of the lineup. Banks had batted but 52 times for the season (getting just nine hits), and Williams, Santo, and Pepitone combined for just six home runs and 40 RBI for July. Santo's one homer and seven RBI marks were especially disturbing.

Hands went 0-4 for the month, losing several tough-luck decisions, while Holtzman was 1-4. Fergie's 6-1 log and Pappas's 4-2 work helped make July a 16-13 success. Moreover, now deep into the season, Durocher clearly had not developed any real pitching depth. After the Big Four, Regan's 49⅔ innings out of the pen led the team, followed by Bonham's 37⅔.

On August 1, with game 2 of a scheduled twin bill in New York postponed, 34-year-old left-hander Juan Pizzaro outdueled Met ace Tom Seaver 3-2. Pizarro, who had spent the early part of the season pitching 127 innings for Tacoma in the Pacific Coast League, was now 2-1. Typical of Durocher's bizarre pitching strategy, Pizarro hurled all 9 innings, despite not having pitched in 12 days.

By August 5 the Cubs were showing signs of life at 60-50, still in third but now 8½ behind 69-42 Pittsburgh, as Pizarro fired a 1-hit, 3-0 shutout at the Padres in Wrigley Field. The team had now won four straight and had held the opposition scoreless for 33 innings (6 by Jenkins, backed by complete games from Hands, Pappas, and Juan Pizarro). As for newfound hero Pizarro, "He knows how to pitch, he's hungry," said the fiery manager. For his part, Pizarro snuck in a suggestion for optimal usage. "I never say anything, I jus' do my job and try my best for whatever they want," the Puerto Rican southpaw explained, "but I always know I pitch better as starter."

After an off day on the 6th, Ferguson Jenkins labored through his 22nd complete game before 36,715 at Wrigley Field, winning 6-5. Jenkins was fortunate to have lasted 9, as home plate umpire Ed Sudol tossed him in the 4th after arguing a strike call when hitting, only to reconsider his decision and reinstate him.

"It was nothing but a struggle all the way," said Fergie. Claiming his slider and curve had been ineffective, "I guess my fastball probably saved me," the right-hander concluded. The 61-50 Cubs were now just seven down as the 69-44 Pirates lost.

The next day, 43,066 believers piled into Wrigley to see the Cubs play two with the Giants. After Bill Hands lost 4-2 in 11 frames to Gaylord Perry in the opener, Milt Pappas salvaged a split with an 8–0 shutout in the nightcap. Billy Williams hammered three circuit shots in the twin bill, giving him 21 for the campaign.

After an off day, the Cubs—still seven out—headed to Pittsburgh for a key showdown with the divisional frontrunners. Juan Pizarro took the hill in the series opener, winning 2-1 on an impressive seven-hitter. Durocher spoke boldly. "There's no way I'm going to take the cream out of my rotation now, Holtzman [on reserve for the weekend] will have to fight to get his job back, although I could go with a five-man rotation when the schedule calls for it," he announced. As for Pizarro, he was now 4-1, with a 2.41 ERA, having scattered a mere 26 hits over 41 innings. He and Brock Davis (still hitting .281), the other refreshing contributor, were giving Cub fans reason to hope yet again.

The Pirates then pinned an agonizing 3-2 setback on the Cubs, as a bases-loaded Richie Hebner single off Regan (3-3) gave the Bucs the win in a game Jenkins started. Dock Ellis, 16-6, won. Pittsburgh (71-46) was again seven ahead of the 63-52 Cubs.

Milt Pappas followed a loss to the Reds with a strong 3-1 conquest on the strength of Williams's 22nd home run, and the Cubs were just 5½ out. Moreover, rightfielder Johnny Callison made a circus catch, temporarily restoring Leo's confidence in the outfielder.

On August 15, despite another super catch by Callison, lousy hitting coupled with three errors by Santo resulted in a 5-1 defeat at the hands of Reds' rookie Ross Grimsley, who tossed a 4-hitter.

Juan Pizarro took his second loss. The defeat left the Cubs 64-54, still 5½ behind the 71-50 Bucs, and 1½ down to the Cardinals, who had swept the first-place Bucs. Despite the hitting woes, three Cubs were still batting over .300, with Beckert at .351, Pepitone .307, and Williams .304.

The Cubs went on to win three of their next four, moving within just 4½ of Pittsburgh. When Jenkins won his 20th on the 20th of the month, from outward appearances the outlook seemed bright. Appearances, however, were deceiving, as Leo's style of static strategy was now wearing dangerously thin with this largely veteran bunch.

"The tension between Leo and the players kept building," noted Jenkins. "Guys were saying all kinds of things behind his back, things that could not be said to the press because to do so would have been to write your own ticket to be traded.

"Leo reacted by becoming more and more dictatorial. He was always shouting at players and chewing them out in front of the twenty-four other guys on the club. Leo would drag out all the dirt he knew about a player when he got into a rage, things that should have been said only in the privacy of his office, if at all.

"The continual yelling at the young pitchers and at young outfielders such as Brock Davis and Cleo James got on everyone's nerves. Fellows on the ball club were saying, 'We're going to have to get rid of Leo if we're going to win. Let's talk to the front office.' But that would have been wrong. We held meetings among ourselves, and some of the cooler heads pointed out, 'Let's forget about Leo and concentrate on winning for ourselves. We're big league ballplayers and it's up to us to win. Leo isn't playing for us. If he puts nine guys on the field, there is nothing we can do about it, even if they aren't the guys who should be out there. We'll just have to do the best we can and win it for ourselves.'

"We said these things because Leo would use players who were injured or tired, and he seldom substituted. The extra men rusted on the bench. Durocher was continually shuffling the batting order and shifting players from position to position. A man often would not be sure what position he was playing or if he was playing at all."

Then disaster hit.

With Durocher's increasingly acrimonious relations with players threatening to become ever more the story of 1971, an August 23 confrontation made it *the* story. With 37 games remaining, the team was still just 4½ out but had failed to pick up ground by losing two straight to Houston at Wrigley Field. The latter defeat was unforgivable by the dyspeptic skipper's standards because it occurred when Milt Pappas gave up a 0-2 checked-swing double to Doug Rader. Though the pitch was outside, Durocher insisted it had been right over the plate. The next day, an angry Durocher called a clubhouse meeting, an event that so much marked the 1971 season that few events other than JFK's assassination have been more chronicled.

Durocher—in his somewhat self-serving description of the rendezvous, from which much of the following dialogue was taken—claimed the Pappas pitch was one of the things he brought up in the course of the meeting. "We aren't hustling," he told them, "we aren't bearing down. We're slipping back into the sloppy, uncaring ways that had beaten us for three straight years now.

"There are some who don't seem to care." After chewing out the entire team, he leveled a few parting shots at Pappas's performance and then disarmed the gathering by extending a disingenuous olive branch to his players. Adopting a paternal tone, he set them up by saying, "I get the feeling something is wrong here. For some unknown reason, maybe it's me. This is an open meeting, man-to-man. There's no manager here. Look on me as if I were a player, not a manager, fellas. We're all equal. Everybody is free to say exactly what he thinks. If there's anything on your chest, now is the time to get it off."

Pappas took the bait, quickly entering the fray. "The whole trouble in this locker room is that you don't know how to handle us," stated the right-hander. "I don't think the things that have been going on here for the last year have helped us. We don't need all the shouting you've been doing and all these meetings. If you'd just let the ballplayers play, we could do the job. Why don't you give the guys on the bench a chance? They have to play to stay sharp."

According to Durocher, Pappas went on "lecturing" him in front of his players, focusing on the manager's deficiencies in dealing with players.

"I don't need you to call the pitches in the late innings," offered Holtzman. "I think I've proven that I'm a big league pitcher and that I don't need your help. If I needed help, I'd ask for it. I try to pitch my own kind of game, but every time I let a runner or two get on in the seventh-inning, you take me out. I want to know why."

Pepitone also spoke up. "I want to say something. Why are you always blaming people? Pappas didn't mean to throw that pitch. Santo didn't want to be in a slump. Look, I've been down that road before. But Ronnie can't take it. You got to rub Ronnie. You got to pat him. All you ever do is criticize players. You know, I played for the Yankees with some very good clubs, and Ralph Houk is just a super guy. He let you play. The trouble with this club is if a guy makes a mistake on the field, you talk about him on the bench. Houk never did that."

Pepitone went on extolling Houk's virtues before returning to Santo. "Houk and [Yogi] Berra never shouted at the young players. It's getting to the point that when a guy is called to pinch-hit, he's carrying lead in his bat and lead in his stomach, because you've got him so tight from the pressure of having to get the job done."

After several other players spoke, an enraged Leo, neck veins bulging, took the floor. "OK, now I'm going to speak. Listen, Pappas, I rescued you from Atlanta. I've given you the ball. I don't know what you've got to complain about. You've been winning more games the way I've been handling you than you ever won in your life.

"And what are you, Pepitone, nothing but a rotten clubhouse lawyer. Nobody wanted you when I picked you up off the trash heap. The only reason you are on this ball club is me. If it weren't for me, you'd be in the gutter, you worthless bum. We took a chance and brought you here. Who sets any rules for you? You can come and go as you please. Do you mean to tell me when you screw up in the ball game, I don't have the right to criticize you?"

"I knew I should have kept my mouth shut," Pepitone shot back.

Leo, however, was not about to yield the floor. "You had your say, now I'll have mine," the skipper announced. "The guy in leftfield, number twenty-six, I write his name in the lineup every day and forget about him. He's out there taking batting practice. He's out there early, fielding and throwing. I got a guy over here, Beckert, busting his rear end. He's having a super year. Challenging Clemente for the batting title. He's out there every day. He works on his hitting, he works on his fielding. He works on all his weaknesses. He made himself into a player. I'm out there watching the workout, Ronnie [Santo], and you're not even there during batting practice. You're coming out late."

Santo, when mired in a slump some days earlier on the road, had asked out of batting practice. He then began to hit. With the Cubs back home, he was not taking BP, or for that matter, Durocher's criticisms.

"What are you trying to say, Leo, that I don't practice hitting?" challenged Santo.

"Well, that's what I'm trying to say, Ronnie. Maybe if you came out there and practiced, you wouldn't get into these slumps you get into periodically," countered Durocher.

"No, and the reason is that I'm out of my slump and I want to keep the feeling I've got," said a now venting Santo. "That doesn't mean I don't want to improve myself. If I was hitting .300, Leo, you wouldn't care. But I'm hitting .260, so you're all over me. You say we're all the same. It doesn't matter what I do, you're right on my butt, and you use my roommate [Beckert], who's hitting .300, as an example. That's a great example."

Things were getting out of hand. "The only thing I'm trying to tell you is that you got to go on the field and practice. If nothing else, the fans come out early to see you, and you don't hit, you're not even there, and they're disappointed," Leo claimed to have said.

Santo, in a full lather, was yelling and accusing Durocher of "all kinds of things," according to Leo. With the meeting cycling out of control and Durocher feeling backed against the wall, the Lip started to lay down his trump card.

"Wait a minute. Let me ask you something, Ronnie. Isn't it true that you came to my room in Atlanta about calling off this day [Ron Santo Day] that's coming up this Sunday?"

Santo agreed.

"I didn't want to bring this up, Ronnie, but I'm going to say it. Isn't it also true that you had a problem signing a contract this year and when you couldn't get the money you wanted, you wanted a stipulation that the Cubs would have a Day for you because they gave one to Billy Williams and Ernie Banks? You told me you never wanted the Day, and that was an erroneous statement on your part, wasn't it?"

After a moment of stunned silence, the emotional melee was on. Santo leaped for Durocher, screaming at him nose to nose. "You're a liar! I never asked for a Day. You get John Holland down here this instant. You won't embarrass me in front of my teammates."

"Do you want me to get Mr. Holland down here to clear that up, Ron?"

Leo picked up the phone to summon GM John Holland. With that, Leo headed to his office to smoke a cigarette in hopes that things would cool down. A few minutes passed and Santo, with anguished tears rolling down his face, started after Leo, likely out of concern that Leo would talk to Holland on the side and orchestrate the GM's version.

"You get John Holland down here right now!" an out-of-control Santo screamed.

When Holland arrived, Santo wasted no time laying the issue of the hour squarely in front of Holland. "John, Leo says I begged for a Ron Santo Day. You tell him I didn't ask for this."

"Ron, don't worry, I'm going to handle this," a cornered Holland soothed, sending Santo back to his teammates.

A few minutes later the GM and the manager reentered the clubhouse. "John, you tell my teammates that I didn't ask for this Day," commanded Santo, who to this day denies the charge that he had solicited his own day of honor.

Caught between Durocher and the captain, the backing-and-filling Holland hesitated, saying, "I don't know, Ronnie, whether I brought up the idea or you brought it up at contract time."

With that, Santo erupted, calling out Holland for betraying him.

"Fellas, this thing has gotten out of hand," pleaded Holland. "Ron never asked for this Day."

With that, Pepitone was at Durocher again, stating this to be the worst thing he had ever seen. "You see what you've done! You've destroyed him."

"What kind of manager are you?" Pappas shouted in agreement.

Then Durocher cracked. "I didn't know there was this much hatred for me on this ball club. So I've got a solution to the whole thing. I'll see you later! Just get yourself another manager. I quit. I'm walking up these stairs for the last time as Cub manager."

After a few more words, Durocher headed for his office.

"Let him go. Let him do what he has to do. Let him go," Holtzman and Pappas shouted, anxious to see the end of the adversarial manager's reign.

"We can't have this guy leave! We're not out of this race. If we let Leo quit now, the press will bury us," Holland implored.

Quiet Jim Hickman spoke up, "We've gotten this far with him, we can't let him go. He's helped us all and we need him."

Randy Hundley, J. C. Martin, and Jim Hickman urged similar sentiments, saying, "We can't let this happen. It's going to reflect on all of us to have the manager quit before a game. We're going to look worse than he does. It'll seem like mutiny."

Pappas, unconvinced, jumped up and hollered, "Let's take a vote on it." With that, Coach Joey Amalfitano entered the dispute, calling Durocher "one of a kind" and stating that if the players thought they could win without him, they were crazy.

Holland addressed Santo. "We gave you the Day, Ron, but I'm in a bind. Help me out."

"Let me cool off. I'll do it. If someone wants to go up now, fine, but I need some time," replied Santo.

No one volunteered, although the majority of players felt Durocher should stay. The team did lay down certain conditions, including the need for the manager to get off the back of the younger players and to repair relations with the media.

Santo and Amalfitano then went to Durocher's office. Leo was in street clothes, parting company with the position of manager of the Chicago Cubs.

Explaining that Santo had not meant all the things he had said, Amalfitano spoke to Durocher. "What you said, Leo, I don't think you should have said. And the names you called him, Ron, you shouldn't have said, either. Now if you're two adults, like I think you are, you got to apologize to each other and shake hands."

Durocher told Santo he had nothing against him, and Santo hugged the manager and said, "Leo it got out of hand, we both lost our tempers. Let's try to forget it. We're both competitive guys. We need you. If you leave us now, it's going to be bad for everyone."

"Ronnie, I'm not mad at you. You got a right to your feelings. You had a right to pop off. It was an open meeting. So did I. Forget it," the near nonmanager responded.

According to Durocher, he had no such redemptive feelings for Pepitone and Pappas. Moreover, he was still quitting. Amalfitano and Ernie Banks then tried to talk him into staying on, while back in the clubhouse, the usually measured Hickman was dressing down the team in general, and Pappas and Pepitone in particular for the uproar. Durocher later heard that backup catchers J. C. Martin and Chris Cannizzaro had supported Hickman.

"I've been around for a long time, and this is the worst thing I've ever seen," Leo quotes Martin as saying.

John Holland then stepped in and told Durocher he owed it to P. K. Wrigley not to quit. Durocher then put his uniform back on and managed the Bruins to a 6-3 win, with Ron Santo getting three hits—two doubles— and knocking in half the team's runs.

Things were never the same.

Despite Durocher's pleasant spin on the meeting's outcome, the tension remained. "It was like an armed truce," said Jenkins. "The unspoken agreement between Leo and the players was to talk to each other only if the situation demanded it."

The weather was perfect at Wrigley Field that weekend for Ron Santo Day, an event Santo had wanted to benefit the Diabetes Association of Chicago. Not surprisingly, however, the Cubs lost 4-3 to Atlanta before the 34,998 Cub adherents who filled the park. In the next day's *Tribune*, Dick Dozer wrote that "the Chicago Cubs lost a game they undoubtedly wanted more than any other yesterday. They were battling desperately to make Ron Santo Day a complete success, and they had their best man, Ferguson Jenkins, up for the task. But maybe they were trying too hard."

The Cubs were now 70-60 and sinking. They lost three of the last four in August and by month's end, were again in third, at 71-63. Moreover, they were a disconcerting 8½ lengths behind the Bucs, 3½ under St. Louis.

The consensus was that Durocher's days were growing short. In fact, Dozer began his Ron Santo Day article by stating, "In what plainly has become a countdown toward Leo Durocher's retirement—forced or otherwise. . . ."

Few fans then were prepared for September 3. With the team closing the day at 72-65, their on-the-field exploits were hardly noticed. Instead, a near full-page advertisement, taken out by owner P. K. Wrigley in the *Chicago Today* was the talk of the baseball world. It read:

THIS IS FOR CUB FANS AND ANYONE ELSE
WHO IS INTERESTED
It is no secret that in the closing days of the season that held great possibilities, the Cub organization is at sixes and sevens and somebody has to do something. So, as head of the corporation, the responsibility falls on me.

By tradition, this would call for a press conference following which there would be as many versions of what I had to say as there were reporters present; and as I have always believed in tackling anything as directly as possible, I am using this paid newspaper space to give you what I have to say direct, and you can do your own analyzing.

I have been in professional baseball a long time. I have served under the only five commissioners we have had to date and four league presidents, and I must have learned something about professional baseball.

Many people seem to have forgotten, but I have not, that after many years of successful seasons with contesting clubs and five league pennants, the Cubs went into the doldrums and for a quarter of a century were perennial dwellers of the second division in spite of everything we could think of to try and do—experienced managers, inexperienced managers, rotating managers, no manager but revolving coaches—we were still there in the also-rans.

We figured out what we thought we needed to make a lot of potential talent into a contending team, and we settled on Leo Durocher, who had the baseball knowledge to build a contender and win pennants and also knowing that he had been a controversial figure wherever he went, particularly with the press, because he just never was cut out to be a diplomat. He accepted the job at less than he was making because he considered it to be a challenge, and Leo thrives on challenges.

In his first year we ended in the cellar, but from then on, came steadily up, knocking on the door for the top.

Each near miss has caused more and more criticism, and this year there has been a concerted campaign to dump Durocher that has even affected the players, but just as there has to be someone to make decisions for the corporation, there has to be someone in charge on the field to make the final decisions on the spur of the moment, and right or wrong, that's it.

All this preamble is to say that after careful consideration and consultation with my baseball people, Leo is the team manager and the "Dump Durocher Clique" might as well give up. He is running the team, and if some of the players do not like it and lie down on the job, during the off season we will see what we can do to find them happier homes.

(signed) Phil Wrigley

P.S. If only we could find more team players like Ernie Banks.

Ken Holtzman, a long-time Durocher adversary, was offended at the intimation that Banks was the lone team player and demanded to be traded. Moreover, he felt his 9-15 log was as much the skipper's fault as his own.

"Leo is the dumbest manager I ever played for," stated Joe Pepitone. Ferguson Jenkins summed up much of the team sentiment, remarking later, "If only Mr. Wrigley knew what was really going on." Don Kessinger just wanted to "finish the season."

The next day Beckert was declared out for the season, owing to surgery on an injured thumb. He ended the campaign hitting .342, good for third in the league. That same day a bronchitis-weakened Milt Pappas went 6 innings, getting his 17th win in a 7-5 triumph. A similarly afflicted Phil Regan went the final three frames. The third-place team was now 73-65, nine behind the 83-57 Pirates. Pappas, 17-11, would lose his last three decisions.

From there, the team floundered, winning but 9 and losing 14 of their next 23. It took a 5-3 complete game win by Jenkins in the season finale in Montreal to give the Cubs a tie with the Mets for third at 83-79, 14 games behind Pittsburgh and 7 below the Cardinals.

The Cub faithful had indeed been faithful. After two straight severe disappointments, 1,653,007, about 10,000 more than in 1970, saw the Chicago Cubs play baseball in Wrigley Field sunshine.

With Pittsburgh winning it all in 1971, it is easy to close the books on the season by saying it was the year of the Pirates and simply move on. To do so, however, would be to miss several key points concerning the 1971 edition of the Chicago Cubs.

Despite Markus's preseason reference to improvements, the 1971 team was far weaker than the previous year's club. Despite finishing four games over .500, they were outscored 648 to 637 for the season. Applying the research formula, they projected as an 80-82 ball club.

Offensively, those 637 (3.93 per game) runs ranked them sixth in the league, just four over the league average. Considering they played their home games in the most run-friendly park in the league, the team's offense was clearly substandard, generating 56 fewer runs than the average NL team would have tallied playing half their games in Wrigley.

No Cub hit as many as 30 home runs, and none drove in 100 runs. Though ranking in the top five in batting average (BA), slugging, and on base percentage, the runs just didn't come in. Their Clutch Hitting Index (a complex formula that measures actual RBI in comparison to expected RBI) tells much of the story. They were tied with the Mets for worst in the league.

Runs begin with getting on base, and again, Durocher didn't reconfigure the top of the order. Amazingly, their leadoff man, Kessinger, had a .318 OBP, even with the league average, and an incredible nine points below the team's mark. Beckert's .370 OBP in the second slot, mainly owing to his career year (.342 BA), helped counter Kessinger's limitations.

Though much was made of colorful Joe Pepitone's .307 average, it was a rather empty .307. He batted only 427 times, scored just 50 runs, and drove in only 61. Ron Santo slumped to .267, with 21 big ones and 88 RBI. Moreover, only Billy Williams delivered offensively from the outfield, hitting .301 with 28 jacks and 98 RBI, while placing fifth in Total Bases with 300.

Johnny Callison hit only .210, Brock Davis tailed off to .256, the same number as Gentleman Jim Hickman, who split time at first base. These three combined for 974 at bats, the equivalent of nearly two full seasons, but together they hit just 27 homers and drove home only 126 tallies.

Overall, the pitching held up rather well, despite the near season-long absence of Hundley. Though in the lower half in league ERA at 3.61 (0.14 over the NL average of 3.47), the staff actually yielded 52 fewer runs than expected when one factors in the Wrigley Field effect.

Cy Young Award winner Ferguson Jenkins was again the main force in the team's pitching numbers. He led the league in innings pitched (325), complete games (30), and wins (24), while turning in a 2.77 ERA. He was number 2 in TBR (Total Baseball Ranking), behind the Mets' Tom

Seaver, who many felt should have been granted the Cy, despite Fergie's brilliance.

Milt Pappas (17-14, 3.58) had a solid year, hurling 261 frames and delivering 5 shutouts. Bill Hands turned in a reputable 3.42 ERA, but won only 12 of 30 decisions doing it. For Ken Holtzman, other than his magic night in Cincinnati, 1971 was a bust. He went 9-15 with a 4.48 ERA. Together then, the Big Four went just 62-60. The only other Cub pitcher to throw more than 100 innings was Juan Pizarro (101), who finished 7-6 with a 3.48 ERA.

Yet, again Durocher did nothing to solve the bullpen problems, which once more turned out to be his team's undoing. He simply loaded down his starters with innings. Jenkins, Pappas, and Hands combined for 828 innings (over 57% of the team's 1,444 innings). No other threesome in the NL even totaled 800 frames. Add Holtzman and Pizarro's totals and essentially half the staff started 152 games and threw 1,125 innings, nearly 78% of the team's total.

As a result of such disproportionate overwork, the Cubs registered a major league high of 75 complete games against only 13 saves for the entire season (second lowest in the majors and well under 40% of the average of over 34 per team). That, as much as anything, probably accounts for the reason that this quintet could on one hand post a combined ERA of just 3.44 (three points better than the league, truly outstanding considering the Wrigley factor), and on the other, go just three games over .500 at 69-66.

Moreover, for the third straight unsuccessful season, Durocher only had eyes for one reliever, Phil Regan. The 34-year-old, who had but three strong seasons in his 13-year career, was now more prey than predator. Regan appeared in 48 games, pitching 73 innings, going 5-5 with just 6 saves and a 3.95 ERA, numbers hardly associated with the relief ace on a contending team. The rest of the staff worked just 246 innings with an ERA of 4.28. Again, no young hurlers were developed. Bill Bonham, who started only twice in his 33 outings, topped the youth charts working just 60 innings.

Indeed, the evidence continued to accumulate that the game was moving well past the 66-year-old Durocher. If, in fact, Leo was influencing the personnel calls, as John Holland indicated in his 1970 exit conversation with Ted Abernathy, he was doing little to build the ball club.

For a manager who made his name by gambling hard and effectively, the lack of creativity was painfully on display. Other than a bit of lineup and position shifting, there was a deadly sameness to the players and strategies Leo employed. Offensively, he found no combinations that would deliver runs, while doggedly staying with Kessinger at the top of his lineup. Admittedly lacking speedsters, the team attempted only 76 stolen bases, dead last in the majors. In addition, he remained an archconservative in handling his pitching. Once a keen-eyed scavenger for young talent, Durocher gave over 82% of the team's innings to five veteran starters and one ineffective fireman.

Worse, his relationship with the players was irretrievably damaged. "Later on, in 1971, Leo got to the point where he often did not post the lineup card until ten minutes before the game," reported Jenkins. "The players did not know whether they were going to play that day. They could not get themselves up for the game."

"In 1971, we were still playing over .500," wrote Santo, but the cracks were beginning to show." It was now twilight time for Durocher's Cubs, as the fans had come to know them over the past six years. Banks's career ended. Hundley had two bad knees. Santo was slipping. Regan was finished, and Holtzman wanted out.

Twelve

STUNNER

This is the best team I've ever managed.
Leo Durocher on the 1972 Cubs

It was an election year, and the beginning of a political upheaval summarized in a single word—Watergate. Presidential hopeful George McGovern surprised the electoral world by upsetting heavily favored front-runner Edmund Muskie for the Democratic nomination. Meanwhile, the Republican Committee to Reelect the President plotted a break-in at the Democratic national headquarters, an act that would lead to the imprisonment of high-ranking governmental officials, shatter an administration, and unseat a president—Richard Nixon—less than two years after registering a smashing victory at the polls.

In Chicago, Leo Durocher decided 1972 would be different. Predicting the Cubs would win a pennant, Leo, ever the actor, worked at changing his image. "Durocher worked hard at patching up his relations with the players," noted Ferguson Jenkins. "He shook hands with Ron Santo at spring training camp, and the two smiled for the photographers. Leo assured everyone that he would be more understanding and that there would be no more ranting and raving. There would be a new Leo.

"Wrigley and Holland made Durocher promise to get closer to the players and be more patient with the youngsters," wrote Fergie. Wrigley, however, went further. The architect of the ill-fated college of coaches designed another new baseball position, Information and Services Coach. Its occupant, former Cub southpaw Hank Aguirre, was to act as communications liaison between Wrigley's embattled manager and the rest of Western Civilization, particularly the press and his players.

"I don't think anyone really believed that Leo had changed," claimed Jenkins, "but the players decided that since he was there to stay, they had to make the best of it."

Aguirre did share the Lip's optimism, later telling writer Talley, "I really think that 1972 club could have been the best of all of them."

It was in much respect a substantially different team from that of previous seasons. GM John Holland had peddled Brock Davis, Jim Colborn, and pitcher Earl Stephenson to the Brewers for fleet rightfielder Jose Cardenal, while disgruntled Ken Holtzman headed for Charles Finley's Oakland A's in exchange for centerfielder Rick Monday. Cardenal supplanted Kessinger as the Opening Day leadoff man, while he and Monday added much-needed speed to the North-siders' lineup. These two, with slugging Billy Williams, solidified the Bruins outfield.

Johnny Callison was dispatched to the Yankees for reliever Jack Aker. In addition, the Cubs worked further at bolstering their bullpen by picking up two other relievers, Dan McGinn and veteran Steve Hamilton, both southpaws. Five days into the season, the team acquired right-hander Tom Phoebus from San Diego. Better yet, these pitchers would be throwing to Randy Hundley, who was now healthy enough to handle the catching chores.

The season did not start on time. On April 1 the Players Association struck with demands for increased benefits. The owners dug in their heels and the work stoppage lasted nearly two weeks, pushing back the season's start to April 15.

The opener went to Steve Carlton and the Phillies 4-2, on a costly two-run gaffe by Cardenal in rightfield who lost a fly in the sun. Bill Hands took the loss in relief of Ferguson Jenkins. Leo Durocher, suffering from a throat virus, was not in the dugout for the curtain-raiser, turning the managerial chores over to coach Pete Reiser, who had returned to the Cubs.

The following day young Burt Hooton, making just his fourth major league start, confounded Philadelphia with his knucklecurve, no-hitting the Phils 4-0. Only 9,583 fans witnessed the classic on a cold, wet day. According to Hundley, Hooton—who both walked and struck out seven—was baffling with his unique pitch. "You have to compare his knucklecurve with a Sandy Koufax curveball," the receiver raved, with a bit of exaggeration. "It starts at your head and winds up on the ground."

As for Hooton, the anxiety over the impending no-hitter accumulated between innings. "I kept looking up after each inning and seeing they had no hits on the scoreboard," said the right hander. "Nervous? No, not while I was pitching. I started thinking about it sitting on the bench, though, and took some deep breaths."

After the Cubs won their next game behind Milt Pappas at Pittsburgh, 6-4, with Williams and Cardenal going deep, they began an eight-game skid, with Pizarro losing to Nelson Briles and the Pirates 5-2.

On April 20 Durocher, now back in the saddle, replaced Monday in center with 23-year-old speedster Bill North, claiming Monday was not hitting the ball well. The move was most puzzling to the outfielder, who was hitting .308 with four hits in his first 13 at bats. "Nobody said a thing to me," a bewildered Monday said, echoing a common sentiment among players Durocher had benched in recent seasons. The Pirates prevailed over Jenkins 7–5, with North getting two hits in five trips.

Hooton then lost to Seaver in New York, 2-0, as Leo—now suffering from an infected gum—turned the reins over to Pete Reiser for the third time.

With the team having lost three straight and faced with a day of rain, the *Tribune* took the opportunity to charge the club with a lifeless defeatism. "The gloomy weather outside was positively cheerful compared with the mood in the [New York] Waldorf-Astoria," reported the writer of the baseball obituary, Bob Logan on April 23.

"Like the aging hotel, the Cubs have seen better days. They spent the first four of this road trip trying to nurse some ailing batting averages back to health, but must wait a while to try the new treatment prescribed by Dr. Leo Durocher."

The team was hitting just .205, with none of its regulars blazing away. Pepitone and Beckert were each just 3 for 25, and Kessinger just 2 of 18. Durocher spoke of benching Pepitone and placing Monday at first base.

Things only got worse the next day. "AILING LEO GOES HOME; CUBS LOSE PAIR 8-2, 7-6," blared the *Tribune*. Pappas was hammered in game 1, while Regan—who would pitch in just five games before Durocher backed up the truck and had him shipped to the crosstown Sox—yielded four hits in an inning and third, losing game 2 in the 9th.

By April 25, with Durocher, nearing 67 years old, now hospitalized with what was termed persistent fatigue, the club lost two straight 1-run decisions to Houston, stretching the losing skein to seven straight.

Frustrated, managerial stand-in Pete Reiser described the team's problems as a lack of toughness. "They're trying hard not to make mistakes, and as a result they get timid. We're going to have to get tough—knock some people down if we have to—but that's another story." Reiser may well have been taking indirect swipes at Randy Hundley for not tagging a sliding Jerry Reuss hard enough on a safe call at the plate and at the usually competitive Bill Hands for failing to pitch inside.

Another day, another killer loss. Reliever Dan McGinn (0-1) took a 5-4 defeat as a Kessinger relay plateward managed to hit the back of the mound, hop upward, and allow the winning run to score in the 10th.

After an off day, Durocher returned to the dugout and the team snapped the eight-game streak at Wrigley Field, beating the Reds 10-8. Amazingly, Jenkins went the distance, yielding seven earned runs in gaining his first win. Jim Hickman, who had been on the bench for the first seven games, smacked two 3-run homers.

April ended with a 6-4 win over the Reds, giving the Cubs a last-place (sixth) 4-10 mark for the month—four of the losses were by a single run. They were 5½ behind the surprising 9-4 Expos.

It also ended with Durocher having had a bellyful of his own in regard to Joe Pepitone's alleged stomach disorder. The skipper, having to scratch Pepi from the lineup on a day when he neither showed up nor called the ballpark, seized control of the situation by phone, making certain the "ailing" first sacker received the requisite medical attention.

In and out of Wesley Memorial Hospital with "gastritis" as the game raged on four miles north, Pepitone was back home that evening. His prescription—antacid tablets—hardly suggested a life-threatening medical emergency for the mercurial Pepitone. Leo smelled a "blue flu," on the part of the slumping first baseman, having sat him down the previous Friday in favor of Jim Hickman.

"Pepi told all you fellows he was feeling fine Saturday—right?" queried the Lip, building his anti-Pepitone case with the writers. "After the day Jim Hickman had on Friday [two homers], I wasn't about to take him off first base. But today I had Jose Cardenal out of the lineup, with Hickman in right and Pepi back at first base."

GM John Holland, who was informed by Durocher of the skipper's actions, termed Pepitone's failure to call in "inexcusable."

The soap opera was not over. By May 2, the Dennis Rodman-like Pepitone left the team, claiming the game was no longer fun. He was placed on the Voluntarily Retired list. Meanwhile, the diamond fortunes of the Cubs had perked up.

A win on May 16 behind Hooton's pitching and three homers by Rick Monday gave the team 10 wins in its last 13 outings and a more respectable 12-13 log for the season. Four players were carrying the team offensively. Monday was out of the gate at .375, Hickman at .333. They and Santo each had five homers. Cardenal (.276) led the club with 16 RBIs, followed by Monday and Hickman with 13 each and the .290-hitting Santo with a dozen. Williams was struggling along at .257, with just two homers and 12 RBIs. Kessinger was dragging the anchor at .228, and Beckert and Hundley were hitting .238 and .234, respectively.

On the slab, Fergie, Pappas, and Hooton were each 3-3, and pitching well. So was Hands. Pappas had a 2.25 ERA, Hooton 2.93, with Jenkins and Hands at 3 even. There was no real bullpen, as Phoebus, McGinn, Regan, and Hamilton combined to pitch just 31⅔ inning over the 25 games, the latter pair working just 6⅓.

On May 17 the team reached the .500 mark with a 9th inning victory at Philadelphia, 3-2. Two weeks later the month closed with the final classic Bob Gibson/Ferguson Jenkins matchup, this one going to the Cardinals 1-0 in just 1 hour and 47 minutes at Wrigley Field. Jenkins actually out-dueled the great Gibson head-to-head over his career, going 5-3 against the Cardinal legend.

By winning 7 of their final 12, the team finished May in third place with a 20-18 mark, eight games behind the Mets at 29-11. Despite Jenkins's tough luck 1-0 loss to Gibson in the month's final game, the Cubs went 16-8 in May.

On June 15 when Hands (6-2) downed the Padres 10-1 in Wrigley Field with the aid of Williams's 11th homer, the Cubs (29-22) had won 9 of their first 13 during the month and had closed to just 4½ behind Pittsburgh (34-18).

Although Hooton outhurled LA's Claude Osteen 4-0 the following day and Williams hit a homer in his fourth consecutive game, there was perhaps more intriguing news off the field. The word was that Joe Pepitone had decided to return at the end of the month, at which time he could be taken off the Voluntarily Retired list. With the team having gone 25-12 in his absence, it was hard to see how the club had missed him.

In the next game, Jose Cardenal was Leo's "King for a Day," with a homer (his eighth), a single, and a stolen base. "He's a manager's dream," exulted the Lip. "There isn't a player in either league playing better than Cardenal [hitting.308]. He does everything. I can't figure out where those stories came from that said he was a moody player—tough to handle."

Of no small significance, Pappas (5-4), who had been struggling with arm miseries since May 18th in Atlanta, picked up the 7-2 win over the

Dodgers. The Cubs had now won four straight. Fully 32,065 paid to see the Cubs run their record to 31-22, just 3½ behind the 35-19 Bucs.

A clutch two-out single by Kessinger off former Cub Pete Mikkelsen in the 11th made it five in a row before the season's largest crowd, 35,018. Despite winning this squeaker, it was clear what the undoing of the 1972 Cubs had been thus far. The team was still just 2-4 in extra innings, and 5-12 in one-run tiffs. They were a robust 27-10 in games decided by two more tallies.

The superstitious Durocher, who had taken over as third-base coach a week ago in an effort to shake off the team's ill fortune, now received grudging admiration from *Tribune* columnist Robert Markus. Markus's column provides insight into the difficulty for a member of the Chicago media to offer Durocher anything approaching unqualified praise.

"One of the questions I am asked most frequently is, What is Leo Durocher really like?" wrote Markus. "If I am to be honest about it, I have to answer, I don't know."

Before offering the skipper any commendations, Markus could not resist taking a couple of shots at the Cubs' field general. First, he alluded to Durocher's aggravating antics of keeping the press off balance by departing from his announced lineups and pitching assignments. Leo was said to be driving beat writers "to distraction by the way . . . [he] 'changes his mind' about such things as lineup and his pitcher for the next day." Moreover, echoing a charge by Jerome Holtzman, Markus claimed "the less charitable" were "apt to say bluntly: He's a liar."

He followed by noting that "some have been waiting vainly for six years for Durocher to make his first appearance at the pitcher's mound with the Cubs behind," while frequently appearing to offer "the hurler a pat on the fanny when the team is leading." This, Markus charged, is regarded by many as "a lack of intestinal fortitude."

Nonetheless, Markus acknowledged that "this puzzling man has placed himself on the third-base coaching line all this past week, has been making his own pitching changes, and even admitted making a terrible mistake by sending Ferguson Jenkins in to try to score from first on a double. He has been nakedly exposing himself to the very type of criticism he had apparently been ducking all these years."

Markus finished with another jab, however, this time at Leo's lack of cooperation and personal disclosure. "He is not an easy man to figure out. He wants it that way. About his personal life, he is as tight-lipped as a spinster at an X-rated movie. Ask him anything at all outside the realm of baseball and more often than not, he'll say: 'That's a personal question; you know I don't answer personal questions.'"

Markus then related an incident in which he overheard Durocher regaling several female flight attendants in a hotel bar with a story in which he witnessed his "friend Frank" throw a pie in the face of a man who had come over to Sinatra to introduce himself and his wife. Markus used that mean-spirited event, in addition to Durocher's ungracious attitude toward autograph seekers, as insights into the Lip's character.

The Cubs, however, kept rolling along. With an 11-inning win over San Francisco on June 19, the Bruins were now .600 ball, with a 33-22 mark. A rookie named Rick Reuschel made his major league debut in the victory.

The team then exploded for 18 hits, including a Hundley grand slam, as Reuschel picked up his first win, permitting only two runs in 6 innings of relief. Hundley (3), Santo (8), and Williams (13) went deep in the 15-8 win.

The streak ended as Pappas lost 4-0 to San Francisco's Ron Bryant. As for the skipper's tenure as third-base coach, "I may let Pete go back," said Leo. "I'll make up my mind Friday." Despite the defeat, the third-place Cubs (34-23) were just two games behind the Pittsburgh Pirates (36-21), who were coming to town for a three-game set.

Maybe 1972 would be different, many fans began thinking. The North-siders had won 32 of their last 45 games with some new contributors—Monday, Cardenal, Hooton, Reuschel, and a trumpet-playing utility third baseman named Carmen Fanzone—in the mix.

On June 22, with the Cubs enjoying an off day before opening the key series with the Pirates, the *Tribune*'s Markus reflected the guarded optimism and emotional conflicts felt by Cub fans nationwide. "I promised myself I would not get too enthusiastic about the Cubs," he confessed, "but I must not have meant it."

Having recently allowed himself to "to get within fungo distance of Ernie Banks," Markus was finding it difficult to ward off the infectious optimism of "the sunshine man," who, unlike other optimists who regularly see "a silver lining in every cloud," simply did not see any clouds. Admitting that he tabbed the perpetual wait-until-next-year Cubs as a third-place ball club in the preseason, Markus was beginning to rethink his assessment and allow some Banks-like optimism to bloom. Recognizing the Bruins' newfound capacity to come from behind such that "the Cubs have finally begun to believe that favored cliché of the radio men that the game is never over until the last man is out," along with the success of Leo's bullpen by committee, Markus (and legions of other Cub fans) felt that this might indeed be a team to be reckoned with.

"Ever since the big collapse of 1969, the Cubs had been a front-running team," explained Markus. "Get ahead of them anywhere from the middle innings on and you could pack up the bats and go home a winner." Furthermore, "If the starting pitcher didn't last the whole way, there was always the danger that the bullpen would fritter away a lead in the late innings."

But the times appeared to be changing. Recognizing a fresh offensive spunk and an ability to close out a game from the pen, Markus mused that "maybe this is next year, after all." Markus, nonetheless, delivered a parting shot at Durocher. After quoting Banks as saying that everybody was "enjoying the game, again," Markus followed with, "Well, not everyone of course. There are some members of the team who are still a little wary. Some think Durocher still does not use his relief pitchers properly." He quoted one Cub as saying that Jenkins would be posting "24 and 8 instead of 24 and 17" records if Leo had consistently removed him when wilting in the late innings. Another had told Markus, "Everything is going great now and I think we have the personnel to win it; let's hope the manager doesn't do something to mess it all up."

Despite those disclaimers, the writer was coming down with pennant fever. Admitting that "thus far the manager had done nothing to mess it all up," Markus declared that despite his best efforts, "the Cubs have got me excited again. I should know better, but as Marlene Dietrich lamented musically in 'The Blue Angel':

> *Falling in love again,*
> *Didn't want to.*
> *But what can I do?*
> *Can't help it.*

Indeed, Markus should have known better. The three-game Pittsburgh was a bust. After Jenkins (8-6) lost to Steve Blass 4-3 before 39,193 in the Friendly Confines, Hands (6-3) was beaten by Nelson Briles, and Hooton (6-5) by Dock Ellis. The three Pittsburgh winners in the series had now registered 19 straight winning decisions over the Cubs—Blass (5), Briles (8), and Ellis (6). Broomed by the Bucs, the Cubs tumbled to 34-26, five full games behind the Pittsburghers and a pair under the 37-25 Mets.

The loss in the finale was particularly unnerving, with the Pirates scoring 4 in the 8th, then 4 more in the 9th. Hooton (6-5) actually was up 2-1 with 2 out in the 8th before the floodgates opened. A crowd of 35,099 watched in dismay as seeming victory turned into a 9-2 blowout.

Despite the sweep, Rick Monday was undaunted. "We have the same club today we did before Pittsburgh came in," he asserted. "If anybody thinks we don't have a chance, they're front-runners."

When young Rick Reuschel—who hailed from the farm country near Quincy, Illinois—filled in for the ill Pappas on June 26, and pitched the team to an 11-1 win over the Phillies, Durocher mused, "He may change the outlook around here."

The Cubs divided a pair with the Phils the next day. The opener went to Jenkins (9-6) by a 6-3 margin. With Pappas still out with the flu, Juan Pizarro was pressed into duty as an emergency starter in the 7-4 loss in game 2. Pizarro, who gave up four runs on four hits and two walks in his 3 innings of work, was "wilder than I ever saw him," observed Leo.

In St. Louis the Cardinals bombed Hands (6-4) and the Cubs 8-4 on 15 hits and followed that with a 4-2 victory over Hooton (6-6) the next night. The latter saw all the Cardinal runs crossing the plate in 6th inning misadventures with Williams letting a single fall in front of him, Beckert getting his feet tangled on a pop fly, and Santo committing an error.

The Cubs closed the books on June with a 4-3 win at Pittsburgh. Promising rookie Rick Reuschel pitched into the 8th, giving up just a pair of singles before leaving with a twisted ankle. Despite the recent sag, the Bruins (17-11 in June) were 37-29 and still within striking distance (3½ games) of the 40-25 Pirates and 41-26 Mets. In the 41 games since May 16—when the team was 12-13—the Cubs had gone 25-16.

Three players had picked up offensively. Kessinger, who had hit just .228 over the first 25 games, delivered at a .297 rate since then. Beckert had hit .285 in the past 41 outings; only .238 in the first 25. The real offensive force, however, was Williams. Billy delivered at a .333 rate in the 41 games, with 11 homers and 28 RBIs, after just .257, 2, and 12 numbers earlier.

The pitching, though already strong, continued to be remarkably consistent over the month and a half. Jenkins, Hands, Hooton, Pappas, and Pizarro were a combined 18-13 with a 3.14 ERA. None of the five had an ERA over 3.48 for the 41 games, while Reuschel, Tom Phoebus, and Dan McGinn were also contributing.

The Cubs opened July with an opportunity to close further on the Pirates, only to suffer yet another one-run defeat. Roberto Clemente cracked a 9th inning banger off Jenkins to give the Pirates a 4-3 verdict. It was the future Hall of Famer's second homer of the game, the first tying things up in the 7th.

The usually poised Jenkins was frustrated. "There just seems to be something hanging over my head," lamented the big right-hander. Having shut the Bucs out through 5, Fergie was hit hard from the 6th on and Durocher invited criticism by leaving him in. "He's my best," said the Lip, laying it off on Jenkins, "and if he tells me he's strong, I can't do anything about it." Williams smacked his 14th in the defeat.

The Bucs' Bruce Kison dropped the Bruins 5½ off the pace with a 7-4 defeat of Hands (6-5). It was the Cubs ninth loss in 12 games.

On July 3 the painful beat went on. "CUBS BLOW IT AGAIN, 3-2," the *Tribune* trumpeted. Up 2-1 behind Hooton in the 9th, the Cubs had already given one run away on a three-way collision involving Monday, Cardenal, and Beckert, the latter being sent to the hospital and sidelined for several games. Vic Davalillo opened the final frame with a successful bunt, Clemente then popped out. Willie Stargell then settled matters on a 2-2 pitch with a two-run opposite field circuit shot. The third-place Cubs were now 37-32, trailing the 43-25 Pirates by 6½.

There were plenty of fireworks on July 4th in Atlanta. With 50,597 fans anxiously awaiting Denny McLain's Atlanta debut in game 2 of a holiday double dip, Juan Pizarro was pressed into duty in the opener when Reuschel, termed "the mammoth boy wonder" by Dick Dozer of the *Tribune*, was shelved with back problems. Dozer took some thinly disguised swipes at the Lip in his summary of the 5-1 loss. Pizarro "did a whale of a job until warning signs went unheeded again for the Cubs, and the Braves beat him with a 4-run 7th inning."

Dozer, citing the Cubs' scoring drought on the trip, stated that Durocher "saw this as the cause for defeat," rather than some of his own handling, or perhaps more accurately mishandling, of his pitching.

Pointing out that the Cubs and Pizarro had held a 1-0 lead from the 3rd until the 6th, Dozer made clear that the Cubs—more specifically, Durocher—had now permitted a lead to fritter away in five of the previous seven defeats.

Calling the defeat "unnecessary," the beat writer then assailed Leo for his failure to go to the pen when Pizarro was wilting in the humid Atlanta air. "The Puerto Rican lefty denied that he got tired—'just high,' he said. But he had pitched only 3 innings in the last 15 days, and it is becoming increasingly apparent that Durocher is more inclined toward asking pitchers if they feel like continuing than telling them they don't."

Dozer then drove home his point. The erratically used Pizarro had thrown 94 pitches, "by comparison, [rotation starter Ron] Reed threw only a few more [110] in a full-route job after which he said he was 'completely sapped' in the stifling humidity."

Durocher's curt response to queries on staying with Pizarro, "I got a man hurt [Reuschel]. I can't go to my bullpen too soon," had a sadly lame ring to it when weighed against the evidence.

Durocher was now reaping a full and bitter harvest for his shabby treatment of the local media during his tenure. From 1967 through most of 1969, the Lip had been politically bulletproof because of his team's successful diamond fortunes. During those years, Durocher had displayed maximum arrogance in all but publicly reminding the local press of his national stature and popularity and their comparative insignificance. Now, however, with the "dandy little manager" on the ropes, the media snapped back with full force.

Referring to Leo as "old whatshisname," *Chicago Today* columnist Rick Talley had been virtually calling for the skipper's head daily since 1970, but now "the knights of the keyboard," as Ted Williams derisively described the beat writers, were often becoming more editorial than reportorial in their game descriptions, consistently pointing out Leo's strategic gaffes. Cubdom at large—media, fans, and players—had now all but fully rotated away from Leo. Players were grumbling, fans were hollering, and the press was attacking.

But Durocher was a veteran of public relations wars. As such, he rarely allowed booing fans, griping players, or hostile media members to provoke an outburst. Maintaining a superficial cool, he realized that curt responses or none at all were his best defense. His remote style suggested that he was beyond the emotional reach of his tormentors.

Durocher, however, was not cool regarding events surrounding the July 4th nightcap. In quest of a split, Cub fortunes looked very favorable in game 2. Tied 3-3 in the 8th, the little bears had runners at the corners and nobody out. Then, with rain suddenly cascading down, the undermanned Atlanta ground crew failed to cover the infield adequately and the contest was washed out, only to have another doubleheader scheduled for the following day.

Leo was incensed, feeling that at the very least, the game should have been suspended rather than made up. He registered an unsuccessful league protest, based on the "inability of the Atlanta club to provide sufficient men and equipment to keep the field playable."

In any case, with his pitching severely stretched, the skipper faced

Fans wait outside Wrigley Field for the strike-delayed season opener in April 1972.

Contrary to popular belief, Cubs vice president and general manager John Holland was instrumental in acquiring many of the key players for Durocher's teams.

Cubs owner Phil Wrigley, chewing gum magnate and namesake of one of the most famed ballparks in America.

Cubs manager Leo "The Lip" Durocher argues a call.

"Mr. Cub" Ernie Banks, who said in 1968, "Don't fear—this is the year."

Ron Santo, an integral part of the greatest team that didn't win. Of Durocher, he said, "Leo's hiring in 1966 made complete sense. You could see our ballclub was coming together."

Billy Williams salutes the crowd after breaking Stan Musial's National League record 895 consecutive games played.

Glenn Beckert formed the right side of one of the best double-play combinations in baseball during the 1960s.

Ken Holtzman is surrounded by newsmen after he used his dominating fastball to pitch his first no-hitter against the Atlanta Braves in 1969. He was only 23 years old at the time.

Ron Santo leaps onto Ken Holtzman after the final out of Holtzman's no-hitter against the Braves. Santo provided the necessary offense in the game with a three-run homer.

Santo couldn't contain his joy after his sacrifice fly scored the winning run against the Pirates in 1969.

The aptly named Bill Hands, another of the Cubs' young hurlers during the magical year that wasn't, 1969.

Phil Regan was acquired in a trade with the Dodgers in 1968 and quickly became Leo's favorite option in the bullpen for the next two years.

Hank Aguirre was added to the Cubs bullpen in 1969, serving as an effective setup man for Phil Regan.

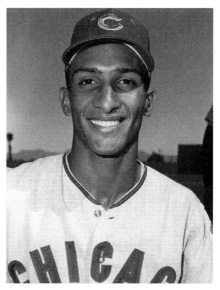

Adolfo Phillips was an immensely talented but flawed player who constantly clashed with Leo before being shipped out of Chicago at the start of the 1969 season.

Fergie Jenkins put together a string of six 20-win seasons for the Cubs from 1967–1972.

When he wasn't injured, catcher Randy Hundley supplied a steady influence on the young Cub pitching staff and some pop with the bat.

Don Kessinger was a slick fielder at shortstop, but his habitually low on-base percentage made him a disappointing leadoff man.

After a long, productive career with the Phillies, outfielder Johnny Callison was traded to the Cubs in 1970. He hit 19 home runs and provided some late-game heroics.

Ernie Banks's 500th homer was a landmark in his Hall of Fame career and seemed to signal good things for the Cubs in 1970.

Paul Popovitch (22) and Ron Santo (10) congratulate Banks after his 507th career homerun.

Joe Pepitone trots into home, surrounded by Don Kessinger (11), Danny Breden (19), Paul Popovitch (22), and Coach Joe Amalfitano (5).

Outfielder Jim Hickman discovered his
power stroke after coming over to the
Cubs from the Mets in 1968, clouting
89 home runs over a four-year period.

Pitcher Milt Pappas, whose
200th career win came in a
Cubs uniform.

**Rookie pitcher Burt Hooton, who pitched his
first no-hitter in 1972 against the Philadephia
Phillies.**

another 2-for-the-price-of-1 on July 5. Jenkins (10-7) notched a 4-1 first game win, with Ron Santo playing second base for Beckert and Carmen Fanzone at third. Fergie triumphed over a shaky start, giving up four hits in the first two innings. "Randy and I couldn't get together on what we wanted to throw," explained Jenkins. The right-hander then took a leaf from Durocher's book, taking a somewhat out of character shot at plate arbiter Steiner, saying "That Mel Steiner isn't the best umpire in the league, either. The guy won't talk when I ask him where pitches are. I think the cat's got his tongue."

A disgruntled Durocher was clearly unhappy having to start a reliever (Phoebus) in the unsuccessful nightcap—a game he felt should not have been played, owing to the July 4th misadventure. Off the split, the Cubs were down to 38-34, seven behind the 44-26 Pirates. Yet another loss, 4-3, followed on July 6, leaving starter Bill Hands—who yielded four tallies in the 3rd inning—winless over the past three weeks.

The club then broke the losing spell on a 2-1 victory behind Hooton (7-7), only to lose 3-2 behind Reuschel the following day. Monday, all the rage earlier in the season, was now just 1 for his last 28. Fergie made it 2 out of 3, hurling his first shutout, 5-0, in the opener of yet another pair. Milt Pappas, fighting through extreme fatigue, went all 9 in the second game, winning 10-5. Umpiring nemesis Mel Steiner made a pair of infuriating calls at third base, leaving one to wonder whether Jenkins's singling him out publicly just a few days earlier was at all prudent. "Just wish I could find a spot for Fanzone," was the skipper's comment after game 2, in which Fanzone hit his fifth home run and knocked in 5 of the team's 10 runs. The Cubs' record now stood at 41-36, eight lengths behind the 48-27 Bucs.

After an off day, the team split a July 11 doubleheader with the Astros in Wrigley Field. After another killer one-run (6-5) loss in the opener, Hands (7-6) evened things up in the second tilt, 9-5, as Monday—out of his slump—pounded a pair.

The big story of the day, however, was the hitting of Williams, who went a mind-boggling 8 for 8 in the twin bill, hitting a homer in each game. Williams, after taking the second game off in the double bill two days earlier followed by an off day, remarked on how fresh he felt. "The rest was good for me mentally and physically," the sweet swinger said. "Anything to stay away from the ballpark." The remark left one wondering how much better the team might have performed in recent years had Durocher been more conscientious about resting Williams and others of his charges.

Two aggravating losses followed. Billy hit his 19th the following day in a 10-6 setback in which a 5-2 lead was blown. "You can't do much if you can't hold them," was Durocher's less than revealing assessment.

The next day, with Jenkins actually going into the 9th tied at 2, the Astros hit the Bruins with a 5 spot for a 7-2 verdict. Stuck in another wire job, Jenkins, who gave up 11 hits in 8⅔ innings, explained the pressure involved in pitching close games. "You can't afford to throw the pitches you want [in the close ones]. When you're ahead in a ball game, they're taking pitches and it gives you an edge over the hitter." The Cubs record had now sunk to 42-39, 7½ down to the also struggling 48-30 Pirates.

The Cubs welcomed Atlanta with a stirring come-from-behind 9th inning win 9-8 on a windy day at Wrigley. Seven baseballs made their way out of the park, four by the Cubs, including Williams's 20th. The game was marked by controversy, however, as a frustrated Milt Pappas was shown the baseball door after losing his temper over several dubious ball-strike calls in a 6th inning in which Atlanta took a 5-4 lead. "I should have taken him out right there [when the furor began], I knew he'd be a wild man," acknowledged Durocher.

After scoring in the 1st for the sixth straight time the next day, Hands (7-8) parted with four runs in five innings of work in a 4-2 setback. Dubious dugout strategy, however, once again hovered over a Durocher-managed defeat. Down two with Santo on second and two out in the 9th, Durocher summoned right-handed-hitting Fanzone to pinch-hit against knuckle-balling right-hander Phil Niekro. "I wanted the man with the power up there, and he had some good rips," Leo explained. Durocher's defense was less than convincing, because a 12-mph wind was blowing from the west, one which actually favored left-handed hitters. In any case, the team was again just three over .500 at 43-40, now 8½ down to Pittsburgh's 50-30.

The Cubs rendered a humdrum finish to their last seven pre–all star break outings. Splitting their next four, with the highlight a 10-inning, 2-1 Williams-powered (21) complete game effort by Jenkins against the Reds, it was then on to the Astrodome, where they limped into the break losing two of three. After Bill Bonham got his first major league win in the series opener, a 7-2 loss was followed by yet another grinding one-run defeat 6-5, with Jenkins pinned with his ninth loss against a dozen triumphs.

The Cubs stumbled into the break with a 46-44 mark. Though good for third place, they were now 10 games behind Pittsburgh at 55-33, and 4½ in arrears to the 49-38 New York Mets.

The excitement of a month earlier had evaporated. Three days before the break, the team announced that Burt Hooton and Bill Hands would be rested until after the classic. Hooton was suffering from shoulder stiffness, the normally reliable Hands from ineffectiveness.

The prebreak 1972 season had been one of extremes. It opened with the club losing 10 of its first 12 games and performing sluggishly throughout the dreary dozen. The slump was followed by a Lazarus-like baseball resurrection resulting in a scintillating 44-game tear, as the Cubs went an eye-popping 32-12 in the process. Back in contention with a number of fresh faces invigorating the squad, the Cubs—just two games behind powerful Pittsburgh—had the Bucs coming into their lair for a three-game series.

Then, with enthusiasm abounding and pennant fever infecting their fans, the North-siders took a sharp turn to the south, going 12-22 in their next 34 tilts, dashing the title hopes of all but the most diehard of their loyalists in the process. In short, the team was sinking, Durocher was under consistent fire, and 1972 looked like another no-cigar season. No one was having much fun.

And then it happened.

The *Tribune* headline shouted the news:

WRIGLEY FIRES LEO! LOCKMAN IN FOR '72

Thirteen

THE AFTERMATH

**I would be the last to dismiss Durocher with a "Throw
the bum out," and forget that Cub fans do owe him
thanks.**
Bob Markus, *Chicago Tribune,* on Leo's departure

Leo out. Lockman in.

There was no sign. No warning.

Ferguson Jenkins could view it only in retrospect. "Durocher had
been strangely quiet and aloof for the last few [pre–all star break] days before this game." he wrote, "I think he was toying with the idea of retiring
as a manager. He kept to himself more than ever."

The words announcing Leo's exit were carefully chosen. After talking
to "Mr." Wrigley, Leo had agreed to "step aside." Wrigley, for his part, credited Durocher. "After just one year, Leo managed a contending team every
season," lauded Wrigley, "and this is why he always has had 100 percent
support from me."

Indeed he had. Although Leo closed the books in Chicago just nine
games over .500 at 535 up and 526 down, he was a healthy 476-423 from
1967 forward. No Cub manager since has even remotely approached his
success.

Wrigley then laid down the gauntlet to his players. "If there has been
any friction between Leo and the players this year, then Leo's decision will
allow the players to find out for themselves if they can win," added the

frustrated owner, carefully making it clear that Leo's departure was, at least in part, voluntary.

It was obvious that Wrigley's angst was for the players. "Some of them [the players] haven't been earning their pay. They don't have the determination Leo put into them when he first came here," he said. Then, after making clear that Lockman was not interested in a long managerial career, the owner issued a transparent threat. "Next year we'll probably need a different manager. Either that, or Leo will be back. We'll see."

When the surprising announcement of Durocher's leaving was made, Cub fans were stunned.

The city was abuzz.

The players were relieved.

Carefully guarded quotes suggested as much. Though admitting "You can't play for a man seven years and not feel the loss of something when he's gone," Don Kessinger was enthusiastic about Whitey Lockman. "I played for Lockman one year in the Texas League and I know he is an excellent baseball man. I look forward to playing for him, and I hope that in the second half of the season, we can turn things around."

"I know players who played for [Lockman] in the minors and they said he is a good man to play for. So I figure he is well qualified," chimed keystone mate Glenn Beckert.

As for Leo, "I guess Mr. Wrigley thought it was time for a change, and he made it."

"You could see the tension and pressure vanish under Lockman. Everybody felt more at ease and played with greater confidence," Jenkins noted later. And it showed on the field.

After splitting a pair in Philadelphia immediately after the break, the Cubs went on a tear, finishing the season a solid second at 85-70. The Cubs went 39-26 under Lockman, just an eyelash behind the Pirates' 41-26 post–all star mark.

Durocher's adversaries felt vindicated. With the club winning without Leo, Jack Brickhouse, referring to previously voiced concerns on how the Bruins would do without their irascible skipper, stated, with subtle sarcasm while broadcasting a Cub tilt, that things were going "just fine these days, thank you."

The team showed little improvement offensively, scoring at the same rate as they had under Durocher, while the batting average actually dropped five points. Moreover, defensively, they committed miscues at about the same rate.

Billy Williams, however, had a banner year. He swatted 42 homers to go with a league-leading .333 average. It was a prophecy-fulfilling year for the quiet slugger. "When I was in double A," says Williams today, "Rogers Hornsby told me, 'If you keep working, you'll win a batting title.'"

On the mound, however, several hurlers truly stepped up. Pappas went 11-1—including a no-hitter—over those last 65 games, posting a 1.88 ERA over the span. Hands was 4-1 and 2.03; Reuschel 7-4 and 2.74.

"We proved we were a better ball club than people thought," remarked Jenkins in summation. "We were certainly a much happier team."

When 1972 is recalled, however, the delightful baseball turned in by the Cubs over those final two months of the season will not be the story. It was simply the year Durocher left.

When the departure was announced, fans were divided.

Legions of Cub devotees felt the Lip was the best thing that ever happened to North Side baseball fortunes. They recalled only too well the 20 years of slogging through the baseball wilderness, during which their beloved Cubs lived up all too well to their image as "lovable losers" on the field, and the misadventures in the front office that were near annual events. Leo's removal had changed all that.

Many others, myself among them, longed for a change. We knew inwardly that the run was over. With the best years of the Cub stars now safely behind them and a manager in crisis still at the throttle, it was folly even to hope for a championship. It was time to throw open the windows and admit some fresh air.

The analysts in the media, though generally merciful in their handling of the sudden exit of this larger than life adversary, felt the time for change had come. The reasoned reaction of Jack Brickhouse was typical. "I'm not going to gloat over Leo losing his job, he has meant a lot to the game," said a gracious Brickhouse. Then, however, weighing in on the other side of the matter, Brick stated, "My personal opinion is the step was long overdue."

The consensus at the moment was that much of Durocher's undoing was brought on by his '40s and '50s style of management in a new era. "He could not keep up with the times," wrote Markus of the *Tribune*, "but I give him credit. He tried. He tried to understand young ballplayers today cannot be handled the way they were handled when he was young and brash and tough. He knew far better than his old pal [White Sox manager] Eddie Stanky that young players need to be gentled with kid gloves. He changed his viewpoint, but he couldn't change himself."

From the outset in 1966, Leo had paid lip service to the changing nature of professional athletes. "You have to treat ballplayers differently now," he had said. "These kids are educated. You wrap a lot of money up in them, and you have to treat each one in a special way."

"He turned off his players," explains Bill Gleason, who covered Durocher throughout his Windy City stay. "He frequently referred to Kenny Holtzman, one of his three outstanding pitchers, as 'kike.' Any Jewish person would be sensitive to such a slur. It was terrible."

Legendary and ever courteous clubhouse manager Yosh Kawano also bore the brunt of Leo's verbal bigotry, according to Gleason. "'Hey Jap,' Leo would yell at Yosh as he threw a pair of his long underwear at him, 'get the brown out.'

"This was the way of much clubhouse language 20 years previous, but the late 1960s was a much more sensitive time. Leo just didn't realize times had changed."

Moreover, Durocher was hardly as color-blind as he loved to portray himself. "Leo did not like black players," is a quote easily attributable to any variety of players and media of that era. Willie Mays, on whom Durocher founded his reputation as a genuine liberal, was hardly a rebel; certainly Ernie Banks, Billy Williams, and Fergie Jenkins were scarcely typical of the angry black players of the era. "Williams never created a scuff and Jenkins was similar," says Rich Nye. "They hardly ever complained." Other African Americans, from the hostile Lou Johnson to the young Oscar Gamble, did not fare so well with Durocher.

In the early years, Durocher had done well in bridling his tongue and avoiding the management-by-intimidation approach under which he spent his playing days, opting rather to teach, encourage, and inspire his charges. As the team became more successful and Durocher older, however, he reverted to the roaring lion image from his early years. Then, as the walls of pressure began closing in after the 1969, 1970, and 1971 debacles, the aged mentor tried to reinvent himself.

Instead of nurturing young players, he broke their spirit. Instead of ingeniously extracting the most from each one, he divided his team into those he liked and those he didn't. "Durocher gained a reputation for having pet athletes who could do no wrong as well as a collection of scapegoats who could do no right," offered Dick Dozer.

"Leo Durocher in the later years provided no leadership in the club he was hired to lead," noted Markus, referring to the Lip's losing control at the wheel and his club then turning against him. Markus's words were echoed by Rich Nye nearly 30 years later, in saying that after 1967 Leo had become "distracted," and no longer "put in the effort" he had earlier.

Whether due to age or complacency, Durocher's losing his grip was evident to beat writer Dozer. "Durocher didn't eat and sleep baseball as he once did, harboring the false security perhaps that he didn't need to anymore," he noted. Moreover, the very element Durocher had stressed upon his arrival in 1966 began lagging. "There came a laxity in fundamentals with the Cubs—not so much because Leo and his lieutenants didn't think they were important. It was merely because he believed—with some justice—that kids making top dollar ought to know what to do when they got in the big leagues."

"The pressures started to get to him after the 1969 failure," noted Santo. He acknowledged that Leo "had brought us closer to a pennant than anyone else had in a generation. But he also brought disruption and chaos; anyone who was in that turbulent clubhouse mess that brought us to near blows could support that."

Markus took the players' side in the divide. "There are many fans who cannot understand why ballplayers will not produce their best for certain men. They're getting paid well, aren't they?

"If ballplayers were mechanical robots, I could buy that. But they are just as human as anybody else. Secretaries get paid, too, but I warrant they do more and better work for a boss who treats them with understanding. And if they don't like their boss, they can quit and find another job. Ballplayers [in this pre-free agency era] can't."

In little more than a year, Durocher was out of baseball, and as defiant as ever. In his autobiography, he all but admits that he had had enough of the modern ballplayer, closing the volume thusly: "It's a different breed, boy, and they're going to keep right on doing it their way.

"Well, I'm a guy who has to do it my way.

"Whether you like it or not."

Fourteen

DUROCHER'S CUBS LIVE!

**The Durocher-era team is the most popular
Cub team ever.**
Les Grobstein

Of wins many, of championships none. The winning, however, stopped after 1972. In fact, it was a dozen years before the organization posted another plus-.500 season.

"I knew that 1971 and 1972 were our last gasps," wrote Santo. "On paper, we were still a first-division team the next three years, but I knew we were on a downward spiral. We had a lot of enthusiasm under Whitey Lockman, but the atmosphere was much different from our peak years with Leo."

In addition, 1972 was not merely the final year for Durocher. By the end of that season, four key performers were gone. Banks had retired, and Holtzman had gone to Oakland in exchange for Rick Monday after the 1971 season. In 1972 Regan finished out his career with the White Sox, and Bill Hands was traded to Minnesota at the close of the season.

The 1973 season was the last campaign for five more Bruins. After the season, Ron Santo was traded to the White Sox and his roommate, Beckert, to San Diego. Jenkins was dealt to Texas and his batterymate, Hundley, was sent in trade to Minnesota. Before the following season opened, the Cubs traded Jim Hickman to St. Louis.

At the close of 1974, the Cubs dispatched 36-year-old Billy Williams to Oakland in a multiplayer trade. The following season was the last for Don Kessinger, who was traded to the St. Louis Cardinals in October of that year. By the end of 1975, all the key figures were gone.

With that, Durocher's Cubs were no more.

• • •

Gone for more than two decades, Durocher's Cubs have maintained an un-breakable grip on the memories of baseball fans nationwide. So popular that they constitute the genesis of the current Adult Fantasy Camp rage. The camp concept was much the brainchild of catcher Randy Hundley who, disillusioned after being exiled from the Cub system when Dallas Green took over in the early 1980s, seized on the idea when it was sug-gested to him.

"Well, there was no question but it hadda be a Cub camp," the for-mer backstop told writer and camp participant Jeff Guinn for the latter's book *Sometimes a Fantasy,* "because I knew what the '69 Cubs meant to Chicago fans." That Cub camp, now more than 15 years old, has become so popular that it has given birth to clones throughout the baseball world, none of which, however, match the Cub original in appeal.

The Cubs won a division title in 1984, again in 1989, and made the play-offs as a wild card entrant in 1998. One night at dinner, a friend of mine, Jeff Magill, who works at Chicago's famous Billy Goat Tavern, dis-cussed the hold on the baseball consciousness the Cub team of 1967–1972 maintains. What Jeff said struck me. "Many adult baseball fans would be hard-pressed to name even half as many regulars from any of the more re-cent play-off teams as they likely could from that earlier one," he stated.

Indeed the former remains so memorable, the latter forgettable.

There are many reasons. One obvious one is Durocher himself. For the better part of seven years, the little man veritably towered over the era, dominating the baseball news, conversations, and events like no other in baseball.

As a player, Leo was a member of Ruth and Gehrig's 1927 Yankees and the Frankie Frisch/Dizzy Dean Gashouse Gang in St. Louis. He man-aged the 1951 Giants when Bobby Thomson hit the "shot heard round the world" and also the 1954 Giants who swept the incredibly favored 111-43 Cleveland team in the World Series. He followed that with a stint in the broadcast booth.

Given his insatiable ego and electric personality, the Lip was the Cubs' mouthpiece, its driving force, the very core of its identity. Durocher put Cub baseball back on the major league map nationwide. Coming to Chicago as one who already loomed large in baseball lore, he was the Windy City's national claim to sports prominence. Leo Durocher was Billy Martin before there was Billy Martin. For Chicago sports fans, he was Mike Ditka before there was Mike Ditka.

Furthermore, it was a stable team from a pre–free agency era. With minimal player movement, quality players all but seared their identities in the memories of a team's fans over a period of years. Certainly this was true of the 11 principal figures on the Cub team from 1967-1972. Below, rounded off to full seasons, are the number of years each of these key players spent with the Cubs.

Ernie Banks—18
Billy Williams—14
Ron Santo—14
Don Kessinger—10
Glenn Beckert—9
Ferguson Jenkins—8
Randy Hundley—8
Bill Hands—7
Ken Holtzman—6
Jim Hickman—6
Phil Regan—4

Note that none of the 11 spent less than four years with the Cubs, and all enjoyed some or all of their best years in Chicago. Banks hit 512 home runs and drove in more than 1,600 runs, all while wearing the Cub uniform. Santo and Williams each blasted more than 300 homers and knocked in over 1,200 runs for the North-siders. Kessinger and Beckert combined for over 3,000 hits for the Bruins. Hundley caught 149 or more games (160 in 1968) for four straight seasons, and Jim Hickman had as big a career year in 1970 as any player of his time. On the mound, Jenkins won 167 games for the Cubs, Hands 92, and Holtzman 74. Regan won 32 and saved 60 more.

In regard to the key six seasons, infielders Beckert, Kessinger, and Santo played regularly through all six, as did leftfielder Billy Williams and (when not injured) Randy Hundley behind the plate. Moreover, Mr. Cub gave the team an intact all-star infield from 1967 through 1969. Jim Hickman, though acquired in 1968, lasted past the 1972 season.

Fergie won 20 or more in each of those six seasons, Hands—also there for all six—had 20-, 18-, and 16-win seasons. Holtzman, twice a 17-game winner, threw two no-hitters and was present for all but the final season, and Phil Regan, who was acquired with Hickman, did not leave until two months into the 1972 campaign.

The 11 were more than merely professionally associated with the Cubs. "Many of the fans' heroes lived in Chicago year-round," George Castle points out. At the same time, the 11 were national baseball figures. From just 1967-1972, they made a total of 22 all-star appearances. When stretched beyond just those years, the group made fully 41 such appearances representing the Cubs.

When asked these days about that collection of players, Santo's summary is succinct and powerful. "A very strong-willed team with about eight leaders."

Furthermore, there is little question that 1969 itself seals the team in memory. Coming as it did amid the upheaval of the late 1960s, the year remains fresh in the minds of many. In addition, unlike the Phillies of 1964, this was not a one-year wonder or disappointment. Jim Hickman and Ron Santo, in conversations with Guinn, focused on that.

For Santo, it's a painful set of memories. "I wanted us to win the pennant, to play in the World Series," he confessed. "Sixty-nine, that's the one everybody talks about, but there were other years we could have won, too. We just didn't."

"Sometimes there's talking about us alongside the '64 Phillies and other clubs," Hickman stated. "But for other teams like those Phillies, there was just one season when they came out of nowhere and contended. Sixty-nine wasn't the only year that happened to us. In '70 and '71 we came right back and almost did exactly the same thing."

Hickman's point is well taken. The Cubs finished third in 1967 and 1968. After that fateful second-place divisional finish in 1969, the team then came in second in two of the next three years (1970 and 1972), and tied for third in the other (1971).

Testimony to the enduring power of that Cub era is the degree to which the very image of Cub baseball was forever transformed in those years.

When, as I have, a fan stands on one of the rooftops across from Wrigley Field—jammed with people, food, and drink—and looks out at stands teeming with people, often rooting for a going-nowhere Cub team with a losing record, he or she realizes it all started with Durocher's Cubs.

As that era dawned, the Cubs most certainly were not a happening. Games were played in near secrecy, often before "crowds" of fewer than

3,000. An annual gate in excess of a million was not even hoped for. Fully 22,000 unreserved and bleacher seats were on sale the day of each game for walk-up patronage. Often, during the first game of a twin bill, Cub announcers would say, "Hey, if you're in the area, come on out, there's plenty of baseball left and good seats available." The former may not always have been true, but the latter was. Moreover, the neighborhood around Wrigley Field, awash with nonowner-occupied brick apartment buildings, was in obvious decline.

Not so after Durocher's Cubs. Every year after 1967 (save the strike-shortened 1981 obscenity), attendance figures have exceeded seven figures. In recent years a gate of over 2,000,000 spirited onlookers is hardly a noteworthy achievement. "Whether you're playing well or badly, you're still playing in front of sellouts," says current Cub star Mark Grace. "Everybody's friendly and everybody's pulling for you. That's what makes it so much fun."

Former Cub Luis Gonzalez echoes Grace's sentiments. "It's the fan atmosphere," he says. "The fans get into every game. It's exciting to run out and know there are a lot of businessmen skipping work, hiding from the cameras, and people just enjoying themselves at the ballpark. That's what makes it so much fun."

Tickets are now sold in advance in a community alive with Cub culture. The neighborhood of Clark and Addison—now actually called Wrigleyville—is peppered with sports bars and other Cub-oriented establishments. So heavy is the commercial traffic in this still largely residential community, that a person has to have a special city-authorized window shield sticker to be permitted to park in the neighborhood during Cubs games.

No longer are all the brownstones across the street from the park privately owned, so that residents and their friends can go at their leisure up to the roof to view a game over the right-field wall. Many of the buildings are now owned by bar/restaurants that rent out the rooftops to business groups, catering amenities to those who have reserved their place overlooking the Friendly Confines.

In addition, the Wrigley Field complex openly celebrates the history of Durocher's Cubs. Before even entering the park at the Clark and Addison entrance, one encounters the Cub Walk of Fame. Begun with the Class of 1992, stars bearing the names of Cub greats are emblazoned onto the sidewalk in Hollywood style. Of the first 16 players inducted, six—Ernie Banks, Ferguson Jenkins, Ron Santo, Billy Williams, Don Kessinger, and Glenn Beckert—are from the Durocher era.

Inside the park, beginning with the ancient Cub clubhouse, the taste of previous eras continues to be evident. The "lockers" in the cramped Yosh Kawano Clubhouse, simple open cubicles with hooks and shelves for occupants' belongings, are reminders of baseball past. Other than the person's name above the cubicle, and a blue-and-white chair adorned with the Cub logo, little distinguishes the sanctuary from an old high school locker room.

Next to a metallic board on which "It takes a little more to make a champion" is scrawled—and a jokester has wedged the word "coffee" between "more" and "to"—the past leaps out more directly in the form of a picture and article about Hack Wilson. The words "Talent Alone Not Enough to Succeed" headline the sad story of the Cub outfielder of seven decades ago whose fame as a player was exceeded only by his renown as a career-destroying alcoholic.

The one white-painted wall, not cluttered with lockers, provides a virtual stroll through Cub history with huge photos of team greats. Underneath each black-and-white photo—in red handwritten script—is the player's name, along with his position(s), and years played. In similar blue script is an inscription, summarizing his contributions to Cub glory. Rogers Hornsby, Kiki Cuyler, Cap Anson, and Frank Chance are featured, as are no less than four of Durocher's Cubs.

An almost rookie-appearing Ernie Banks, posing in his stance, peers out at the viewer. Underneath is the inscription:

> When you think of great players in Cub history, you think of Ernie Banks. Mr. Cub spent 19 seasons with the club, hitting 512 home runs and winning back-to-back MVP awards (1958–1959), driving in over 100 runs eight times and playing more than 1,000 games at shortstop and first base. A 14-time all-star, Banks was elected to the Hall of Fame in 1977.

Below a very young Ron Santo, looming large in his third base crouch, is written "Ron Santo was a career .277 batter with 342 home runs and 1,331 runs batted in. He hit 337 home runs with the Cubs, the third highest total in Cub history, and led the National League in walks four times. The former third baseman won five rive Rawlings Gold Glove awards during his 15-year major league career and a National League All-Star nine times."

A powerful-looking Ferguson Jenkins, full stride in game action, is

pictured with the inscription "Fergie Jenkins was one of the most dominant pitchers in Cub history. He won at least 20 games in six consecutive
seasons (1967–1972), going 127-84 with a 3.00 earned run average during that span and averaging 39 starts, 23 complete games, and 306.0 innings pitched per season. Jenkins, who was elected to the Hall of Fame in
1991, is the only pitcher in major league history to have more than 3,000
strikeouts and less than 1,000 walks."

Below Billy Williams, photographed in the middle of his esthetic
swing, is written "Billy Williams was elected to the Hall of Fame in 1987,
following an illustrious playing career. He won the Rookie of the Year
award in 1961, a National League batting title in 1972 (.333), and six all-
star selections. Williams batted .296 as a Cub, with 392 home runs, and
played in a one-time National League record 1,117 consecutive games."

Once on the field, there are visual reminders of Durocher's Cubs.
Flying atop the left-field flagpole is the #14 set against a blue-and-white
Cub-striped flag, commemorating Mr. Cub. On the right-field pole, near
the locale of many of his home run sailing balls, is the #26 for Billy
Williams.

Among the figures celebrated throughout, Durocher is conspicuous
by his absence, likely the price the dyspeptic mentor paid for his bridge-
burning behaviors.

Nonetheless, the convergence of the past with the present is inescapable at the old ballpark. Jim Riggleman, the final Cub manager of the
millennium, puts it well: "The experience of Wrigley Field is unique," he
says, standing on the grass near third baseline. "It consumes the pregame,
game, and postgame moments. You can't help but feel the history of the
great players who have played here through the years. Visually, the archi-
tecture, the uniqueness of the ivy, the manually operated scoreboard—
there's so many things that distinguish it from the new ballparks.

"I take the el to or from the park once or twice a week," said the manager, just after an elevated train audibly clattered by on the tracks over the
right-field wall. "The el, the horns blowing, and the traffic around the ballpark all remind you that you are near the downtown area, something other
cities are trying to incorporate into their stadiums."

The park is particularly precious to people like Billy Williams and
Randy Hundley. "I love this ballpark, it's where I wore my first big league
uniform," says Williams, unabashedly sitting in the dugout. "There are very
few changes. The ivy is still on the wall. The scoreboard is still manually
operated. They haven't disturbed the beauty of time past."

"The scoreboard, the ivy, the location, the skyline, the playing field. How do you describe it to someone?" says Hundley, in a moment of reflection. "There's a lot of nostalgia here."

Don Baylor, Riggleman's successor, made no secret of the effect that the colorful team history, in addition to the charm of Wrigley Field, had on his decision to accept the team's offer to take over managerial duties at the outset of the new millenium.

As much as anything, however, the team stays together in memory because it has stayed together in fact. Years after their run has been over, the annual fantasy camp regularly attracts many of the main figures of the era who return to coach the campers largely because they enjoy being together.

Guinn talked with a number of them. Jenkins acknowledged that he would have come for free, even were he not one of the coaches. "It's special to come back and spend time with the guys you used to play with. Hey, I played seven or eight years with some of these guys—Beckert, Santo, Randy."

Remembering the roles his teammates played, he recalled his pitching days, "I always had the idea of what I wanted to do, but then I had good individuals playing behind me. Hundley calling great games, Beckert and Kessinger making double plays, Billy Williams and Ernie and Ron Santo getting me runs to work with. We complemented each other, really."

Hickman, while initially uncertain about what kind of experience coaching campers would be, "still wanted to go back to Arizona and see some of the guys."

"The biggest part is being with the guys I played with for so many years," Williams explained. "You know, I can make ten times this money just by taking one or two autograph shows every off-season. I come here to enjoy being with the guys."

Reflecting on his relationships with his teammates, Santo said, "I didn't play in a World Series, but I got to be around all these other guys who've stayed close friends. Some teams, you know, split up after the season and nobody ever talks to anybody else until spring training. Guys play for years together, retire, and don't stay in touch. We have. I think we're all happy about that."

Santo's one-time roommate Beckert also affirmed the unity of the team. "What you see with us [in the fantasy camp] is just the way it was in the clubhouse when we really played. Some guys are outgoing, some more inward. But the closeness is real, maybe because we played together so long. We saw our families grow up together. . . . This free agency means there isn't the bonding between players like back then. Plus the money in the game now is so big—players spend more time with their agents than with each other. They work on a different level than we operated on. Nobody talked about salaries then. You usually didn't think about what you were making compared to the other guy, not during the season, at least. You had a team idea."

The now departed Hank Aguirre, who spent just 2 of his 16 big-league seasons in Chicago, felt a lifelong connection with the '69 team. "I come to do Randy's camps when he asks me and when I've got the time," explained the highly successful Detroit businessman. "And I do see the rest of the guys some other times. I saw some of the rest of the '69 guys— Willie Smith, Nate Oliver—just before Christmas. This guy flew all the '69 Cubs in for a show, put us up in a hotel, promised us $1,500 each. Then he ended up saying he hadn't made any money himself so he couldn't pay us. What could we do? At least we got together, got to see each other."

Even the colorful Pepitone felt the pull. "It's to be around the guys," responded Pepi to the question of his fantasy camp participation. "Beckert, Williams, Santo, Hundley, Jenkins, Ernie Banks—those Cubs shoulda been winnin' every year."

For Hundley, no one cemented the team in perpetuity more than Durocher himself. Randy, who appreciated Leo's public endorsement of him as worthy of being a major league manager, recalled for Talley the evening when the 78-year-old Durocher—recovering from recent cardiac surgery—spoke at the camp.

Biographer Gerald Eskenazi's claim that even as an old man, Leo could light up a room was evident that night when the aged skipper stepped to the microphone as the camp's speaker.

After saying a number of kind things, the still magnetic Durocher seized the moment as only he could. "I want to apologize to Ron Santo," said the now mellow and repentant skipper about the 1971 imbroglio. "I made a mistake, and I've been wanting to say so to Ronnie and his family for the longest time."

Eyes filled with tears as disappointments and bitter feelings of the past dissolved in an air of reconciliation and affection.

"You ask about what kind of bond our team has?" said Hundley. "I don't have the vocabulary to express how we all felt that night."

$$\bullet \quad \bullet \quad \bullet$$

Durocher died in 1991 in Palm Springs, California. Though not elected to the Hall of Fame in his lifetime, he had made peace with his team. He also made peace with the Lord. Leo spent the closing years of his life faithfully attending church, regularly going to confession, and trying to rid himself of his lifelong habit of cursing. Sharing with once adversary Talley an experience he had at the confessional, Durocher provided a rich insight into how he looked back on his life.

The priest, noting the regularity of his visits, had said to Leo, "What are you doing here, you haven't done anything."

"Well, Father," Durocher replied, "if you want to go back a few years, I have done a few things."

Bibliography

Brickhouse, Jack. *Thanks for Listening*. South Bend, Indiana: Diamond Communications, 1986.

Castle, George, and Jim Rygelski. *The I-55 Series*. Champaign, Illinois: Sports Publishing, 1999.

Durocher, Leo. *Nice Guys Finish Last*. New York: Pocket Books, 1976.

Eskenazi, Gerald. *The Lip*. New York: William Morrow, 1993.

Guinn, Jeff. *Sometimes a Fantasy*. Fort Worth, Texas: Summit Group, 1994.

James, Bill. *The Bill James Baseball Abstract*. New York: Ballantine Books, 1985.

James, Bill. *The Politics of Glory*. New York: Macmillan, 1994.

Jenkins, Ferguson. *Like Nobody Else*. Chicago: Henry Regnery Co., 1973.

Langford, Jim. *The Game Is Never Over*. South Bend, Indiana: Icarus Press, 1982.

Santo, Ron. *For Love of Ivy*. Chicago: Bonus Books, 1993.

Talley, Rick. *The Cubs of '69*. Chicago: Contemporary Books, 1989.

Thorn, John, Pete Palmer, Michael Gershman, and David Pietrusza, eds. *Total Baseball*. New York: Total Sports, 1999.